The Last Sermon I Would Preach

If Jesus Were Coming Tomorrow

Forrest Pollock

Encouraging Word ◆ Brandon, Florida

To Dawn

The Last Sermon I Would Preach If Jesus Were Coming Tomorrow
Copyright © 2007 by Forrest Pollock
All rights reserved
ISBN 978-0-6151-5940-9

Requests for information should be addressed to:
Encouraging Word
2102 Bell Shoals Road
Brandon, Florida 33511

Printed in the United States of America

Cover designed by Lee Snow

Edited by Jeffre Littleton & Barbie Frost

Contents

PREFACE

Sadly "hereafter" preaching has too often been replaced with the "here-and-now." Whereas preachers of yesteryear fervently and frequently pointed to the rapture and the new world to come, too many of preachers today are content to deliver feel-good pulp and pop-psychology clothed in biblical dressing.

Thankfully, there remains a remnant of thundering and prophetic voices faithfully proclaiming the imminent return of Christ. In powerful pulpits across America, God-called preachers are sounding the claxon bell of alarm that God's "Spirit will not contend with man forever." Their message: Jesus is coming soon!

Recently, I invited some dear friends to contribute the last sermon they would preach if Jesus were coming tomorrow. In the days that followed, the manuscripts and recordings that flooded our offices were as different in style and content as the men who delivered them. But the crimson thread weaving its way through each message is an undying optimism that Jesus is returning soon and that everyone must give an account before God. This volume is dedicated to these faithful and prophetic servants of our Lord.

This compendium has two purposes: First, it is hoped that these messages will encourage believers to share the gospel with renewed passion and conviction. As theologian Martin Marty once said, "If people really believed in hell, they wouldn't be watching basketball games or even the TV preachers. They'd be out rescuing people." I couldn't agree more.

Second, this volume is a call to arms to evangelize with urgency. When Jesus returns, pulpit witnessing ceases. Therefore, we must make "the most of every opportunity, because the days are evil." I would add that the days are also few.

If our Lord should tarry, may you find renewed fervor to look eastward with expectancy, believing that Jesus is coming soon.

And who knows? Maybe tomorrow is the day.

1

THE WHEAT AND THE TARES

Dr. Bailey Smith

Evangelist

Bailey Smith Ministries

Atlanta, Georgia

A FEW YEARS AGO, BILLY GRAHAM was conducting a major evangelistic crusade at a correction center in Oklahoma City. On the closing Sunday morning of that crusade, I was privileged to have him speak for me when I was the pastor of the First Southern Baptist Church in suburban Del City, Oklahoma. We were all excited to have Dr. Graham at our church since he rarely speaks in local church services.

I had listened intently to Dr. Graham every night during the crusade. Now that we were alone for a moment before the service began, I had the opportunity to ask him a question that was heavy on my heart.

"Billy, why is it that every night during this crusade you have made some reference to lost church members?" I asked.

"Bailey," he responded, "I still preach what I did when we began our crusades years ago in Los Angeles."

"Why is that?" I inquired.

"For two reasons," Billy replied. "First, I was a lost church member myself. I was the vice-president of my youth group at church, but I was not really born again. Second, I remind people that they can be church members and still be lost because the greatest mission field in the world is not the foreign field or the home field, it is the mission field of the membership rolls of American churches!"

There are 160 million church members in America. If they were all truly saved, this country would not be in the spiritual mess in which it finds itself today. Opinion polls continually tell us that the number of professed believers is growing and that more Americans claim a born-again experience than ever before in our nation's history. Yet America is overrun with immorality, pornography, alcohol and drugs. Robbery and murder are on the rise. Teenage pregnancies are epidemic. Over one million babies are aborted every year. Something is deeply wrong with the moral fiber of our nation.

I am convinced that one of America's greatest problems is that of unconverted church members. Our churches are filled with people who profess Christ, but who do not possess Him. They claim His name, but they have never submitted to His Person. They want His blessings without His authority. They want His favor without His leadership. They want to accept their own will for their lives instead of submitting to His will for their lives.

There is no one I respect in the ministry more than Billy Graham. God has used him mightily for six decades to proclaim the gospel of Jesus Christ to our generation. Millions have come to Christ in response to his preaching. Yet one study reported that 70 percent of those converted in his crusades are church members. I thank God that He is using Dr. Graham to reach the lost within the church as well as those who have had no church affiliation.

The sad condition of our churches is the inevitable consequence of weak preaching and a lack of spiritual leadership. Divorce and immorality are rampant in the 20th-century church. John MacArthur has said, "I am convinced that the popularized gospel of the 20th-century church has made all this possible, even inevitable." MacArthur further asks, "If repentance, holiness of life, and submission to the Lordship of Christ are all optional, why should we expect the redeemed to differ from the heathen?"

In the parable of the wheat and tares (Matthew 13:24-30), our Lord Jesus vividly depicts the distinction between the saved and the lost. The saved are pictured as bearing fruit, and the lost are pictured as being without fruit. This is identical to what Jesus said in the parable of the sower (vv.3-9), where He stated that believers might vary in the amount of their fruitfulness "some an hundredfold, some sixtyfold, some thirtyfold" (v.8). But notice that He did not allow for a true believer who produced no fruit. Some believers might prove to be more fruitful than others, but no true believer is totally fruitless.

Jesus said,

"The kingdom of heaven is likened unto a man which sowed good seed in his field: But while men slept, his enemy came and sowed tares among the wheat, and went his way. But when the blade was sprung up, and brought forth fruit, then appeared the tares also. So the servants of the householder came and said unto him, Sir, didst not thou sow good seed in thy field? From whence then hath it tares? He said unto them, An enemy hath done this. The servants said unto him, Wilt thou then that we go and gather them up? But he said, Nay; lest while ye gather up the tares, ye root up also the wheat with them. Let both grow together until the harvest: and in the time of harvest I will say to the reapers, Gather ye together first the tares, and bind them in bundles to burn them: but gather the wheat into my barn." (vv. 24-30)

Parables are designed to teach a lesson by illustration or example. However, they can be easily misunderstood if we try to press every detail of the story. This parable serves a warning to the "laborers" (evangelists) in the "field" (which Jesus interpreted as the world in v.38). We are sent by Christ to proclaim His gospel throughout the world. Those who are genuinely converted are represented as "wheat," but false "converts" are depicted in the parable as "tares."

The tares (the Greek word is *zizanion*, denoting "darnel" or "ryegrass") are indistinguishable from real wheat. They look exactly alike. I have often had farmers bring me both a shock of wheat and a shock of tares after hearing me preach this message. As I take them both in my hands, I cannot tell them apart. They appear to be identical. Even the farmer cannot tell the difference until be breaks open the head to see which contains the grain of wheat. The one with the fruit is the wheat, and the one which is empty is the tare.

In the parable, the "kingdom of heaven" refers to the church, which is the subject of all of the parables in Matthew 13. Thus, while the gospel is to be preached in the world, it is among the believers (symbolized by wheat) that the enemy (Satan) sows his tares (fake converts). Since the tares are identical imitations of the true wheat, it only stands to reason that they simply profess to be real.

In commenting on this passage, Ed Hindson observed:

> "Unlike the Jewish form of the kingdom in the Old Testament where citizens could be easily recognized, during the Church Age converts will be made from all over the world and received upon their profession of faith. Thus, it will be easier to slip in some counterfeits who profess what they do not possess."

The key to understanding the parable of the wheat and tares is the interpretation that Jesus Himself gave in Matthew 13:36-40. Our Lord identified the sower as Himself, the "Son of man," and the enemy as the devil. The wheat represents the "children of the kingdom," in contrast to the tares who are the "children of the wicked one." The harvest is at the "end of this world" (literally, "this age"), when the angels will serve as God's reapers. The clear implication of the parable is that God alone knows who are His actual children. In the end, the saved will be taken to heaven, and the unsaved will be burned in fire, an obvious reference to hell.

In 2 Corinthians 13:5, the apostle Paul challenged his readers: "Examine yourselves whether ye be in the faith." One of the most important questions you can ever ask yourself is whether or not you are truly saved. Our churches are filled with people who seem to be living for themselves and seem not to have a heart for the things of God. They are not always the worst church members. Sometimes they are the best church members. I'm not talking about those "church bunnies" who hop in only on Easter. Nor am I referring to those who live in open disobedience to their profession of faith. It is easy to distinguish that kind from truly committed believers. I'm speaking of those who attend every service, sing in the choir, teach in Sunday School, tithe, serve in the deacon body and outwardly appear like the "real thing." But inwardly, they have never been born again by the Spirit of God. These are the tares, if you will. Outwardly they look exactly like the genuine article, but they produce no spiritual fruit.

The Bible tells us that at the judgment, Jesus will be the Great Separator. He will know the true believers from the false professors by their fruits. In the meantime, it is the task of the evangelist to challenge the "tares" in the church to become "wheat." In our crusades across America, we have seen 57 pastors, 69 pastors' wives, 17 missionaries, 139 deacons, 171 deacons' wives, and a host of others find new birth in Jesus Christ. The powerful conviction that results when a lost church member is saved causes two things to happen: (1) other lost church members begin to examine their lives and come to Christ, and (2) truly saved people in the church gain an even greater assurance of their salvation.

In light of the biblical command to examine the genuineness of our faith, we need to do two things. First, go back in your mind to that time you professed Christ as Savior. What really happened then? Did Christ become real to you and did your life begin to change? Don't rely on what others said happened to you. Ask yourself what happened. Second, examine the fruits of your life since your profession of faith. Have you developed a heart for God and His Word? Are you growing spiritually, producing the fruit of the Spirit and giving evidence of new life in your walk with God? Remember there is a significant difference between human works and spiritual fruit. Anyone could go through the motions of being an usher or singing in the choir without experiencing a new heart from God.

SOWING OF THE PRODUCT

The severe situation that occurred in the parable of the wheat and tares is that the two were planted together in the same place. While the field represents the world in the broad sense that the converts of Christ are won to Him in this world, the specific place within the world where Satan plants his tares is where the wheat is – namely, within the church.

No farmer ever arose in the morning and announced to his wife that the farm needed a few acres of weeds and then set off to plant them. Jesus said that the enemy, the devil, planted the tares "among the wheat" to disrupt the crop. That is exactly the situation in our churches. The wheat and the tares are intermingled. It is possible for someone to walk the aisle, profess Christ, be baptized, and join the church without being truly born again. They enter the baptistry dry sinners and go home wet sinners.

I was holding a crusade in El Dorado, Arkansas, a few years ago, when a pastor gave a startling testimony at our Monday morning pastors' meeting. He announced, "Men, we had 140 people saved yesterday." Then he added, "But I was not one of them!" A few people started to laugh until he added, "But I should have been." Then he proceeded to relate his story. "Last night," he explained, "I went home under deep conviction. At 3:00 a.m. I awakened my wife, told her I was not really saved, and asked her to pray with me."

As we all rejoiced with him over his new experience with Christ, he said, "Let me tell you how I became a tare in God's field. I was brought up in a church in the city. One Sunday I vividly recall the pastor pleading with people to come forward. I left my seat and walked the aisle, but that is all I did. I never prayed or called upon the Lord to save me. No one talked to me or prayed with me personally. Later I graduated from a Southern Baptist college and a Southern Baptist seminary. Then I entered the ministry and became a pastor – all without ever having been born again!"

I remember preaching for Dr. Ron Herrod at the First Baptist Church in Fort Smith, Arkansas. During the invitation, an elegant 69-year-old woman came forward to talk with me. She had five sons in the ministry.

"I've known for 30 years that I was lost," she said soberly, "but pride kept me from admitting it," she added.

During the invitation that night, she explained that she could picture herself in the intense flames of hell, screaming, "At least I kept my pride!"

"It was as though God said to me," she went on, "What good is pride in the lake of fire?"

My friend, you can go to hell because of your pride if you want to, but it won't lower the temperature one degree! Ultimately, it doesn't matter what others think. It only matters what God thinks. The Bible says, "God resisteth the proud, but giveth grace unto the humble" (James 4:6). Whenever we let God break our pride, He will always give us grace to live for Him.

Tares can appear anywhere that you find true believers. Wheat and tares sit in the same choir loft. They serve on the same committee. They belong to the same denomination. Tares can serve as pastors, deacons, missionaries, evangelists, singers, ushers, youth workers, or in a host of other positions. Tares and wheat always appear side by side.

SIMILARITY OF THE PROGRESS

Wheat and tares look so much alike that it is impossible to tell them apart. They grow in the same field, at the same rate, and outwardly appear to be identical. Trying to distinguish the one from the other merely by sight would be like trying to tell the difference between a glass of artesian well water and a glass of city water without tasting either. Similarly, there is no obvious difference between a loaded gun and an empty gun until you pull the trigger!

Outwardly, there is often no obvious difference between a heaven-bound church member and a hell-bound church member. But the eternal consequences are so great that it is not worth taking the risk if you have any doubts about your ultimate destination.

"How can lost church members appear to be saved?" I have often been asked. They can tithe, increase their missions giving, become more faithful in attendance, read the Bible, pray and even witness to others – all in the arm of the flesh. People often serve God out of a mere sense of religious duty or by outward conformity to the expectations of others without inward response to the convicting ministry of the Holy Spirit.

A well-known and highly respected woman in one of my previous churches came under such conviction. She had all the outward appearance of being a dynamic and growing Christian. Her husband was a prominent denominational leader. She told me that she knew something was wrong in her life. Even her church work had become a perfunctory labor of self-effort, but when she admitted that she was a tare in God's wheat field, she was gloriously saved and transformed.

I am seeing this kind of conviction repeated again and again across America. A gospel singer once grabbed me by the arm and confessed with tears in his eyes, "If it were not for you, I would be headed straight for hell." He went on to explain that someone had given him a tape of this message, he had listened to it on the bus, and trusted Christ as his personal Savior.

Such is the convicting work of the Holy Spirit. He uses the truth of the Word of God to convict us of sin and unbelief and draw us to Christ who alone can save us. All the working, serving, singing and preaching in the world will not transform your life. Only Jesus Christ can regenerate your heart.

SOURCE OF THE PROBLEM

Both the wheat and the tares were planted to good soil and shared the same atmosphere, nutrients, and growth. But only one had the kernel of grain. The other was an empty sham.

Jesus taught that the tares were planted by the enemy, the devil. They came from the wrong source; therefore, they produced the wrong results. Both were planted, but only the wheat was planted by God. The real source of the problem was Satan. He planted the tares among the wheat. I am convinced that many church members are going to hell because their faith is in their faulty experience and not in the finished work of Christ. The Bible tells us that salvation is of grace. We cannot earn it, and we do not deserve it. Therefore, we can only receive it by faith in the death of Christ as the sufficient payment for our sins.

I was a pastor for nearly 30 years. I have heard hundreds of personal testimonies – some good, some not so good. Many times someone would say something like this: "When I was a child, I attended a revival where they preached about hell. I went down the aisle that night and took the preacher's hand. Afterwards the stars seemed brighter, the grass was greener, and the flowers, more radiant. It was glorious!"

How many times I wanted to interrupt them and ask, "But what about Jesus?" What people are often describing in testimony is an emotional experience. No matter how exhilarating one's experience may be, it is not the experience that saves one but the *fact* that Christ died for one's sins. Satan doesn't mind a person having euphoria over an emotional moment, just so long as they miss Jesus in the process.

Our crusade team was at a church a few years ago, when the music director's wife made a public profession of faith in Christ. She explained that as a child she walked the aisle to receive Christ and someone handed her a packet with a form letter inside which said, "Welcome to our church family. Be here tonight at 6:30 p.m. with a change of clothing to be baptized." She stated that no one talked to her about repenting of her sins or receiving Christ by faith into her life. No one prayed with her or helped her in any way to understand *what* to do to be saved. She was baptized and received as a member of the church without ever being born again.

The goal of the ministry is not to enlist people for the church but to introduce them to Jesus! He will get them into the church and eventually into heaven. All the emotional experiences or good intentions in the world will not save your soul or change your life.

SORROW OF THE PROCESS

In that fateful Day of Judgment, God Himself will separate the wheat (true believers) from the tares (unbelievers). Only God knows the hearts of men and women. Therefore, He alone can examine our lives and discern the saved from the unsaved. You and I can never know for certain that someone else is truly saved, but we can come to know for sure whether or not we ourselves are saved.

Too many people try to usurp the Holy Spirit and say, "Oh, I know that he or she is saved." No, you do not know that for sure! Only God knows who is truly saved. It is not our job to decide who is or is not saved. It is our job to help every professing believer to examine himself to see whether or not he is truly born again. Only the Spirit of God can reveal to you whether or not you are the wheat or the tare.

Some will always argue that the devil is only trying to make them doubt their salvation. Now it is certainly possible that Satan would tempt a true believer to doubt his conversion. The longer one wrestles with such doubts, the more he will expend his spiritual energy struggling with doubts rather than serving God. Many a Christian has been bogged down in what Bunyan called the "slough of despond" in the *Pilgrim's Progress*.

It has been my observation, though, that many people who struggle with doubts about their salvation have good reason to struggle. They are keenly aware that something is missing in their lives. They could be going through all the outward motions of Christianity without having the risen Christ within their hearts. The devil certainly doesn't want unsaved church members to doubt their salvation, repent, and receive Christ.

I have witnessed to people who were Mormons, Jehovah's Witnesses, Moonies, and a dozen other cults, and every one of them was convinced they were right with God. Satan had so blinded each one that none of them wanted to believe he was lost or in need of a Savior. They had no doubts about their beliefs, but they were lost because they were trusting the wrong thing to get them to heaven.

"How does one become a tare?" you may ask. I believe the devil deceives people in three different areas: good works, good faith and good people.

Some are depending on their *good works* to get them to heaven. "I'm just as good as the next guy," they will alibi. "I'm doing the best I can" is another excuse. The problem is that works cannot save us because none of us is good enough to work our way to heaven.

Even *good faith* won't save you if the object of your faith is anything other than Christ. You could believe in soap and die dirty. The Bible reminds us that even the devils believe God's truth, but they aren't saved by it (James 2:19). You could believe in all the "fundamentals of the faith" and still be lost. Believing that Christ died as a fact of history is not the same as believing that He died personally for your sins.

Being around *good people* will not save you either. Some take comfort in being in church because they feel safe around God's people. But when the judgment comes, they will have to stand there all alone, facing God in their sins. Unfortunately, some people become tares by the mistakes of good people. I will never forget a young woman who came forward with her father, weeping as she walked. "Daddy," she said, "When I was twelve I came forward to receive Christ. You met me and prayed for me, but you never let me pray and ask Christ to save me. All these years I've known I really wasn't saved."

Her father did not mean to give her wrong advice. He so desperately wanted her to accept Christ that he tried to do it all for her. Can I remind you that no one can pray the sinner's prayer for you? *You* must pray it for yourself!

The young woman's father later told me that his first instinct was to try to tell his daughter that she was already saved. "But if at the judgment," he said, "I learned that she had already been saved, I could live with that. I would be glad that she made sure of it." Then he added, "But if I learned at the judgment that she had never truly been saved, and I talked her out of it and she died lost, I couldn't live with myself!"

My friend, eternity is too long to be wrong. A few years ago, one of our greatest crusades was held at the First Baptist Church in Tampa, Florida. On the closing Sunday morning, Dr. Marvin Gibson baptized 121 people. As the pastor extended the invitation, one young man came forward and said, "I almost didn't come because I was 99 percent sure I was saved, but God convicted me that I wasn't 99 percent sure, I was just 99 percent saved, and that meant I was 100 percent lost!"

Only you can decide with the help of the Holy Spirit whether or not you have ever really been saved. Salvation is a life-changing experience that occurs at the moment of faith when you repent of your sins, believe that Jesus died to save you, and submit your life by faith to Him. The Bible says, "For Christ also hath once suffered for sins, the just for the unjust, that he might bring us to God" *(1 Peter 3:18)*. He suffered and died for you so you could know for sure that your sins are forgiven and that you are on your way to heaven.

Don't be content to be almost sure you are saved. Remember, a king named Agrippa once told the apostle Paul, "Almost thou persuadest me to be a Christian" (Acts 26:28). "Almost" wasn't good enough for Agrippa, and it won't be good enough for you either. Make sure today that you are really saved. Examine yourself to see if you are in the faith.. Don't wait for the day of judgment when the wheat shall be separated from the tares.

Then, it will be too late.

2

IT'S STILL THE CROSS

DR. JOHNNY HUNT

Senior Pastor

First Baptist Church

Woodstock, Georgia

IN 1 CORINTHIANS 1:18, THE BIBLE SAYS that,

"For the message of the cross is foolishness to those who are
perishing, but to us who are being saved it is the power of God. For
it is written: 'I will destroy the wisdom of the wise, and bring to
nothing the understanding of the prudent.' "Where is the wise?
Where is the scribe? Where is the disputer of this age? Has not God
made foolish the wisdom of this world? For since, in the wisdom of
God, the world through wisdom did not know God, it pleased God
through the foolishness of the message preached to save those who
believe. For Jews request a sign, and Greeks seek after wisdom; but
we preach Christ crucified, to the Jews a stumbling block and to the
Greeks foolishness, but to those who are called, both Jew and Greeks,
Christ the power of God and the wisdom of God. Because the
foolishness of God is wiser than men, and the weakness of God is
stronger than men."

In 1 Corinthians, chapter one, verse 17, Paul clarified the nature of his mission, namely to teach the gospel. He proceeded to identify the central feature of the preaching of the gospel, namely the cross of Christ. For over 2000 years now, the sign and symbol of the Christian faith has been an old rugged cross. It is the message of the cross which is the heart of the gospel. Some of the church's greatest hymns and songs are about the cross; for instance, "The Old Rugged Cross," "At Calvary," "At the Cross." And my wife's favorite, "When I Survey the Wondrous Cross." Paul made a tremendous statement concerning the cross in Galatians 6:14. He said, *"But God forbid that I should boast except in the cross of our Lord Jesus Christ, by whom the world has been crucified to me, and I to the world."* Someone said to Charles Haddon Spurgeon, "Mr. Spurgeon, all of your sermons sound exactly the same, why is that?" Spurgeon responded, "Because I just take a text anywhere in the Bible and then make a beeline straight to the cross." With that in mind, I want to take a moment and give you a couple of truths about the cross – "It is still the cross."

First of all, let me talk to you about the dynamics of the cross. In verse 18, the Bible says that *"the message of the cross is foolishness to those who are perishing."* In the first part of this phrase, the word "message" is a little word that translates "word." It is the exact same word we find in John chapter one for the word *logos*. It means the whole totality of truth. So, the cross is the heart of the gospel and the central theme of Christianity. The word of the cross includes the entire gospel message and work. God's plan and provision is for man to be saved, so Christ's work on the cross is the pinnacle of God's revealed word. No wonder Paul said in Romans 1:16, *"For I am not ashamed of the gospel of Christ, for it is the power of God to salvation for everyone who believes; for the Jew first, and also for the Greek."* Now in this dynamic of the cross, I want to show you three different views.

First of all, there is the foolishness of the cross. Now pay attention to this absolutely accurate statement: The Lord Jesus Christ has called me not to foolish preaching, but to a message that is foolish. The word "foolishness" in our Greek New Testament is where we derive a little word in the English language *moria*. It means that the message God has called me to preach is a message of absurdity. It means that it's nonsense. It is absolutely accurate when an unbeliever comes to our services and hears how the cross has changed someone's life. He said to a man who has never been saved, who is perishing, this message is absurdity. That anything significant should be accomplished through the death of a carpenter of Nazareth was sure absurdity to the Greek and Jewish minds. That one man, even the Son of God, could die on a piece of wood, a stick, on a nondescript hill and in a nondescript part of the world, and thereby determine the destiny of every person who has ever lived, seems stupid. It allows no place for man's merit, no place for man's intelligence, no place for man's understanding, and no place for man's pride. "It is still the cross." So this is how the cross is viewed by unbelievers who rely on their own wisdom.

One of our families once brought some non-church attenders and non-believers to our service, which is not unusual. They were nervous, and they said that they prayed, "Lord, ask Pastor Johnny to have kind of a toned-down message. Ask him not to offend in anything he says, and, you know, just sort of have a sweet little message where you can go to hell comfortable." It just happened to be that day that I was waxing the elephant; I dealt with about every issue you can deal with. That couple bowed their heads and thought, "Oh, Lord, they will be offended and will never come back." During the invitation, that couple told me they bowed their heads, and when they looked up, their guests were at the alter giving their lives to Jesus Christ. "IT IS STILL THE CROSS!"

So what is foolishness to this world are the power of God and the wisdom of God according to the Scriptures. Now, let me just make a statement to you.

If you ever bring a guest with you to church, and on your way home in your automobile, you ask, "How did you like the message?" and they reply, "Nonsense," don't you ever try to defend me, don't you ever try to defend this message. To the unbeliever, this message, until you embrace the cross, is absolute absurdity. How could someone who lived 2000 years ago, born supposedly of a virgin, in a stable, raised in an obscure village of Nazareth, born in an obscure town of Bethlehem, live a sinless life for 33-1/2 years, die on Good Friday, and then get up from the dead on Sunday morning? How in the world could someone 2000 years ago change me today? That's absurdity! But once you come to Christ, it is the power of God and the wisdom of God, and so the Bible speaks of the foolishness of the cross.

Let me go a step further. There is another dynamic I noticed in this text. It is what I call "the force of the cross." The Bible says that the message of the cross is foolishness, but to us who have been saved, it is the power of God. A man might ask, "How could the blood of such a person remove my sins, give me perfect righteousness and guarantee me hope beyond the grave?" Well, sir, the power of God, the dynamic of Jesus Christ and the vindication of the cross are not wisdom, but it makes sense. That power, it works. It changes lives! I have not been able to explain how God can do it. But God changes lives through the power of the cross. Some people say, "Well, I'll tell you one thing, you'll never convince me of that message until I can figure it out." But you will never figure out the message of the cross; and by the way, there are lots of things that I can't figure out that I enjoy every day.

On one occasion I flew over to Dallas, and I got this little phone the church provided for me, small enough to fit down in my pocket. I took it out, pushed the power button and talked with somebody back in Atlanta. I do not understand how that gadget works, but I am going to continue to use it even though I don't understand it. I got up this morning early, it was dark, so I turned the switch and a light came on. I don't understand that. The only thing that I understand is, if it doesn't come on, change the bulb, if that doesn't work, call the electrician. But I will tell you something, I don't plan to sit in the dark until I figure out electricity, I just thank God for it, and I am going to use it. Seriously, I don't understand how, on a chilly Sunday night, 27 years ago, on my way to hell, lost, with no focus and direction in my life, I don't understand how I could in simple and childlike faith say, "I'm a sinner, and I embrace Jesus Christ as my Savior, I believe He died on the cross, I believe in Good Friday, I believe in resurrection Sunday," and He could change my life. I don't understand it, but I have been experiencing the life of Christ for 27 blessed years. It is the power of God. It makes saints out of sinners, makes preachers out of blasphemers. The cross is the manifestation of the power of God at work in our lives.

Second Corinthians 5:21 puts it this way, *"He made Him who knew no sin to be sin on our behalf, so that we might become the righteousness of God in Him."* Listen to Paul's testimony found in 1 Timothy 1:12-13, *"And I thank Christ Jesus our Lord who has enabled me, because He counted me faithful, putting me into the ministry, although I was formerly a blasphemer, a persecutor, and an insolent man...,"* which means he was arrogantly proud, *"...but I obtained mercy because I did it ignorantly in unbelief."* And so we see in our Bibles that there is the foolishness of the cross. You just can't understand it.

But there is another dynamic; it is what I call the force of the cross. When Paul is preaching, he reaches back 600 years to Isaiah chapter 29, verse 14, and there is one verse that gives a story of the power of God.

"Therefore, behold, I will again do a marvelous work among this people,
a marvelous work and a wonder; for the wisdom of their wise men shall
perish, and the understanding of their prudent men shall be hidden."

Now what does this verse have to do with the power of God? The verse speaks of an event in Israel's past. The Assyrians were threatening the southern kingdom of Israel, known as Judah. The counselors of the Jewish king came and advised that he have an alliance with Egypt. They said the only way to defend against the Assyrians was to bring in the allegiance of another nation. But then, there was a preacher there by the name of Isaiah, and God spoke to him and said in effect, "Go tell that king that I oppose his alliance with Egypt and appeal to that king to trust in Me alone." Well, the Bible says that the king and the people who advised the king began to mock the name of God. And they said, "Are you crazy? There is no way that we, a small nation in the southern part of Israel, can go against the entire Assyrian nation!" However, history tells us that Egypt never came to their rescue, but God did. You know what happened? They lay down, planning to go to battle the next morning, and my Bible records that when they got up there were 186,000 Assyrians slain by – listen – by one angel of God. You see, men had devised a program for personal assistive redemption in which they tried to save themselves, to trust themselves, and not God. A lot of people, instead of coming by way of the cross, would say, "You know what I am going to do? I'm going to do a religious thing. I'm under conviction; I am going to join the church." You can join the church, but when you die, you'll spend eternity separated from God. Some would say, "You know something? I am just gonna get baptized." You can be baptized so many times that it equals your Social Security number and spend eternity separated from God. Baptism will get you church membership, but it won't get you the cross. IT IS STILL THE CROSS. And so today, what I am telling you, what you need in your life is the power of God to change your life.

Proverbs 14:12 says this, "*There is a way that seems right to a man, but its end is the way of death.*" Reread that statement. Not only is there the dynamics of the cross, let me for just a moment talk to you about the dividing of the cross. Did you know that the cross is a great divider? Focus your mind on that cross for just a moment. Listen to this statement, "The cross either stands between you and heaven or between you and hell." For instance, the cross stands between me and hell, I cannot go to hell because I have embraced the cross, THE CROSS is keeping me from going to hell when I die. It does more than that, but it does that. However, the cross also stands between some of you and heaven because you cannot go to heaven but by way of the cross. It is the CROSS that leads home. The way of the cross leads home. So, if someone says, "I've been a good person, I've pulled myself up by my own boot straps, I am not going to bow down and acknowledge that Jesus is Lord and come by way of the cross," the Bible says that the CROSS stands between that person and heaven. The cross, if you have embraced it, stands between you and hell, or if you have not embraced it, stands between you and heaven. And so the cross is a great divider.

The Bible says that the cross divides, first of all, those who are believing. The Bible says in verse number 18 that "the cross is the power of God" – focus on these words – "*to those who have been saved.*" In the Greek text, it is a present tense verb there that says "whom I do save." God is doing a work in my life, and one day He will bring it to fruition and bring it to total completion. There is a present tense verb there, but it is a passive voice. "Pastor Johnny, why are you telling me this?" A passive verb in the language of the New Testament indicates the inability of those who are being saved to accomplish that end in their own strength. It is God who is acting to save them through His own power. Here is what it means, watch carefully; this verse here means that apart from God coming into my life, I have no hope of ever going to heaven. It means nobody can get there on his own. It means you must be acted upon by an outside force. So, somebody that knew me 27 years ago maybe said, "Man, you were a drunkard, you were running a pool hall, and you have been an alcoholic since you were about eleven years old, which is hard to believe, you had no purpose, no direction in life, a high school dropout, and now you are preaching the gospel." IT IS THE CROSS! IT IS THE POWER OF GOD that changed my life! It is the wisdom of God, but He did just that. I was acted upon by another. Someone says, "Man, what happened to you?" God got hold of me, God gave His ability. Someone says, "Oh, you can't change your life," and they are exactly right. You can turn over a new leaf, but Jesus Christ can give you a new life, and that is what it is all about. It is the cross! It says that the cross is the power of God to those who are being saved. Let me illustrate: When I was under conviction of the Spirit of God, although I was not a Christian, I was 20 years old…I heard the message of the cross…I was concerned…I knew I needed to be saved…I knew I needed Christ. I knew there was a hole in my heart and there was a fire in my belly that nothing could quench. And I was told by the preacher, and I was told by my wife, that I should get right with the Lord, that I needed the Lord. But I began to say to my wife, Janet, "I know this is what I need, but honey, you need to realize, I am going to the Red Sox saloon regularly; I am gambling as heavy as I ever have on the pool table," and I said, "I just want to say to you, that I am going to go to church, and I am going to make a decision for Jesus Christ, but listen to this, if God does not change me, don't you get on me about going back and getting drunk; don't you get on me about going back to the bar."

But I am telling you, on that Sunday night, God met me right back there, and by the ability of heaven, God through the CROSS changed my life. And if not, I would be a hypocrite today to stand up here and preach about something that influenced and affected my life. It takes Him changing it!

Some of you say, "I am going to change my life and start being a good person." If you change your life, you'll go to hell good. It is only through the CROSS, it is only through the CROSS that a man comes to God.

One of my favorite old hymns simply says, "Years I spent in vanity and pride, caring not my Lord was crucified, knowing not it was for me He died at Calvary. Mercy there was grace and grace was free, pardon there was multiplied to me, there my burdened soul found liberty at Calvary." It is still the cross. Let me say two things about the cross today that have not been said.

I want you to see a certain verse because you are going to think, "Man, is that in the Bible?" Notice what it says in 1 Corinthians 1:21, "...*the world through wisdom did not know God...*" Is that not amazing? Did you see that? "...*The world through wisdom did not know God.*" You can have four Ph.D.s from Harvard University and not know God. Listen, you can be a person who can't read and you can know God. You don't come to God through human wisdom. As a matter of fact, the Lord Jesus Christ, God in the flesh, once took a child and put him on His knee, and said to the disciples into whose lives He poured three and one-half years, "Except you become like a little child and be converted, you cannot enter the kingdom of God." Jesus invited the adults to come like children. But we are inviting children to come like adults. He was saying it is not based on human wisdom, He was saying that through wisdom they did not know God. Somebody says, "I'll tell you what I am going to do; I am going to research religion." I have an uncle who is into comparative religion. He is more confused than a termite in a yo-yo. You don't come to God with human wisdom. You come to Jesus by embracing the cross in faith.

Some might say, "Man, that sounds stupid, but I tell you what I am going to do; I am going to get up out of my seat, and I am going to trust Jesus Christ as my personal Savior. And if He is not who He says He is, and He doesn't change my life, I have lost nothing." Thirty years ago Jesus changed my life. So, I got hooked, and I have been preaching and telling people all over the world. And you know what? Thousands, literally millions, literally billions have trusted Him and have found Him to be true.

Now consider this, "It pleased God through the foolishness of the message preached to save those who believe." Salvation comes only through faith in the message of the cross. It is not foolish preaching that pleases God. It is the preaching of a foolish nothing. There is a bunch of foolish preaching out there. I remember when I got saved and God called me to preach, I was 22 years old, had only been a Christian two years, and God called me to preach. So I thought I needed to go up to a Bible college, which I did. I went to seminary. And God used that in my life. But I remember when I got ready to go get my education, somebody asked me, "So why are you going to school?" I said, "Man, I just need to know the Bible better." And he said, "Oh, if God called you to go preach, boy, go preach!" What that meant is, don't study, just open the Bible and whatever comes to mind, say it. I want to tell you something, folks, if I did that, that would be some pretty doggone foolish preaching. God has not called me to foolish preaching; He has called me to preach a foolish message. Now, somebody may say, "He is a foolish preacher," but it is really not that I am a foolish preacher; I'm just preaching a foolish message. And so then people just say, "You know what? We are living in a sophisticated nation now; instead of having this foolish message, why don't we just dress it up some? Let's make it easier for people to accept." Look, a lot of people try to dress it up, and what they do is dress it down, and they are preaching, but they are not preaching the gospel, and they are not preaching the cross, and it is the cross that still changes lives. That's where the power of God lies. You explain to me how I could have a father who left me when I was seven years old, how I started drinking when I was eleven, was raised in the government projects, had no focus and no direction in life, managed a pool room for four years, and now I preach the gospel. The only explanation is the power of God.

So, it is not foolish preaching that pleases God, it is the foolishness of the message being preached. The preaching does not refer to the act of declaring the message, but to the content of the message. Friends, the content of God's message is the gospel of the power of the Christ, the word of the Christ, the power of God. It does not refer to a special technique of oral communication; rather it pertains to the content of the message that is declared.

I was greatly honored once to preach at the First Baptist Church of Dallas, Texas. Sitting down in front of me was Dr. W. A. Criswell, Pastor Emeritus, and a lifelong buddy to me. He came to hear me preach and sat on the front row. He was 90 years old. They wheeled him in with a wheelchair. He asked me if he could pray for me before I preached, and the building was standing room only. He began to pray for me, and I was standing beside him, he was patting my leg, and he said, "Preach it Lord, preach it." And it finally occurred to me that for 55 years he was the pastor of that church, and that pastor was bigger than life to me. He was such an eloquent preacher. I remember when he preached, he had a golden tongue, and he had mastered the vocabulary, something I have never been able to do. He was such a great preacher, he was so intimidating, and I was so intimidated. You know what I wanted to do? I wanted to throw my Bible up and ask that man if I could carry his briefcase, and say that I was not worthy to be in the ministry. But then God said to me, "It is not in the oral communication, it is not your ability, it is not whether you have veins popping out and your face turning red, and you sweat and you stomp and you run. That's not it." He said, "It doesn't matter what style you use, what really matters is the content of your message." It is not rip- roaring preaching that saves, it is the power of God, and God is the only one who can change somebody's life." That's the bottom line!

Somebody says, "I like somebody who is calm." That's fine, as long as he preaches the CROSS. Another says, "I like a more subdued service; this service is too noisy, and that doesn't matter as long as they're preaching the CROSS.

But, if they are not preaching the cross, I don't care about it! They are not giving you the truth!

About those who are believing, I want you to consider this: The Bible is divided not only to those who are believing, but to those who are perishing. Do you see that same present tense verb form? Do you see it in your Bible, in verse 18? He said that to those who believe, it is the power of God, who are believing, who are being saved. But do you also see that the message of the cross is foolishness to those who are perishing, present tense. I want you to pay close attention to my heart. The word "perishing" does not describe a future possibility, but a present reality. I've always been a witness for Jesus Christ. When I am with someone socially, if I am ever invited to go to lunch with you or something, and you and I are talking, most likely I make you this commitment, sometime between our time of meeting and departure, I am going to talk to you about your relationship with Jesus Christ. I'm just going to get bold and say, "Is there a time in your life that you've trusted Jesus Christ?" I mean, I'm just going to tell you, I'm just going to be honest, I have no close associate in the world to whom I have not presented the gospel. I'm serious, under God. But here's what it says, "It is not a future possibility, it is a present reality." When I got burdened over my family, it was not because I said, "I better get to them or one day they will perish." No, the Bible says they are already in the process of perishing. So, it is a present reality. Some of you have family members that have never been saved, and you are thinking, "Look, they are going to perish." No, they <u>are</u> perishing. Do you remember what Jesus Christ said in John 3:18? He said, *"He who believes in Him is not condemned; but he who does not believe is condemned already..."* By the way, do you know what the previous verse says? *"For God did not send His Son into the world to condemn the world, but that the world through Him might be saved."* You know why He didn't come to condemn the world? It was already condemned! How can you condemn something that is already condemned?

So, if somebody says to me, "You know, Brother Johnny speaks kind of harsh, and is kind of condemning." No, this is not a condemning message; this is a saving message about preaching protection in the cross. You are already perishing! So, you can't blame me for what is already happening in your life. You are already perishing.

Now, do you remember a moment ago I told you that the word for being saved is present tense, that it is in the passive voice, that it was acted upon by an outside force? Let me just ask you a question: Have you been changed by the power of God? All right, let me just say this to you, do you know how that happened? God did it. Give credit where credit is due – God did it.

And if your life has not been changed, it is because you have resisted the power of God. Now, that's the passive voice. But now we've got a different voice here. And you just find this in the Greek text. When the Bible says you are perishing, it is now an inner voice. You are not perishing from the outside; it is an inside decision. It is the same exact Greek word (and I am not much on Greek words, but this is one of five I know that I have memorized), *apolluma*. Let me tell you why I memorized it. "For God so loved the world that He gave His only begotten Son, that whosoever believeth in Him should not perish – *apolluma* – but have everlasting life."

Somebody says to me, "Brother Johnny, I tell you one thing, God would never send anybody to hell." High five, my man, I am with you! He would never, and never has sent anybody, but allows them to *apolluma* in their own little voice, inside themselves. God has been trying to save them, but they chose in and of their own volition to say, "I refuse to know Christ, I want to go to hell, I want to be a crispy critter." Well, act upon yourselves. Somebody may say, "I tell ya, I'm perishing because my mom and dad turned me off, that's my truth." And as soon as somebody tells you that, it's a lie of hell. "So how did they turn you off?" "They made me go to church." "I see; are those the same ones who made you brush your teeth? Did you go shoot the dentist?" By the way, most likely your parents made you do some things far more difficult in your life than go to church. Are those the same ones who made you wash behind your ears? Did you say, "I'll show them, I'll never wash again!" Don't ever go to hell because of something so stupid. Now the message I am preaching may be absurdity, but it will become the power of God in your life when you embrace it. So now, to be saved, there must be an outside power to change you. Someone asked me once, "What do you believe somebody's got to do to go to hell?" And I said, "Nothing! Absolutely nothing!" Some would say, "Man, he deserves to go to hell, you know what he did?" Well, we all deserve to go to hell if you want to get down to the bottom line. Jesus Christ took our hell on Himself at the cross so that we can know Him and be changed by the power of God.

I close with this. The Greek word *perish* means to be loosed from something. In other words, those who refuse to believe are being continually loosed from any relationship with God. I have been a minister for 28 years. People call me every now and then and say, "Hey, I want you to pray for my husband, he is getting close." And I say, "Well, praise the Lord!" They say, "He's getting close, he is starting to come, he is getting close to making a decision." A year later, I ask, "How's it going?" and they say, "Well, I don't know what happened, but he is just further and further away." You see, the more you say no to receiving Christ and embracing the cross, the easier it is to say no the next time. And the greatest the need in your life may be what you are resisting more than anything else in your life.

So, the only way you will go to heaven is by embracing the cross of Jesus Christ. Jesus Christ said, "I am the way, the truth and the life. No one comes to the Father except through Me." I believe that with all of my heart. And I'll tell you why I believe it, not because I can explain it, and not because it makes sense, but because it has worked. I am a satisfied customer. I embraced the cross 30 years ago and I have been changed. I was not a good man to be around. As a matter of fact, when I went to Janet's house to meet her daddy, he was not a happy camper. I was not a Christian. I'm not the type of guy you want your daughter to bring home, but within two years, Jesus radically changed me. God changed my life. That's what I want to say to you, Jesus Christ, through the cross of Christ, changed my life. And thanks to Calvary, I am not the man I used to be. The same thing can happen to your life.

3

GOD'S WAKE-UP CALL

Dr. Steve Gaines

Senior Pastor

Bellevue Baptist Church

Memphis, Tennessee

SEVERAL YEARS AGO THE ASSOCIATED PRESS released a story about a 20-year-old man named Gene Tipps of Seymour, Texas. On May 21, 1967, Mr. Tipps was involved in a very serious automobile accident in which he suffered severe head injuries. He was in a coma for three weeks, after which he remained in a state of unconsciousness for eight solid years. During that extended period of time this was his daily routine — his parents would prop him up in bed, move him to a chair, brace him up by putting pillows around him, and then feed him. They would usually have to open his mouth and help move his jaw so he could chew the food. He would then swallow. When he finished eating, they would comb his hair, talk to him for a while, and then put him back to bed. For eight long years that was his daily experience. Then, one day after all those years of slumber Gene Tipps woke up! His nurse was startled because she was trying to give him some medicine when he awakened. His parents ran to him and shouted for joy. They called the doctor. Everyone was thrilled and shocked simultaneously.

Later someone asked him, "What was it like to be asleep for eight years?" Tipps replied, "It's all very strange. My girlfriend is now married and has children. The war in Vietnam is over. To everyone else I am 28, but in my mind

I am still only 20."

As I thought about that time period, I realized that he slept from 1967 until 1975, the year I graduated from high school. He went to sleep when Lyndon Baines Johnson was President of the United States and woke up with Jimmy Carter smiling in the White House. He slept right through Richard Nixon!

Can you imagine sleeping for eight years? But I know a group, dear friends, that has been asleep five times longer than that. I am talking about the Church of the Lord Jesus Christ in the United States of America. Since the 1950s, we have been asleep.

Some of you can remember back to the 1950s. That is the last time God moved on a large scale in our country, except for a little blip on the radar screen of revival we call the "Jesus Movement" at the end of the Sixties and the early Seventies. The Fifties were post World War II days. The economy was good. Patriotism was high. Billy Graham began to fill stadiums as he preached the gospel of Jesus Christ. Southern Baptists were aggressive soul winners. We didn't have to worry about moderates and liberals. We were focused on winning "A Million More in '54."

But toward the end of that great decade, the churches across this land said, in effect, "We have worked hard. Let's take a rest." And when God's people went to sleep, the devil began to prowl and ravage our land. The 1960s were the most turbulent years of our nation's history. We expelled God, prayer, and the Bible from our public schools. The hippies ushered in the drug culture. We were sending our boys to the rice patties of a little country called Vietnam. The Beatles brought modern rock 'n roll to our shores. Racial violence rocked our inner cities. The three tragic assassinations of John Kennedy in 1963, Bobby Kennedy in 1968, and Martin Luther King, Jr. in 1968 sent our nation into a tailspin.

As we continued to sleep, the 1970s dawned. With them the radical feminist movement emerged. The Supreme Court decided that unborn babies have no rights, and abortion on demand was legalized. The Watergate scandal prompted President Nixon to lie to us all on television. As a high school senior, I listened by radio as he resigned from the presidency. Inflation was high, and morals and patriotism were at an all-time low. Our soldiers had returned from Vietnam ashamed because our politicians did not allow them to win the war. We had an energy crisis that ushered in a flood of Japanese automobiles. A small country called Iran held some of our citizens hostage. In doing so, they held the greatest nation in the world hostage as well. We tried to send two helicopters to rescue them, but they crashed in the middle of the desert. It seemed that nothing in America was going right. Yet, despite the moral decay and corruption in our nation, the churches hit the snooze button, turned over in bed, pulled the covers over their heads, and continued to sleep.

Then came the 1980s. The New Age Movement emerged. There was widespread interest in the occult. Witchcraft, psychics and Satanists abounded. As America studied the horoscope, the churches were rocked by the moral failures of Jim Bakker and Jimmy Swaggart. Crack cocaine polluted our cities. Pornography polluted our minds. Gangs ravaged our inner cities. But the Church refused to wake up.

As we entered the 1990s, the Church, rather than getting out of bed, put a "Do Not Disturb" sign on the door. We elected a President who was pro-homosexual, placing gays in prominent positions throughout his administration. Mr. Clinton was also pro-abortion. Our Senate and our House had passed a bill that would have banned partial birth abortions. But our President vetoed that bill, indelibly staining his hands with the blood of all the innocent babies who have been butchered through that barbarous procedure. He appointed a Surgeon General who did not want our children to smoke cigarettes, but she didn't mind if they engaged in what she called "safe sex." After all, her boss, the President himself, was having sex with an intern inside the Oval Office! Meanwhile, the President's wife proposed the idea that our children would be better off if they were reared in a socialist "village" rather than in a normal home where one man was married to one woman for life.

Now we are in a new millennium. Is the Church waking up? The verdict is still out. A group of militant Muslims threatens our national security. On September 11, 2001, they brought the battle to American soil by destroying the Twin Towers in New York and by attacking our Pentagon. Bin Laden continues to make threats against all decent people who would oppose him. Our soldiers are fighting a bloody war in Iraq with the hopes of helping those desperate people to become a free, democratic society, instead of a nation in bondage, held captive by fundamentalist extremists.

On the home front, radical homosexuals and lesbians seek to take over our nation. You cannot watch television without being subjected to gay propaganda. They seek to brainwash our citizens so they can make same-sex marriage the law of the land. Homosexuals and lesbians cannot reproduce biologically so they prey on the children of normal people, seeking to entice them into being trapped in their perverted lifestyle. They want to silence Baptist preachers and others from denouncing their sinful lifestyles by making it an illegal "hate crime" to point out what the Bible says about their wicked practices. Regardless of what anyone says about the goodness of being "gay," the Bible still calls it "degrading, unnatural, indecent, and depraved" *(Romans 1:26-28)*. Homosexual practice always has been, is, and always will be "an abomination" in the sight of Holy God *(Leviticus 18:22)*. By God's grace, homosexuals can be saved and set free from their sinful lifestyles because the blood of Jesus can cleanse anyone from any sin. But they must first repent of the sin of homosexuality and denounce their ungodly homosexual behavior.

Are you aware that we have major problems in the United States of

America? We are a nation divided morally, spiritually, intellectually, and politically. Jesus Himself said in Luke 11:17, "Any kingdom divided against itself is laid waste; and a house divided against itself falls." Our churches as a whole have been asleep for over 50 years! It is time to wake up!

The Old Testament prophet, Joel, preached to God's people in Judah just before the Babylonian armies came and destroyed Jerusalem and took God's people into exile. He cried out for them to repent so that God could spare the land from the coming invasion. His words of warning are very pertinent for us today. I personally believe that if America does not repent, she is headed for national disaster. Hear the Word of the Lord:

> "Yet even now," declares the LORD, "Return to Me with all your heart, and with fasting, weeping and mourning; and rend your heart and not your garments." Now return to the LORD your God, for He is gracious and compassionate, slow to anger, abounding in loving-kindness and relenting of evil. Who knows whether He will not turn and relent and leave a blessing behind Him, even a grain offering and a drink offering for the LORD your God? Blow a trumpet in Zion, consecrate a fast, proclaim a solemn assembly, gather the people, sanctify the congregation, assemble the elders, gather the children and the nursing infants. Let the bridegroom come out of his room and the bride out of her bridal chamber. Let the priests, the LORD'S ministers, weep between the porch and the altar, and let them say, "Spare Your people, O LORD, and do not make Your inheritance a reproach, a byword among the nations. Why should they among the peoples say, 'Where is their God?'" *(Joel 2:12-17 NASB)*

God desires to send spiritual awakening. He is sounding an alarm. He is crying

THE LAST SERMON I WOULD PREACH

out to His people in America, saying, "It is time to get out of bed!" Let's look at our text and analyze God's wake-up call. Notice that it is a gracious call, a demanding call, and, thank God, it is a rewarding call.

A GRACIOUS CALL

First of all, we see that God's wake-up call is a gracious call. Notice what the Bible says in verse 12. "Yet even now," declares the Lord, "Return to Me." God was saying through His prophet, "Even now, Judah, though your women have poured out libation offerings before idols made of wood and stone; though your men have taken your little children down to the Valley of Hinnom in Jerusalem, where Molech the demon-god has an altar, to sacrifice your babies in the fire; even though your priesthood is corrupt, your politicians are scandalous, and your hands are stained with innocent blood; yet even now, return to Me with all your heart." *That*, my friend, is a gracious call!

In verse 13, God's gracious attributes are mentioned. It says that God is gracious, compassionate, and slow to anger. Aren't you glad He doesn't have a short fuse? Aren't you glad He is slow to anger? He is abounding in loving-kindness, He is relenting of evil. And notice verse 14 – "Who knows, if you will repent, He might forgive you." He doesn't have to. You don't deserve it, but He just might. "Who knows whether He will not turn and relent. Maybe He will leave a blessing behind Him, a grain offering and a libation for the Lord your God." Joel indicated to the people of Judah that God's wake-up call was a gracious one. I believe God is saying the same thing to America.

When I think about the grace of God, I think about another Old Testament prophet, Hosea. Hosea's life is a beautiful picture of the grace of God. Most of you know his story. The prophet found out that his wife, Gomer, was unfaithful to him just before she left him to become a street harlot.

He continued to preach, though his wife had abandoned him and their three small children. In all of that shame and humility, one day as he prayed, God said, "Go downtown, Hosea." As he walked along the streets, he came upon a very dangerous part of town where they sold slaves. The Lord said, "Hosea, I want you to go down this street today." He never asked a question. He simply obeyed the Lord. As he walked down that horrid street, he looked upon the disgusting sight of people being sold like cattle — human flesh being marketed like animals. As he looked, someone suddenly caught his eye. Could it be? There was a woman who looked a little bit like his wife, Gomer. Could it be that Gomer was still alive and now she was a slave? Sure enough, she was. This woman who had left in all of her pride, arrogance, and rebellion had been humbled by years of sin. Sin always fascinates, but then it always assassinates. The devil will promise you gold but he gives you dirt. Her head was hanging down in despair. God said to Hosea, "Buy her back. Pay whatever the price is. Buy her back and bring her home, Hosea. I want you to love her and protect her, and I want you to be kind to her. For just as she has been unfaithful to you, My people, Israel, have been unfaithful to Me. Even as she has committed physical adultery against you, My people, Israel, have been committing spiritual adultery against Me. Buy her back because I want to buy My people back. I want to use what is happening in your life as a prophetic illustration of My grace."

Now before you get too mad at Gomer and before you say that Hosea should have never bought her back, you had better realize that you and I are Gomer in that picture. We are the ones that Jesus bought when we were nothing but slaves to sin. Thank God for the grace and forgiveness of God. And God is saying to our country today, "America, you are wicked. America, you are secular. America, you don't pray any more. America, you have 'In God We Trust' all over your public buildings and even your currency, but you have turned your back on Me. Yet even now, I am gracious, compassionate, slow to anger, and abundant in loving-kindness. I will relent of evil if you will turn. I will forgive you." It is a gracious wake-up call.

A DEMANDING CALL

Not only is God's wake-up call a gracious call, but it is also a demanding call. God is not in the asking business. He is in the telling mode. Have you found that out? Sometimes I see children who are disobedient. I see parents letting their children hit them and talk back to them. Do you know what those children need? An old-fashioned spanking right on their bottoms is what they need. You might say, "Oh, but my pediatrician says that is wrong." Well, tell your pediatrician that he is wrong, because the Bible says that children should respect, honor and obey their parents. I have to tell our people that all the time. Just as a parent has the right to tell his children what to do, God has the right to tell His people what to do.

God wasn't asking Judah – He was telling them. God didn't ask them to wake up – He told them to wake up or else. He was very specific. Notice what He said. Turn back to chapter one of Joel and look at verse 13. He said "Gird yourselves with sackcloth and lament, O priests; wail, O ministers of the altar! Come, spend the night in sackcloth O ministers of my God…" In verse 14 He said, "Consecrate a fast, proclaim a solemn assembly..." Notice – sackcloth, lamenting, weeping, wailing, spending the night, fasting, solemn assembly – it is very serious. And those are the things He wants us to do as well.

Look at chapter two, verse 12 again. He said that He wanted "fasting, weeping and mourning." God was saying, "I am ready for you to get serious about this, Judah." Underline those words, "fasting, weeping and mourning." I will talk more about them in just a moment. That is *how* He wanted Judah to awaken. And then He said *who* He wanted awakened. Look at chapter one, verse 13 again. He said, "Wail, O ministers of the altar" and "lament, O priests." And look at chapter two, verse 17. He said, "Let the priests, the Lord's ministers, weep between the porch and the altar." Revival must start with the leadership. Revival will come only when the preachers and the leaders get right before God. But also the laity. Look at chapter 2, verse 16. He was saying, "Sanctify the entire congregation, assemble the old people, the elders and the children and even the nursing infants." In other words, "Get everybody together, it is going to take pulpit and pew, leaders and laity." That is *who* needed revival.

And then, God told them *when* they needed to be awakened. Notice verse 12 in chapter two. "Yet even *now*." Have you ever told your son to do something and he said, "Okay, I'll do it," but then you come back an hour later and it hasn't been done? Again you say, "Now, son, I want you to do this." And he replies again, "Okay, okay, I'll do it." But when you return, it is still not done. Then you have to be explicit. You say, "Come here, son. I want you to do it *now*." He replies, "Oh, *now?*" "Yes, *now, now, now, now!*"

God was saying to Judah, "Repent now!" How serious and urgent was it? Look at verse 16. "Let the bridegroom come out of his room and the bride out of her bridal chamber." Break up the wedding. There is something more important than two people getting married here, and it is revival.

And notice what He said in chapter two, verse 12. "Rend your heart and not your garments." And then He said in chapter two, verse 17, "Weep between the porch and the altar." Repent in your hearts and also at the place of prayer in your sanctuaries. And what were they to say to God? "Spare Your people, O Lord, and do not make us a reproach among the nations."

We can't continue to do the same old things and expect revival. Here is the difference — "fasting, weeping and mourning" and asking God to forgive you. You say, "Brother Steve, I have never fasted in my life." Well, it is time you learned how. God called me to a 40-day fast one summer. I fasted and got alone with God. God got a hold on my life and convicted me of some things and cleansed my heart. While I was fasting, my associate pastor fasted for 40 days, another staff member fasted for 21 days, and a host of people fasted for three and four days at a time. I don't know how to explain it, but the glory of God came down on our church when we fasted, prayed, and asked God to forgive our sins and the sins of this country. That is *how*.

And *who*? First, the leaders, the pastors. It starts in the pulpit. Can I tell you what would help America? If we could have some men who would stand in the pulpits and be more afraid of God than they are of their congregations, we could have revival in our country. I pray that God will rid us of wimpy preachers. Some of these guys come up and they are so pretty, and they are so polite, and they are so sweet, and they are telling everybody how good they are. I heard W.A. Criswell say, "I like to come up behind them and say, 'Boo!' and watch those sissies jump! It scares them to death." We need some men of God back in our pulpits. We don't need preacherettes preaching sermonettes to Christianettes. God give us some prophets who will preach and say, "Thus, saith the Lord," and let the chips fall where they may. If some deacon doesn't like it, good. If some Sunday School teacher doesn't like it, so what? We must preach for an audience of one – the Lord Jesus Christ! And not only the leaders but also the laity. You are going to have to get filthy magazines out of your home. You are going to have to get Hell's Box Office (HBO) out of your home. Consecrate yourself before God. Leaders and laity, everyone involved.

And *when*? Right now! Break up the wedding if you have to. There is something more important than your getting married. We need to have revival. We need to wake up.

And *where*? In our hearts, and in these beautiful sanctuaries of our churches. Thank God for prayer rails. I pray that God will let these beautiful wooden and carpeted steps and these rails be stained with hot tears for revival. I am convinced that if the Lord could awaken a few of our larger churches, He could send revival to the entire Southern Baptist Convention and then through all of America. If we will allow God to get a hold on our hearts; if we would rend our hearts and not our garments; if we would weep and fast and pray and say, "O God, spare Your people," I tell you, He would do it!

A Rewarding Call

God's wake-up call is a gracious call and a demanding call, and thirdly, it is a rewarding call. Look at chapter two, verse 18. It begins with the little word, "Then." Thank God that word is there. In other words, after you have done all this, "then" this is what the Lord is going to do:

Then the LORD will be zealous for His land, and will have pity *(mercy)* on His people. The LORD will answer and say to His people, "Behold I am going to send you grain, new wine and oil, and you will be satisfied in full with them; and I will never again make you a reproach among the nations. But I will remove the northern army far from you, and I will drive it into a parched and desolate land, and its vanguard into the eastern sea, and its rear guard into the western sea. And its stench will arise and its foul smell will come up, for it has done great things. Do not fear, O land, rejoice and be glad, for the LORD has done great things. Do not fear, beasts of the field, for the pastures of the wilderness have turned green, for the tree has borne its fruit, the fig tree and the vine have yielded in full. So rejoice, O sons of Zion, and be glad in the LORD your God; for He has given you the early rain for your vindication and He has poured down for you the rain, the early and latter rain as before. The threshing floors will once again be full of grain, and the vats will overflow with the new wine and oil." *(Joel 2:18-24 NASB)*

Now look at verses 25 through 27:

"Then I will make up to you for the years that the swarming locust has eaten, the creeping locust, the stripping locust and the gnawing locust, My great army which I sent among you. You will have plenty to eat and be satisfied and praise the name of the LORD your God, who has dealt wondrously with you; then My people will never be put to shame. Thus you will know that I am in the midst of Israel, and that I am the LORD your God, and there is no other; and My people will never be put to shame." *(Joel 2:25-27 NASB)*

God can make up for the 50 years we have been asleep if we will repent and let Him send revival!

Several years ago, my family and I were in some of the great cities in the northeastern part of our nation. We went to Washington, New York, Philadelphia and Boston, to name a few. In all of those cities, I saw many church buildings, but virtually none of them had the power and presence of God. Most of them were more like museums than churches. By the time we got to Boston, I was absolutely convinced that our nation was no longer a Christian nation. In Boston, we toured the Freedom Trail. We saw the home of Paul Revere, his statue, and the old North Church ("one if by land and two if by sea"). I was pushing our three-year-old daughter in a stroller as we were coming back to the parking lot. We were about to go up to Plymouth,

Massachusetts where the Pilgrims had landed. In a state of despair, I started praying, "God, what can we do?" I had seen homosexuals, every kind of immoral person, and people with rings all over their bodies. I prayed, "O God, our nation is so secular. What can we do?"

Suddenly, in the background, in Boston, Massachusetts by the harbor walk, I heard the bells from one of those old churches starting to ring out. And do you know what those bells were playing? *"Sweet hour of prayer, sweet hour of prayer, that calls me from a world of care, and bids me at my Father's throne, make all my wants and wishes known. In seasons of distress and grief, my soul has often found relief, and oft' escaped the tempter's snare, by thy return, sweet hour of prayer!"* The Holy Spirit brought to my mind that verse out of Ezekiel which says that God searched for a man among them in Ezekiel's day who would build up a wall, and stand in the gap before Him for His land so that He should not destroy it. But in Ezekiel's day, alas, God had to say, "But I found no one." Then I prayed, "O Lord, I don't know if you mean just 'one' or not, but I will be one. I for one am going to pray for revival!"

Don't you want your children to grow up in an America where Jesus Christ can be worshipped? Don't you want your grandchildren to live in an America where God is moving? Wouldn't it be wonderful if God sparked a revival even here today? Wouldn't it be wonderful if God sent another spiritual awakening to America? If He does, it will come with fasting, it will come with weeping, it will come with brokenness, it will come with repentance, and it will come by getting right with God. Christians, hear me today. God is not playing games. God is not asking you to wake up, God is saying, "Do it or else! I will give you over to My wrath if you don't!" Thus saith the Lord. He that has ears to hear, let him hear what the Spirit is saying to His churches.

4

JESUS' BLOOD: THE PRICE OF TRUE SALVATION

DR. TOM ELLIFF

Senior Vice President for Spiritual Nurture and Church Relations
International Mission Board of the Southern Baptist Convention
Richmond, Virginia

WHY DID GOD DO IT THAT WAY? Why did God determine that the death of His Son, Jesus, would be required for the salvation of any person? And not just any death, but death on the cross; the most cruel, painful and shameful death-dealing device ever conceived in the twisted mind of sin-cursed humanity.

The answer to this perplexing question can be found in the words of our Lord Himself when, only a few hours before His crucifixion, He said to those seated with Him at the Passover Feast, "...this is the blood of my new testament which is shed for many for the remission of sin" (Matthew 26:28). What did Jesus mean by "new testament?" And what was the Old Testament or covenant that it was meant to fulfill and replace?

I. THE OLD TESTAMENT

The Bible contains two libraries of books. Each speaks of a unique covenant, or means of establishing fellowship between holy God and sinful Man. Because of what Jesus did on the cross, one library is called the *Old* Testament, or covenant, and the other is called the *New*.

Consider the Old Testament. In its most broad, sweeping terms, the Old

Testament can be said to address three basic issues…God's sovereign creation, Man's sinful conduct, God's saving compassion. In its opening pages, we are immediately confronted with the work of our Sovereign God in His act of creation. First we see the broad, telescopic view of this awesome event. Then with microscopic precision, we focus on a remarkable place called the Garden of Eden in which we find the crowning glory of God's creation, the first man, Adam, and his companion, Eve, created in the very image of God.

In Adam and Eve, God reveals the breathtaking reality of what it means to be *alive* in every sense. They are alive *physically*, seeing, hearing, smelling, tasting, touching. In a way that separates them from all other creatures on earth, they are alive *spiritually*, created in the image of the One Who, Himself is Spirit, and is to be worshipped in Spirit and truth. And they are alive *soulishly*, they can reason, they have emotions and they possess a will with which they can make independent choices. They are experiencing real life!

But it was through the exercise of their will that Adam and Eve introduced sin and rebellion into the world God created. Satan entered the Garden of Eden. Judged for his own rebellion in heaven, he was still seeking a kingdom to call his own. Adam and Eve had been charged by God to fill the earth, to subdue, and to have dominion over it. That awesome responsibility also afforded Satan an opportunity to establish his own kingdom, to become "the god of this age."

First, however, Satan had to entice Adam and Eve to surrender their will to him, ignoring the stewardship assigned them by God. Standing with them before the "tree of the knowledge of good and evil," he promised that if they would but disobey God, they could become gods themselves. Lured by the physical attraction and the soulish appeal, Eve at first is deceived and then disobeys. But then Adam, the original overseer, the first man and the one out of whom Eve was fashioned, the one upon whom was placed the ultimate responsibility, made the deliberate choice to sin.

The moment they sinned, Adam and Eve died, for indeed God had said that to eat of the tree of the knowledge of good and evil would be to incur the judgment of death. They didn't die physically (They continued to exercise their physical senses.), nor did they die soulishly (They continued to reason, experience emotions and exercise their will.). But they died a spiritual death, a death that impacted every realm of the universe. It was a death that would ultimately affect even their bodies and souls, as well as those of all their descendants. They were immediately cut off from fellowship with God. Until then, they had lived in perfect harmony with Him, but now, having lost their innocence, we see them hiding from God, seeking to cover themselves and their guilt.

It is important to remember here that, as descendants of Adam, we have inherited their sinful nature, "All...have sinned," (Romans 3:23). And, like them, we justly deserve God's judgment of death, "For the wages if sin is death" (Romans 6:23a). As the prophet Isaiah said, we are all like sheep that have gone astray (Isaiah 53:6). The sins we commit are simply outward manifestations of the sinners we are by nature.

In the garden, God dealt with Adam, Eve and Satan, both personally and prophetically. Passing judgment upon their wickedness, He prophesied that one day a man would be born of woman who would strike the deathblow to Satan ("He will strike your head" (Genesis 3:15)). Then, in a stirring manifestation of God's saving compassion, He used a physical illustration to establish a remarkable spiritual principle. He revealed that the only suitable substitute, as payment for our sin, is another life. It must be life for life. Because the life of the body is in the blood (Genesis 9:4, Leviticus 17:11), it follows that "Without the shedding of blood there is no remission (or, forgiveness) of sin (Hebrews 9:22).

And what was the physical illustration of this spiritual principle? There in the garden, God performed a sacrifice, making for Adam and Eve a "covering of skins" to hide their shame and nakedness, something possible only by the sacrifice of animals or the shedding of their blood (Genesis 3:20). It was at this moment that the practice of a blood sacrifice was introduced as a reminder that, for payment of sin, it must be life for life. This, in fact, is why God accepted Abel's offering, but rejected Cain's. The first represented a man's inability to pay for his sin, while the second was an attempt to be justified the basis of human effort.

Throughout the balance of the Old Testament, we find continual evidence of God's saving compassion, evidence that always pointed toward the cross upon which the ultimate and only truly satisfactory payment for sin would be made. It was by the shedding of the blood of a lamb and its application to the doors of Israelite homes that the sentence of death was not imputed to them and their deliverance from Egyptian bondage was insured. Soon after their deliverance, it was through the celebration of the Passover Feast that Israel was to be in constant remembrance of that event. Later, in the wilderness on the Day of Atonement, it was the sprinkling of the blood of a lamb on the mercy seat that brought the atonement or covering of sin, so that God and Israel might walk in fellowship.

We are not told that God sacrificed lambs for Adam and Eve but, if so (and that would seem reasonable) we could think of the sacrifice there as a "lamb for a man," or a life poured out for each *person*. The deliverance from Egyptian bondage was accomplished by the sacrifice of a lamb for each *family*, as they ate of the sacrifice, standing in their homes, ready to go out to the Land of Promise. Later, in the wilderness, it was a lamb for a *nation*, as the High Priest annually made atonement by the blood on the Mercy Seat, covering the Ark of the Covenant in the Holy of Holies. But where is there a lamb for the whole world? The inability of sinful humanity to abide by the principles of God is glaringly obvious. There must be another way, a way that relies on God's mercy and grace rather than human effort.

II. THE NEW TESTAMENT

It is in the New Testament that we discover how all of the sacrifices in the Old Testament were simply pointing toward an ultimate, final sacrifice. In the broadest of terms, the first four books of the New Testament, or gospels, speak of the Savior's coming, His confirmation, and the consummation of His substitutionary work by His death on the cross and subsequent resurrection. Jesus, God's virgin-born and thus sinless Son, after 30 years of silence, appeared at the Jordan to be baptized by John. "Behold," exclaimed John, "the Lamb of God Who takes away the sin of the world" (John 1:29). Jesus, the Savior, had come in the fullness of time. What an astounding confession! John acknowledged that Jesus was, in fact, God's answer for our sin, "The Lamb, slain before the foundation of the world" (Revelation 13:8).

Jesus confirmed John's declaration by both His conduct and His confession, constantly referring to Himself as "The Son of Man." In essence, He was painting a bull's-eye on Himself, saying to the world and to Satan, "I am that Man born of woman who will strike the death blow to Satan and to sin." No wonder Satan constantly hounded Jesus, seeking by every means to entice Him to compromise His unique sinless nature and thus His ability to save.

Seated at the Passover on the eve of His crucifixion, Jesus stated that while in the past the Passover had been implemented as a reminder of Israel's deliverance from the bondage of Egypt, its observance was also a picture of Him and His redeeming work, His body that was broken, His "…blood of the New Testament shed for many for the remission of sin" (Matthew 26:26). The Passover of the Old Testament had now become the Lord's Supper of the New Testament. From there, Jesus went first to Gethsemane, then to judgment, and finally to the cross.

THE CROSS

It was not an easy thing for Jesus to die on the cross. Consider the grueling events which preceded His crucifixion. In the Garden of Gethsemane, He experienced such tremendous anguish and torment that He literally sweat drops of blood. In His agony, Jesus cried out, "Father, if it be your will, let this cup pass from me. Nevertheless, not My will but Thine be done."

During this time of turmoil, His disciples offered no help. Finding them sleeping, Jesus asked, "Couldn't you stay awake one hour?" Then He said, "For the spirit is willing, but the flesh is weak." He was not speaking of the disciples and their weakness; He was referring to Himself, His "flesh." He was saying that His spirit was willing – that which is divine was saying, "Not My will but Thine be done" – but His flesh was literally in torment, oozing drops of blood and crying out, "No, don't go to the cross!"

In the Garden of Gethsemane, Jesus was arrested and taken to the house of Annais, who was the former high priest and father-in-law of Caiaphas. As high priest, it had been Annais' responsibility to examine the sacrifices offered in temple worship. It's interesting to note that here Annais was looking at the true Sacrifice – the Lamb of God. He was probably inches away from Jesus, and yet he didn't recognize Him. Likewise, you can be very close to Jesus and know a lot about Him, but close is not the same as being born again.

Then they took Him to the house of Caiaphas, the high priest. Caiaphas said, "I can't have anything to do with this man, because this is Passover, the town is full of people, and this is a holy Sabbath day. You'll have to take him to the legal authorities." So they took him to the house of Pilate.

Pilate normally lived on the Mediterranean Sea, but he was in Jerusalem at this time. He was the Roman representative, or Governor, over the area that included Judea and the city of Jerusalem. After interrogating Jesus, Pilate said,

"I can't find any fault with Him." When someone said, "You've got to crucify this Galilean," Pilate said, "Oh, if he's a Galilean, then Herod (who had the same position in Galilee as Pilate had in Judea) must judge this case." So they took Jesus to Herod. Herod questioned Him, had Him beaten, and returned Jesus to Pilate. Then Pilate, weakened by pressure from the Jewish leaders, had Jesus scourged.

The act of "scourging" was sheer agony. Professionals at this kind of punishment could strip off so much flesh that to hit a man one more time meant he would be disemboweled. The phrase "beaten to within an inch of you life" comes from this practice.

The victim was taken to a doorway or a post where his hands were tied and his body was raised up so that just the balls of his feet touched the floor. One man started at the ankles, another at the neck, and throwing leather straps (into which were woven pieces of stone, glass and metal) around the victim, they would plant their feet, turn around, and with a fierce jerk, literally shred off the flesh. Occasionally, they would stop and throw salt water on the victim.

In this manner, Jesus was scourged. They even added insult to injury when they put a robe on Jesus, placed a scepter of wheat in His hand, and mocked Him as king of the Jews.

Jesus' beard was pulled out and blood flowed down his face. A crown of thorns two inches in length was pressed into His scalp. The Bible says that if you had known Him before He was scourged, you would not have recognized Him when they finished, because He was so disfigured. Then, they made Him carry His cross through the streets of Jerusalem, out through the Damascus gate, to a place called Calvary.

Contrary to what you may think, Calvary was not a beautiful, lush, green hill. It was a filthy, foul-smelling place, where the worms crawled, gnats and flies buzzed, dogs prowled and dust flew. It was the highest place in the city, so this execution could be seen by all. It was to serve as an example to every person under the oppressive rule of Rome

They stretched His body out on the cross and drove spikes though His extremities. Then they raised up the cross and dropped it with a thud into the ground, which caused His bones to come out of joint. Jesus hung there with only His sinews holding his body together.

In crucifixion, if a man didn't die from the loss of blood or the fever of infection, he would gradually drown in the fluids of his own body; a man could inhale, but because of the way he was pinioned on the cross, he could not exhale completely. Gradually, the body would fill with fluid. This is why, when they pierced Jesus' side, blood and water poured out.

But remember, in addition to the physical sufferings of Jesus on the cross, He also bore the weight of the sins of the world. Think of how bad you feel when you sin against God; then multiply that feeling times every sin you've ever committed; then multiply that feeling times everyone who has ever lived, is living, and will live. Take all that shame and guilt and put it in one man's heart and you will only begin to understand the spiritual weight pressing down on Jesus' heart. The sin was so great that His Father could not look at the sin; God turned His back on Jesus, causing the Son to scream out, "Why have you forsaken Me!"

The consummation of our Lord's substitutionary work took place on the cross within hours after that observance of the Passover. There, after enduring an unrelenting physical assault, Jesus cried out, "It is finished!" or "It is paid in full!" Jesus had become "sin for us that we might be made the righteousness of God" (2 Corinthians 5:21).

After His death, Jesus' followers buried His body in a borrowed tomb located in a nearby garden. But the evidence that His death had paid for the sin of Man is that just as He had prophesied, three days later, God the Father raised up Christ the Son from the grave (I Peter 3:18)! Jesus had purchased our redemption by His blood, the pouring out of His own life for us.

III. YOUR TESTAMENT

The important issue facing you is not *why* did God do it that way but *what* will be your response. A testament is a formal declaration of your beliefs, a statement of what is true, and the acknowledgement of a covenant relationship. What is your testament? Have you entered into your own covenant relationship with God through Christ?

FOUR QUESTIONS

I have just given you a biblical, historical summary of the importance of blood and, in particular, the shed blood of Jesus. Now I want to ask you four questions about the blood of Jesus:

1. HAVE YOU PLED THE BLOOD?

Have you come by faith to Christ alone? Have you received His blood as payment for your sins, trusting in Him as a resurrected and living Savior to give you eternal life? Have you come to that point in your life where you are not trusting in church attendance, good works, your family or your familiarity with the Bible? Have you come to Christ with the attitude of the songwriter who said, *"Nothing in my hand I bring, Simply to Thy cross I cling, Save me Jesus is my cry, Save me Jesus lest I die?"*

Have you come to the place in your life where you realize that it is only through the blood of Jesus that you can have God's gift of eternal life? Have you pled the blood?

Many people, when asked if they are a Christian, will answer "Oh, I go to church a lot," or "I'm trying real hard," or "I hope so," or "I've gone through all the rituals of my church." But that's insufficient. Dear friend, unless you come underneath the blood of Jesus, and plead his sacrificed life as God's payment for your salvation, you will spend forever in hell separated from God. Have you pled the blood?

2. HAVE YOU PICTURED THE BLOOD?

This is a question for those who have already pled the blood of Jesus as their payment for sin. God doesn't want you ever to forget what He has done for you. He wants you to remember His gift. He wants you to confess your belief openly to others.

Two symbols are provided for you to picture that moment when you passed from death to life:

The first is baptism. Of course, you don't have to be baptized to have eternal life. Eternal life comes when you receive Jesus Christ by faith as your Savior. God is not going to leave your eternal destiny up to whether it's convenient to be baptized, or whether there's somebody else around who can baptize you. But God wants believers to be baptized as a way to openly confess their new life in Christ.

I don't have to wear a wedding ring to be married. But as a married man, I love wearing my ring. The ring doesn't make me married, but it's a good way to show that I am a married man. I love my wife, and I wear this band proudly because I want everyone to know that I'm a married person. Likewise, baptism doesn't make you a Christian, but it does show that you belong to God, you are the "Bride of Christ," the church.

Salvation is by grace through faith alone and not through an ordinance such as baptism. But on the other hand, you cannot come to God and say, I will be saved, but I refuse to be baptized." You cannot receive salvation with that attitude. When you come to God, you don't come on your terms, you come on His. You receive Him not only as Savior but as Lord and, therefore, you cannot select beforehand what you will do and what you will not do. You must say, "God I give you myself, and if baptism is what your Bible says believers should do, then I will be baptized, because You are my Lord!"

The second is the Lord's Supper, the Christian's equivalent of the Jewish Passover. For the Jew, the Passover represented deliverance from Egyptian bondage and pointed to a coming messiah. For the Christian, the Lord's Supper is a way of remembering Christ's death until He returns for His people.

The Lord's Supper doesn't save you, but it pictures the Lord's death until He comes (1 Corinthians 11). It is a way of remembering that Jesus' body was broken and His blood was shed.

Have you pictured the blood?

3. DO YOU PRIZE THE BLOOD?

Do you think it would be fitting to place on your mantle the weapon used in the murder of your dearest friend? Of course not! But in a sense, your sin and mine is what brought Christ to the cross upon which he died. Do you prize the blood of Jesus so much that as a blood-bought child of God you want to flee from sin…you want to run from whatever resulted in his death?

Years ago in Chicago, there was a terrible accident. A young boy on his way home from school was struck by a car and killed. His father, coming home from work, saw the crowd gathered around his son who was lying on the pavement. Realizing that time was of the essence, the father picked up the boy's mangled body in his arms, put him into the car, and raced to the hospital. But the boy was dead on arrival.

The father was joined at the hospital by a broken-hearted mother, and together they wept their hearts out in grief. Later, as they were driving home, they came to the intersection where their son's life had been taken. Out in the middle of the intersection was a pool of blood from the accident. Motorists were unknowingly driving through the blood. The broken-hearted father slammed on the brakes, jumped out of the car, took off his coat and stood astride the puddle of blood shouting, "You can't drive through my son's blood! You can't drive through my son's blood!" The police had to escort this grief–stricken man from the street.

In a similar manner, a careless attitude toward the presence and practice of sin in your life shows an arrogant disregard for the blood of Jesus. He gave His blood, His life, so that you could be set free from sin. Should you not prize the blood of Jesus so much that you seek, by God's grace, to live a holy life, living the life of victory He has purchased for you? Will you prize the blood?

4. WILL YOU PREACH THE BLOOD?

It seems that this message on the blood of Jesus is not popular with our generation. But the blood of Jesus has always been an offense to those bent on sinning. The Bible never said it was going to be popular to preach the gospel. Jesus said, in fact, that in this world, we would have tribulation.

Everywhere I go, I have a compulsion down deep in my heart from God's Holy Spirit to ask this question: Will you preach the blood of Jesus, *the cost of true salvation?* Preaching the blood of Jesus can be as simple as sharing the gospel with your neighbors. Or it may be as profound as answering God's call to some specific ministry. But one way or the other, you can be assured that it is His plan, His commission, that you declare to your world that the blood of Jesus, His very life, is the cost of genuine salvation.

"What can wash away my sin?
  Nothing but the blood of Jesus.
What can make me whole again?
  Nothing but the blood of Jesus.

Oh! Precious is the flow
  That makes me white as snow;
No other fount I know,
  Nothing but the blood of Jesus."

Have you pled the blood of Jesus? Have you pictured the blood of Jesus? Do you prize the blood of Jesus? And will you preach the blood of Jesus – the price of true salvation?

5

THE UNPARDONABLE SIN

DR. JOHN BISAGNO

Pastor Emeritus

Houston's First Baptist Church

Houston, Texas

MATTHEW 12:22-34 SAYS,

22"Then was brought unto him one possessed with a devil, blind, and dumb: and he healed him, insomuch that the blind and dumb both spake and saw.

23"And all the people were amazed, and said, Is not this the son of David?

24"But when the Pharisees heard it, they said, This fellow doth not cast out devils, but by Beelzebub the prince of the devils.

25"And Jesus knew their thoughts, and said unto them, Every kingdom divided against itself is brought to desolation; and every city or house divided against itself shall not stand:

26"And if Satan cast out Satan, he is divided against himself; how shall then his kingdom stand?

27"And if I by Beelzebub cast out devils, by whom do your children cast them out? therefore they shall be your judges.

28"But if I cast out devils by the Spirit of God, then the kingdom of God is come unto you.

29"Or else how can one enter into a strong man's house and spoil his goods, except he first bind the strong man? and then he will spoil his house.

[30]"He that is not with me is against me; and he that gathereth not with me scattereth abroad.

[31]"Wherefore I say unto you, all manner of sin and blasphemy shall be forgiven unto men; but the blasphemy against the Holy Ghost shall not be forgiven unto men.

[32]"And whosoever speaketh a word against the Son of man, it shall be forgiven him: but whosoever speaketh against the Holy Ghost, it shall not be forgiven him, neither in this world, neither in the world to come.

[33]"Either make the tree good, and his fruit good; or else make the tree corrupt, and his fruit corrupt; for the tree is know by his fruit.

[34]"O generation of vipers, how can ye, being evil, speak good things? for out of the abundance of the heart the mouth speaketh."

It's bad enough to think that men would sin against a holy God and necessitate the overwhelming forgiving grace of God. But to think that men would so sin as to never be forgiven is almost beyond the realm of comprehension. And yet the Bible clearly says that one such unforgivable and unpardonable sin clearly exists.

If you knew that this night you would commit a sin that would finally and eternally seal your destiny in hell, would you do it? The answer, of course, is no! Yet, many of you are standing in the very shadows of the unpardonable sin. It is not an uncommon sin; it is not a sin relegated to the archives of antiquity. To the contrary, it is perhaps America's most prevalent sin. It is not adultery, murder, lying, stealing, or drunkenness. It is simply this: "Blasphemy against the Holy Ghost shall not be forgiven unto men."

It is nothing more and nothing less. To this there can be no questions, no controversy. To understand the answer to this tricky question, as to every controversial theological question, one must understand the context in which Jesus said that a man could sin so as to never be forgiven.

One day the disciples brought a man who was blind and mute to the Master. The man was demon possessed. This does not mean that blindness and muteness are always signs of demon possession, but in this particular case, they were. Without prayer lines or healing cloths, Jesus healed the man. He healed him instantly, publicly, and completely. Immediately, all the people were amazed and said, "Is not this the son of David?" Among other things, when the Messiah, the Savior was to come, He was to be called the Son of God, the Son of man, the Son of Abraham, the Son of David and many other names. He was to validate his ministry by the performing of miracles. Verse 23, instead of saying all the people were amazed, literally says, and most all of the people were amazed and said, "See, here is the Messiah. We are convinced by these miracles; we believe His power; we acknowledge Him." In other words, when most of the people witnessed the preaching, the ministry, the miracles in force, the power of Jesus Christ, they were convicted. They said, "We believe He is the Messiah, the Son of God, the Son of David."

Today, it is the same. Most people who continually go to a gospel preaching church and constantly witness the ministry and power of Jesus Christ carried out and attested to by the power of the Holy Spirit are likewise converted. The problem is that most people never hear the gospel of Jesus Christ. They hear positive thinking, good living, history lessons, Ann Landers and weather reports, but few, far too few, ever hear the blood-bought old-fashioned new birth, hell and heaven, crucified, resurrected, interceding, soon-returning gospel of Jesus Christ. Then, as now, when most people were touched by the message and ministry of Jesus Christ, they accepted Him and were saved. But verse 24 continues, when the Pharisees heard it, they said, "Oh no, this fellow, this carpenter has no heavenly power. He is not the Son of God, the promised Messiah; this power is the devil's power." They once and for all crossed off Jesus Christ and the power in Him as being of the devil.

Who were these Pharisees? Were they seeing the power of God and hearing his gospel for the first time? Most people are saved the first time they are touched by the power of heaven, but they had probably been following Jesus every day for three years and the more they heard, the harder they became. Now, remember this, the biggest lie Satan will ever get you to believe is that by waiting and by tasting more and more of the gospel, by coming closer and closer, you will become easier and your heart will become softer. It is a lie; you will not. You get harder. The most easily you could ever have been converted was the first time you heard the gospel. The more you wait, the harder you become. Every passing day brings an increasing resistance to the gospel. The sun that melts the ice also hardens the clay.

Delay is danger and death. Most people are converted early in their lives. I repeat; for your soul's sake, hear it well. When the devil tells you to put it off, it will be easier, he lies! It will become harder. Every day it will become harder. This is the time. Now is the hour; today is the day of salvation. The Pharisees had countless opportunities to accept Christ, but the more the Holy Spirit called them, and drew them through the ministry of Jesus Christ, the harder they became.

The first time you brand a cow, it will writhe in agony. But if you keep hitting that same spot with a branding iron, it will eventually become so hardened, so calloused, that the cow will make no response at all. This is what the Pharisees did and they finally blasphemed, insulted, rejected, and repelled the ministry of the Holy Spirit through Jesus Christ one last time. They got the last call from God, and God gave them up. They crossed the deadline and crossed Jesus off and His whole ministry and power as being of the devil, and

God said, "Let them alone."

There are only two powers in this world, the power of God and the power of Satan. If you honor the power of God, the drawing power of the Holy Spirit pulling you to Jesus Christ by accepting Him, by yielding to Him, you will be saved. But if you insult, repulse, and reject Him, you acknowledge only the power of Satan as the god and the reigning power over your life and commit the unpardonable sin.

Verse 25 says that Jesus knew their thoughts. This is the key to the unpardonable sin. Jesus knew what they were thinking. The unpardonable sin is not in the mouth, it is in the heart. It is not something man says, it is something man does. The mouth is the fruit, but the heart is the root. The unpardonable sin is crucifying the Holy Ghost. It is going to church, hearing the gospel being preached, being witnessed to, and in a hundred other ways being called by the Holy Spirit to repentance and faith in Jesus Christ, and then having the audacity, after hearing, to say no to Him. "No, I am not ready to come; don't crowd me; I'll come when I am ready."

Unfortunately, most people think that the unpardonable sin must be spoken, that it must be a verbal insult of the Holy Spirit. Their reason is that verse 32 says, "And whosoever speaketh against the Holy Ghost, it shall not be forgiven him." But look again at the statement in context. In verse 31, Jesus says simply, clearly, and finally that blasphemy against the Holy Ghost shall not be forgiven unto men. PERIOD! If this were the only verse in the Bible, it should be clear, once and for all, that speaking against the Holy Spirit is not the unpardonable sin, but that it is only a symptom of the fact that the unpardonable sin has already been committed in their heart. Having said, once and for all, in verse 31, that blasphemy against the Holy Spirit is the unpardonable sin, Jesus adds something else in verse 32. He now says, carrying out the thought, "And now I am going to tell you something else in addition to that, not only is blasphemy against the Holy Spirit unforgivable, but if you speak against the Holy Spirit, that is unpardonable, too." Why? He explains in it verses 33 and 34. The man who speaks against Him has already blasphemed against Him in his heart. What men say with their mouth is only the symptom of what they have already said in their heart. To be sure, one who speaks against the Holy Spirit has committed the unpardonable sin, but he is only evidencing the fact that he has already blasphemed him in his heart, not in the mouth. The heart is the root, the mouth is the fruit. He says in verse 33 that with the fruit of their mouth they could not bring forth any good praises to Him. They could say nothing good about Him because their sterile, impotent, empty-hearted hearts could produce nothing good, and He adds in verse 34, "O generation of vipers." Literally He was saying, "Oh, you barrel of rattlesnakes, you are so empty-hearted and empty-headed, so abjectly devoid of everything good that you could not say anything good if you wanted to, for out of the abundance of the heart, the mouth speaketh." It was absolutely impossible from that day to eternity for the Pharisees ever again to say anything good about Jesus. They could not honor Him with their lips, they could not confess Him with their words. They could not confess Him with their mouth because their hearts had crossed the deadline. They had waited too long. They had built up an indestructible, unbreakable resolve against God in their hearts. They were eternally and irrevocably locked in the sin of Christ rejection, forever locked in the condition of their hardened heart, sealed in their own damnation, and forever consigned to hell.

The unpardonable sin is blasphemy against the Holy Ghost. Two questions arise: What is blasphemy? Who is the Holy Ghost?

To blaspheme means to insult something sacred and need not necessarily be spoken. Suppose I were to come inside your church next Sunday morning and roll up the rugs and have a dance and put on a big drunken blast in the sanctuary. I would be insulting your auditorium which has been sanctified to the glory of God. I would be blaspheming the sanctuary, but blasphemy against the sanctuary is not the unpardonable sin. Were I to take the sacred vessels of the Lord's Supper table and desecrate and mock them by getting drunk out of them, I would be insulting, and blaspheming, the sacred vessels. But blasphemy against the Lord's Supper table is not the unpardonable sin. If I were to come into your educational building and write obscene words all over the walls, I would be blaspheming that building, but blasphemy against the educational building is not the unpardonable sin. In every sense, I would be blaspheming without saying a word. Blasphemy is not necessarily what one says; it is what one does. Blasphemy means insulting something that is sacred and holy.

To understand why this final rejection of His ministry is unforgivable, we must answer the question, "Who is the Holy Ghost and what is His ministry?" This mysterious, delicate third member of the God-head has many ministries. To the Christian, He does the actual work of regeneration in the life of the believer. He seals and keeps him or her for eternity. To the Christian, He speaks, comforts, guides, teaches, convicts, helps, and interprets, and performs innumerable other ministries. With the unsaved person, however, He has only one job, just one ministry. The purpose of the Holy Spirit, that only ministry for which He exists with the lost man, woman, boy and girl, is to draw them to Jesus Christ. He exists for no other purpose with you. The unpardonable sin is simply this: If in your pride, your self-sufficiency, your arrogance, and your rebellion against God, you habitually refuse to allow Him to do the one thing He is in the world to do, to draw you to Jesus Christ, eventually He will simply withdraw and leave you alone in your sins, and you will have crossed the deadline.

Contrary to what you may believe, you cannot be saved any time you are good and ready. Over and over the Bible emphasis is on salvation *today!* Today, if you will hear his voice, harden not your heart, as in the day of provocation.

There is no tomorrow on God's calendar, and you cannot be saved just any time. You can insult the Holy Spirit one last time; you can say no to Him so long that He will eventually say no to you. He will eventually reject you. You can crucify the Holy Ghost. In Genesis, God said, "My Spirit will not always strive with man." And Jesus added, "Except the Father that sent me draw him, no man can come unto me."

Three times in the first chapter of Romans, the Bible says, "God gave them up." God gave them up! God gave them up! Do you think you will be saved when you are ready? "Don't push me, I'll come when I am ready," says the lost man. If I have heard it once, I have heard it a thousand times. But what are you going to do if you get ready and he is not ready? There are two points in a man's life between which he may be saved. He cannot come before, he cannot come after. NO man knows where either of them is, that is why the invitation is always today!

The first point comes when you reach the age of accountability. Some come to an awareness of their sins and a conviction of their need of Christ at age six, at seven or eight, or even ten, fifteen, or twenty. No one can say when different individuals reach the age of accountability. The same uncertainty surrounds the unpardonable sin. Can you be sure you will have three chances, or four or five or ten or twenty? Perhaps you can hear the gospel for six months before the Holy Spirit quits striving with you, perhaps it will be a year, or five, or 20, or 50. No one can say. There is only one time that it is safe for you to be saved, and that is now; today; this minute; before you finish reading this page. Even the printed words of this chapter may be the last extended call of the Holy Spirit to your soul. At this moment you may be one step away from committing the unpardonable sin, one page short of crossing the deadline. Today, today, today, receive him today. The unpardonable sin is a sin of delay.

The searching, forgiving Savior is seeking us! Wonder of wonders, amazing grace, how amazing. But if in your pride, you persistently harden your heart, and you the creature have the audacity to say no to the Creator, what He does is simply to abide by your decision and leave you eternally in a condition without Him.

The Hebrew writer has stated, "He that despised Moses' law died without mercy under two or three witnesses. Of how much more punishment supposes ye, shall ye be thought worthy who have trampled under the foot the blood of the covenant and have done despite to the Spirit of Grace?" Man, you would be far better off to bite your tongue in half and spit it out of your head than to say no to God. Does it seem a light thing to you in His sight? You are stomping over the cross and defying, despising the Holy Spirit. I have talked to hundreds of men about Christ and seen them, after hours of pleading, still say no. And though I have never done it, I have felt like saying to them, "Man, if you have made up your mind to go to hell, go ahead; I am through with you." If I can feel that way, when I am not even the one who is being rejected, I can see why the Father would say to the Holy Spirit, "Leave him alone, don't call him anymore. He has insulted me for the last time. He has crossed the deadline."

The unpardonable sin is a sin against light; it is a sin against knowledge, a sin against opportunity. I believe the Bible teaches degrees of punishment in hell. You would be far better off to die and go to hell from the jungles of Africa, where you have had little light, little possibility of salvation, than to go to hell from America, where there is a church on every street corner. Some shall be beaten with few stripes and some with many. To whom much is given, much shall be required.

What about the people of Africa, who have not heard the gospel? Do they have a chance? I do not know! But my question is, "What about you that have heard it ten thousand times? What excuse will you give? Do you really think that when you stand before God and say, 'Lord, there were hypocrites in the church,' or 'Lord, I was a good man.' Or 'Lord, I was going to be saved,' that the Lord will say, 'Is that right? Well, what do you know; then come on in, since there were hypocrites in the church, I'll let you in anyway.'" Of course not! Oh, sinner, I beg of you, be saved today.

The unpardonable sin is a sin of the will. Regardless of what you say, regardless of what excuse you give me, it is not the feeling you are waiting for, it is not anything except one thing: You are lost because you will to be lost! You are not saved because you will not be saved. God has made man above the angels, above animals and matter; He has made you with a will. You can choose to respond to the Spirit's calling or you may choose against Him.

The unpardonable sin is a sin of the will. Jesus wept over Jerusalem in the night of their rejection. Hear Him as he cries, "Oh Jerusalem, Jerusalem, thou that stonest the prophets and killest them that are sent into thee. How oft would I have gathered you unto myself as a hen gathers her brood under her wing, but ye would not." He did not say, "ye could not" or "ye did not" or "you may not," but "ye *would* not." You can be saved if you want to be saved. There is no reason in the world for you to go on lost in darkness, destined to hell. You can be saved if you will to be saved. Stop delaying, quit making excuses; come now. You can be saved if you will!

The unpardonable sin is a sin against compassion. When you cross the deadline, when the burden of the Holy Spirit is withdrawn from your life, it will be withdrawn from others who have cared about you.

Many years ago in a small northeastern city, we had spent over eight hours one week trying to win a man to Christ. He kept saying, "No, preacher, not now, I am not ready." The pastor had tried to win him to Christ for 14 years, his wife for 20 years. Always it was the same, "Not today, I will do it tomorrow." After an all-night prayer meeting one Saturday, I met his wife in the hall during Sunday School, and she looked very refreshed and called to me.

"Thank God," I said, "You've got the victory, your husband is going to be saved this morning?" "No", she said, "And preacher, it's a strange thing, I just don't care anymore. God has removed the burden." Quickly I raced to the pastor's office and said, "Pastor, come quickly, Frank has committed the unpardonable sin. God has removed the burden from his wife. We must go to him one more time." "I can't go," he replied. "This morning, as I was praying, the burden lifted. I am sorry to say it, but I simply don't care anymore." With that he turned and walked away. When you cross the deadline, when the Holy Spirit withdraws from your life and leaves you eternally and irrevocably locked in your decision of rejection, he will remove the burden from the hearts of others who have loved and prayed for you. But remember this: though you will first have every opportunity, you will never know when the last opportunity may come! The Bible tells us that God hardened Pharaoh's heart. Many people have tried to preach around this, to explain it away. The truth of the matter is that God did harden Pharaoh's heart, but He gave him ten chances to repent!

The unpardonable sin is a sin against faith. The biggest lie the devil will ever tell you is that you will know when your time comes to be saved, that you will feel it. Men are not saved by feeling, they are saved by faith. God did not say that we have to have so much money to be saved, for some are rich and some are poor. He did not say that we have to have so much education, for some are educated and some are illiterate. But there is one thing that is common to all men – the ability to believe. You say you do not have faith, but every day you prove that you do. You ate something that someone else grew, cooked, prepared and packaged. There may be poison in it, but still you ate it, in faith. You go to a doctor you have never seen before. He gives you a prescription you cannot read, you take it to a druggist whose name you cannot pronounce, he prepares a prescription you know nothing about, and yet you take it; all in faith. Yes, we exercise faith every day. The capacity to believe in

Jesus Christ, to ask Him to come into your heart by faith, is the most prominent part of your personality. You can do it if you will, but you will never get that feeling you are waiting on. Why would God give you a feeling? What kind of a feeling would it be? How will you know it when it comes? You cannot trust your feelings, you cannot trust your emotions, for they change. Will it be a feeling of elation? But some people do not get happy easily. Will it be a feeling of sorrow; will you cry? But that would not be fair for me, for I do not weep easily, so God would not be fair. Feelings change, they vary from person to person. Some do not show any feeling, so God would not be fair. Some people weep at funerals, some smile from inner peace. Hear me, for your soul's sake, hear me. Different people react to the same situation with different emotions; therefore, feelings cannot be trusted, emotions cannot be relied upon.

The unpardonable sin is a sin against patience. Throughout the history of the world, God has gone to great extent to call man to repentance, to get the good news through to him that He loves him and would pardon him. First, He spoke to man himself. But man blasphemed the Father, and rejected Him. But God is long-suffering. "Perhaps they did not understand," He thought,. "so I will send men to give them the message in their own language." But they blasphemed the prophets, they did not hear Him. Next, God sent the written Word so that men could touch it, look at it, examine it, feel it, and see it, but the Bible says they blasphemed the Scriptures. They rejected even the written message.

Listen to the pathos, the agony from the great heart of God. "I will send my Son; surely they will reverence my Son." Now, they would have seen Him in the flesh. God's love, God's forgiveness, His patience, His compassion, wrapped in swaddling clothes, lying in a manger. Do they now believe? Do they now repent? Listen – "Release unto us Barabbas. Away with Him! Let Him be crucified!"

The Bible says they blasphemed the Son, they rejected Him, and they insulted Him. But oh, amazing grace, how sweet the sound, God has one last offer! Now, He sends the Holy Spirit; and on the day the Spirit of God burst upon the world scene in redeeming, drawing, convicting, saving grace, God began His last appeal to man.

If you are waiting for perfection, it will not come. If you are waiting for emotion, wait no more. If you are waiting for a new way of salvation, a new message, a new method, it is never coming. The Holy Spirit is God's last call.

To convict does not mean "to get an emotional feeling." It means to make aware of. Do you know you are lost? Yes! Do you know Christ died for you? Yes! Do you know you need to be saved? Yes! Do you intend someday to be saved? Yes! You are under conviction, only the Holy Spirit of God can make you aware of your need. Feelings and emotions will not come. Faith in answer to awareness is God's plan for your salvation. There is no other way.

The unpardonable sin is not the final blasphemous, insulting, rejection against the Holy Spirit because He is the greatest. The unpardonable sin is against the Holy Spirit because He is the latest. He is the last. There is no one else; there is nothing else; there will never be another plan, another way of your salvation.

6

WWW.SALVATION.COM

DR. JAMES MERRITT
Senior Pastor
Cross Pointe Church
Duluth, Georgia

IF GOD HAD A WEBSITE ON SALVATION, and you were to pull up that page to find what the God who will decide who gets into heaven and who does not says about salvation, what do you think you would find? Incidentally, there is such a website, because I found it in preparing this message – what they had on several pages I believe God probably could condense down to one paragraph, which is the text I am preaching from today.

> "For by grace you have been saved through faith, and that not of yourselves; it is the gift of God, not of works, lest anyone should boast. For we are His workmanship, created in Christ Jesus for good works, which God prepared beforehand that we should walk in them." *(Ephesians 2:8-10)*

There are three words in my version (the *New King James*) which, taken together, explain salvation completely and totally. They are the words "by," "through," and "for." Those three simple prepositions will keep you straight on this whole matter of exactly how a person is saved, and how a person can go to heaven. There is a debate as old as the New Testament as to whether salvation comes through faith alone, or good works. Even today Americans are split on the idea.

Fifty-five percent of all Americans in a nationwide survey said that a good person can earn his way to heaven. But that's not all. Fifty-eight percent of Episcopalians, 59 percent of Methodists, 76 percent of Mormons, and 82 percent of Catholics agreed. Incidentally, 38 percent of Baptists also said that a good person can earn his way to heaven.

When I was pastoring my very first church, my chairman of the deacons, named Rollie Matthews, a godly old man, invited me to come down one day to see him deliver a calf. I had never seen that done before and it was a fascinating sight. It reminded me of the story of the farmer who was helping one of his cows give birth, and he had the calf about halfway out of that mother cow when he noticed his four-year-old son at the fence soaking in the whole event. That man thought to himself, "Great! Four years old and now I've got to start explaining the birds and the bees." He started to say something, and then he thought, "No, I'll just let him ask questions and I'll answer."

Well, after he had safely delivered the calf and put the calf down, and everything was over, the man walked over to his little boy and said, "Well, son, do you have any questions?" The wide-eyed boy said, "Just one, Dad – how fast was that calf going when it hit that cow?"

When it comes to salvation, the vast majority of this world, and a lot of people in church, have it totally backwards. If you want to keep it straight, keep those three little prepositions in mind, and you will learn what God says about salvation.

I. SALVATION IS A PRESENT OF GRACE

"For by grace you have been saved." *(v.8)* If you don't count the name

Jesus, I think grace is the most beautiful word in all the Bible. It is the Greek word *charis* which gives us the name "Karen." There are some special qualities about grace that make grace *grace*, and unlike anything else in the world.

First of all, grace is something no one deserves. There are three ways that God can deal with you and me. God can deal with us according to justice. That is, He could give us exactly what we deserve. Or, God could deal with us according to mercy. That is, God does not give us what we deserve.

But God has done something totally different. He has chosen to deal with us by grace. Grace is when God gives us what we do not deserve.

As hard as it is to believe, God did not provide a way for us to be saved because we deserved it. He did it in spite of the fact that we did not deserve it. Please understand that the Lord Jesus did not die on the cross for you because of your goodness, but in spite of your badness. "But God demonstrates His own love toward us, in that while we were still sinners, Christ died for us" *(Romans 5:8).*

I read somewhere this definition of grace: "Grace is what everyone needs, what no one deserves, and what God alone can give." No one will ever go to heaven because of his performance, that is, what he has done; or his position, who he is; or his pedigree, who his parents were. Those things are irrelevant. It has nothing to do with either conduct or character.

The only reason anyone goes to heaven is because of the compassion of God, and the cross of the Lord Jesus Christ. Both of these have been provided by God's grace.

But another thing about grace is this: Not only is grace something given to people who do not deserve it, but it cannot be earned. For this salvation is "not by works."

You know the average person has the idea that when Jesus died on the cross, He made a down payment for our salvation, but we have to make the installments. Well, I've got some great news. In fact, the greatest news you will ever hear. Salvation is totally and completely free because Jesus paid it all. You cannot win it as a prize, you cannot earn it as a wage, you do not deserve it as a reward, but you can receive it as a gift.

I read a story about a poor woman over in England whose daughter was deathly ill. The doctor said that she needed the minerals and vitamins that only fresh fruit could give, but there was very little fruit to be found in the city. When this woman went out searching, she had to walk by the king's vineyards, and there she saw cluster after cluster of luscious beautiful grapes. The gate happened to be opened and she walked through and began to pick some.

About that time the king's gardener saw her and came over to her and said, "You cannot touch these grapes. These grapes belong to the king." She said, "Well, I'll pay what little I have." He said, "Lady, you cannot have them for any price. You must leave and leave now."

Well, she began to cry, weep, and beg, but the gardener would not listen to her. About that time, the king himself came walking up and asked what the problem was. When he was told, he said to the lady, "You may have all the grapes you want." She said, "Thank you so much. Here's what little money I have saved up and I'll be glad to pay you." The king looked at her and said, "Lady, these are not ordinary grapes. These are the king's grapes, and they are not for sale. You may have them as a gift or you may not have them at all."

That is exactly what God says to us about His salvation. It is not a bargain, it is an offer; it is not a reward for those who are righteous, it is a gift for those who will admit they are guilty.

There is nothing in the history past or in the future to come like the grace of God. No artist could paint its beauty, no scientist could discover its ingredient, no language could describe its wonder, no imagination could conceive its greatness, no eloquence can explain it, no intelligence can totally understand it.

II. SALVATION IS THE POSSESSION OF FAITH

This salvation that comes by grace is "through faith" *(v.8)*. Now faith is the flip side of the coin of salvation. Salvation is like a gulf. The two rivers that flow into the gulf are salvation, or the river of grace and the river of faith. Grace is God's hand giving salvation, faith is our hand receiving salvation. Faith possesses what God provides.

But even this faith, Paul says, "is not of yourselves, it is the gift of God." Not only is salvation and grace a gift of God, even our faith is a gift of God.

John 6:28-29 records a brief instant in the life of Jesus in which He revealed a great truth. The disciples asked the Lord Jesus, "What shall we do that we may work the works of God?"

Listen to Jesus' answer: "This is the work of God, that you believe in Him whom He sent."

Faith is not a good work you do for God, faith is God's good work in you. Grace is not a reward for faith, faith is the result of grace. When we get to heaven we can't even brag on the fact that we put our faith in God, because that, too, was His gift.

Paul said in Philippians 1:29, "For to you it has been granted on behalf of Christ...to believe in Him..." Faith is God's gift to us.

Now the reason why a lot of people reject this idea of salvation by grace through faith is because it is so simple. It's incredible how we try everything in our power to complicate the matter of salvation, when God has done everything in His power to simplify it.

If the Bible had said that you are saved by grace through intelligence, some of us would have been too dumb. If we were saved by grace through looks, some of us would be too ugly. If we were saved through education, some of us would be too ignorant. If we were saved by grace through money, some of us would be too poor. But all that is necessary for you to be saved is simply faith in the Lord Jesus Christ.

But when I talk about faith, please understand I'm not talking about an intellectual acknowledgement of something in your head. Faith is more than that. It is trusting with your heart. A true-to-life story illustrates what I'm talking about.

A motorcycle officer was moving smoothly through a Los Angeles suburb on his way to work. As he neared an intersection, a red pickup truck sped past without even slowing down for the stop sign. The officer turned on his flashing lights and radioed the station he was in pursuit of the red vehicle.

As his unit pulled up behind the truck, the officer was thinking, "That fellow is just probably late for work." Unknown to the officer, the driver of the pickup had just robbed an all-night grocery store. On the seat beside the driver was the paper bag with the money and the gun he had used. As the officer pulled up beside him, this man put his hand on the gun. The truck pulled to the side of the roadway and stopped.

The officer parked his motorcycle and approached the driver's side of the pickup. He was relaxed. He said, "Good morning sir, may I see your license?" Those were the last words he said. The driver stuck his arm out of the truck and fired his weapon. The barrel of the gun was only two inches away from that officer. The bullet hit the officer in the center of his chest. He was knocked to the ground seven feet away.

For a few moments all was quiet. Then to the horror of the gunman, the officer slowly stood to his feet. The driver couldn't believe it. He said, "This guy must be Clark Kent." In shock, the policeman slowly began to brush the dirt from his uniform.

After two or three seconds the officer regained his wits, pulled his service revolver and fired two rounds into the side of the truck. The first round went through the open window, destroying the windshield, and the second round went through the side of the door and ripped into the driver's left leg. The terrified robber screamed, "Don't shoot!" and threw the gun out along with the bag of money.

That officer's life had been spared because he was wearing a bulletproof vest. Vests are incredibly strong even though they are only about three-eighths of an inch thick. They are made of dozens of layers of an extremely tough fabric called Kevlar.

Well, a few months later another officer, Ray Hicks, and his partner, went to serve a search warrant on a well-known drug dealer in the city of Inglewood. As his partner knocked, Hicks yelled out, "Police!" and started to knock down the door. From inside the shabby apartment four slugs were fired through the door; and one found its mark. The impact was almost exactly where the motorcycle officer had been hit only a few weeks before – squarely in the center of the chest.

Later his partner recalled that Hicks simply said, "I'm hit," and slowly sank to the floor. The coroner reported that the policeman probably lived less than a minute. The bullet had ruptured an artery; and blood to the brain had been stopped instantly.

Police officer Ray Hicks was 27 years old. He left a wife, three children and a bulletproof vest in the trunk of his car parked 30 feet from where he fell. What is the moral of the story? An officer can believe in vests all he wants to, but he must take his belief to the point of personal commitment where he puts that vest on and wears it at all times.

It is not enough just to believe that a man named Jesus Christ lived 2000 years ago, nor even to believe He was born of a virgin, nor even to believe He performed miracles, nor even to believe He died on the cross, nor even to believe He was raised from the dead. Saving faith is when you take your belief to a point of commitment and you put on that risen Christ as your Lord and as your Savior.

III. SALVATION IS THE POWER FOR GOODNESS

People always wonder what the relationship is between goodness and grace, what part do good works play in salvation? This may surprise you, but they do.

The thing to remember is this: Good works are not the root of salvation, but they are the fruit of salvation. They are not the price of salvation, but they are the proof of salvation. Good works do not produce salvation, but salvation produces good works. Works follow faith just like heat follows fire.
A good root sunk into good soil will ultimately grow a tree that will bear good fruit. That's why Jesus said, "A good tree bears good fruit." If you have sunk the roots of your heart by faith into the soil of God's grace, you will bear the fruit of good works. But the thing to remember is that even good works are the result of God's grace.

Martin Luther said it better than anyone:

"No one can be good and do good unless God's grace first makes him good; and no one becomes good by works, but good works are done by him who is good. Just as the fruits do not make the tree, but the tree bears the fruit...therefore all works, no matter how good they are and how pretty they look, are in vain if they do not flow from grace."

When God says to you that He is not finished with you, He has just started with you. He's got great things for you to do. Verse ten says, "For we are His workmanship." The word "workmanship" comes from the Greek word *poiema* from which we get the English word "poem." Now the word 2000 years ago could refer to any work of art: a statue, a song, or a painting. It literally means a work of art or a masterpiece.

A child of God is God's masterpiece, His work of art. He is the poet, I am the poem; He is the painter, I am the portrait; He is the potter, I am the putty.

You see, the world once again has it backwards. It says you've got to work so that you can make something out of yourself. God says, "I've got to make something out of you so you can work." A person is not a Christian because he does good works. He does good works because he is a Christian.

That's why you were created. He goes on to say, "We were created in Christ Jesus for good works." God's will for every Christian is that he performs the good works that He has already planned for him to do.

I'm always wary of anybody who spends more time braging on what they do for God rather than braging on what God has done for them. May I throw a cup of cold water reality in your face today? Every good work you've ever done is not what you did for God. It is what God did through you. Paul said in Philippians 2:12-13:

"Therefore, my beloved, as you have always obeyed, not as in my presence only, but now much more in my absence, work out your own salvation with fear and trembling; for it is God who works in you both to will and to do for His good pleasure."

It just amazes me how many people continue to get it backwards when it comes to God, grace, faith, good works, and salvation.

I read about a man who was on trial for murder, and the tide seemed to be running against him. So he tried to bribe an elderly juror to hold out for a verdict of manslaughter. Well, the elderly man accepted the bribe because it was a great amount of money. The jury was out three, four, five, six days and the accused man found the tension unbearable. But in the end, the jury brought in a verdict of manslaughter.

Well, as the relieved man was being led out of the courtroom, he happened to get a chance to whisper in the old man's ear, and he said, "Thanks so much. Did you have much trouble getting the others to vote for manslaughter?" The man replied, "You bet I did. They all wanted to vote for acquittal!"

So often we go and we try to bribe God with our good works, to maybe get a lesser punishment or maybe to get consideration for letting us into heaven, when God has already acquitted us at the cross. All we have to do is accept it. For by grace, through faith, for good works is what salvation is all about.

7

CERTAINTY FOR AN UNCERTAIN WORLD

DR. ROY FISH

Professor of Evangelism
Southwestern Baptist Theological Seminary
Fort Worth, Texas

FIRST JOHN 5:13 SAYS,

"I write these things to you who believe in the name of the Son of
God so that you may know that you have eternal life."

We live in a day that is filled with unrest. The only difference between
now and the last time I made that statement is that the unrest is just greater
today than it was then. A great deal of the unrest in our world is brought about
by chilling feelings of uncertainty. This is a terribly uncertain world.

I was in our Dallas/Fort Worth airport not long ago, and I was struck by
the headline of a weekly news magazine that said, "Almost everybody in this
country is unhappy." I knew it was the kind of headline they put on paper to
sell the paper, but it worked on me. I bought one. I wanted to see if almost
everyone in this country was unhappy. The article reported that there is more
unhappiness in the United States today than there has ever been in history. It
was a series of statements from people who supposedly were knowledgeable.
One man from Georgia said, "People seem more upset and uneasy than at any
time I can remember. The thing I hear them talking about all over the

country," and he was a traveling man, "is this: that everything is so unstable and uncertain."

Economically, it is always an uncertain age. We have seen our dollar battered about abroad and watched the cost of living spiral upwards in this country. Most of us make more money than we've ever made, but it's not going as far as what we earned ten or fifteen years ago. Economically, it's an uncertain world.

Internationally, it is an uncertain world. It was the *U.S. News and World Report* that suggested not long ago that there are 40 wars going on in our world right now. Someone corrected the statement and said it is more like 70 wars. It is an uncertain world internationally. It appears to me that the world is seated on a powder keg and there are a lot of people running around with blow torches coming dangerously near the fuse.

Physically, it is an uncertain world. As far as your own condition, your life, it is an uncertain world. No one knows for sure that he or she will be here tomorrow. Physically, the world is chilled by haunting feelings of uncertainty. Things we once thought were nailed down are coming apart around us.

I want today to dare to speak to you, in an uncertain world, about certainty, "Certainty for an Uncertain World." A passage of Scripture that speaks of certainty is found in the little letter of 1 John 5:13. "These things have I written unto you who believe on the name of the Son of God that you may know that you have eternal life." That you may *know*, that you may be sure, that you may be certain that you have eternal life. Here is a great word of certainty from God, "I've written to you who believe on the name of my Son that you may *know* that you have eternal life."

The first prayer I ever prayed was one I had committed to memory as a child: "Now I lay me down to sleep; I pray the Lord my soul to keep; if I should die before I wake, I pray the Lord my soul to take." It never occurred to me until I thought of this prayer with reference to my own children that one of the lines in this prayer contains a frightening prospect for some people. It is the line: "If I should die before I wake." Just suppose you should die before tomorrow. What would happen to you? If you should join 150,000 other people in the experience of dying in the next 24 hours, where would you go? If you should die before you wake in the morning, will Jesus receive you unto Himself?

Many psychologists tell us that one of the deepest yearnings in the spirit of man is the yearning for assurance or security. This is particularly true when it comes to things eternal or things spiritual. When it comes to what is going to happen to me when I die, I don't want any hazy question marks hanging over my head. This is something about which I want to know, something about which I want to be sure. This passage of Scripture says, "I've written these things to you who believe on the name of the Son of God that you may *know* that you have eternal life."

What I want to do in this message is very simple. I want to ask you three questions, and I will draw the answers to the questions from this passage of Scripture. Here is the first question: Can you know for sure that if you died today you would go to heaven? Can you know beyond the shadow of a doubt that you have eternal life?

I know there are people who say that it is sheer presumption to say that you know that you have eternal life. You might hope so, you may think so, you may assume so, it might be maybe so, but you cannot know so. I submit to you that it is God Himself who says in this passage of Scripture that "I've written to you that you may *know* that you have eternal life." God says you can know that you have eternal life.

But, someone responds, "You'll never know for sure until you stand before God on the Judgment Day." I submit to you that it will be altogether too late to do anything about it then. God wants you to know that you have eternal life if your faith is in Jesus as your Savior. Not merely does He want you to know that in the sweet by and by, but also in the ugly, nasty here and now as well.

I have thanked God many times that this passage of Scripture did not say, "I have written to you that you may *hope* that you have eternal life, or that you may *assume*, or that you may *wish*, or that you may *think*." I've thanked God that this passage of Scripture says, "I've written to you who put your faith in the Son of God that you may *know* that you have eternal life. Is it possible to know that you have eternal life? God's answer to that question is "yes." I've written to you that you may *know*.

The second question is: Who among us can know for sure that he or she has eternal life? I quickly want to say that this is not a blanket coverage kind of promise. It is not written to all people everywhere; it is written to a select category of people; it is written to a particular group. "I've written these things to *you who believe* on the name of the Son of God."

But what does it mean to believe on the name of the Son of God? When our New Testament uses the word "belief," it might better be translated "trust" or "put your faith in" or "commit yourself to." It is not referring to mere intellectual acceptance of facts. For years I thought I believed on the Lord Jesus Christ because I believed everything about Him, but when the Bible tells us to believe on the Lord Jesus Christ, it is far more than merely believing *about* Him. It is more than intellectual faith. You can believe that Jesus was born of a virgin, that He lived a sinless life, that He was God, that He was flesh, that He died on a cross, was raised from the grave, and someday is coming again. You can believe all of that and still never really trust Him to be your Savior. The Bible uses the word "belief" as more than mere intellectual faith.

Further, it is more than just trusting Jesus to do something for you in a temporal sense. I have asked people about their faith in Christ and they have said, "Oh, yes, I trust Him. When I was sick, I trusted Him to make me well." But merely trusting Him to make you well is *not* saving faith. I believe He wants us to pray to Him when we're sick. I believe He wants us to trust Him with illness. We will call that "healing faith." But "healing faith" is not saving faith. Some of you fly on airplanes a great deal. I fly almost once a week, and I trust the Lord to take care of me when I'm flying. We'll call that "flying faith." I believe we ought to trust Him to take care of us, especially when clouds hang low and there is no visibility, but flying faith is not saving faith.

Sometimes I forget to take the garbage out, and it is midnight, and I realize the next day is trash day. It's a long way from our front door to the curb at midnight. I take one sack in one hand and one sack in the other and make a mad dash to the curb and trust the Lord to take care of me while I make that trip. We'll call that "trash-carrying faith."

Well, you can have healing faith, you can have flying faith, and you can have trash-carrying faith and still not have saving faith. Saving faith is putting your trust in Jesus Christ to give you eternal life. It is trusting Him to forgive your sins. In old evangelical language, it is trusting Him to save your soul. Has there been a time in your life when you put your trust in Jesus Christ to save you? This alone is saving faith.

This passage of Scripture did not say, "I've written to all of you that are doing your best to be Christians that you may know that you have eternal life."

I asked a man not long ago if he were a Christian and he said, "Oh, I'm doing my best to be a Christian." Would you like to know how many people have become Christians by doing their best? Not a one. If you became a Christian just by doing your best, I want to tell you how good your best would have to be. The Bible says, "Be ye therefore perfect even as your Father in heaven is perfect." If you ever got to heaven by doing your best, there could not be one sin on your record, not one fault, not one mistake, not one error. If you're hoping to get to heaven by doing your best, I hope today that hope in you will be blasted because you will never get to heaven by doing your best. Your best simply is not good enough and there's not enough of it.

Sometimes we have a tendency to compare ourselves with other people. We look across the street at our neighbors and think, "I just know if God made a choice between them and me, as to who is going to heaven, I'd get in before they did." We look down the block a couple of houses and think, "There's not even a contest there." God does not grade on the curve. He doesn't say to you, "Look, if you make it up to this point, I'll let you in. But I'm going to cut the curve right here and below that point, tough luck."

God doesn't say, "I'm writing to all of you who are trying to be Christians so that you may know that you have eternal life." I talked to a man working on his car not long ago. In the course of the conversation, I asked, "Are you a Christian?" He said, "I'm trying to be a Christian." Would you like to know how many have become Christians by trying? Not one. This is going to surprise some of you, but you don't become a Christian until you stop trying and start trusting. Trying is self effort. Trying says, "I believe if I worked hard until my fingers are blue to the bone, and I'm really red in the face, if I really try that hard, I believe God will save me." No, never because you've tried. You must come to Jesus Christ and say, "Jesus, I've tried and failed. I trust you to do it for me." That is the only way a person ever receives eternal life.

"I've written to you who believe on the name of the Son of God that you may know that you have eternal life." Has there ever been a time in your life when you put your trust in the One who died for you on the cross? Has there been a time when you nailed it down? Jesus, I trust You alone for eternal life. I put my trust in You to save me. If you can answer "yes" to that, I've got some good news for you. God says, "I've written to you who put your trust in Jesus, that you may know that you have eternal life."

Some of you say, "I really do trust in Jesus as my only Savior. But my faith is very small. I've never been able to shout along with the apostle Paul, "I know whom I have believed and am persuaded that He is able to keep what I've committed to Him against that day." I'm more like the woman who has barely touched the hem of His garment. My faith is smaller than a grain of sand, smaller than a mustard seed. My faith is so small; it is wholly in Jesus who died for me. Will this small faith save me?" Never forget this. It is not the size of your faith that saves you. It is the object of your faith, the Lord Jesus Christ who saves. Faith is not the Savior. Jesus is the Savior. Nowhere does God ever tell you to trust your faith. He tells you to put your faith in Jesus. I'm not asking you today how big is your faith. I'm asking you where *is* your faith for eternal life? Somebody hearing this could have the greatest faith of anybody and be lost forever. If your faith is in your own goodness, your faith is in your own keeping of ethical and moral standards. If your faith is in your church membership or your baptism, you can have the greatest faith of anybody and not be saved. On the other hand, the smallest, most child-like faith in Jesus, the One who died for you on the cross, will save you eternally. I'm asking you today: Has there been a time in your life when you put your trust in the One who died for you?

There is a third question: How can you know for sure that you have eternal life? You may say, "You're talking to me about eternal life. How can I know that I have that? It's outside the realm of my senses; I don't feel it with my fingertips; I don't see it with my eyes; I don't taste it with my tongue. How can I know I have eternal life?" You may respond: "I drove an old car into an automobile agency not along ago. I drove out with a new one. I know I have that new car, as I can look out in the driveway and see the sunlight as it catches it. I get in it, and it even smells new. I put my foot on the accelerator and there's a surge of power. Three hundred and fifty dollars every month come out of my checking account. I *know* I have that new car." Or you stood one day at the altar of a church as an officiating minister said, "Do you take this woman to be your wife?" You said, "I do." You *know* something happened, and you live within that wonderful relationship every day. But you respond, "You're talking to me about eternal life. I don't see that like I see my car; I don't touch that like I touch my wife or husband. How can I know I have eternal life?" Listen to the facts. *"These things have I written* unto you that believe on the name of the Son of God that you may know that you have eternal life." God says you can know it because He has written it.

Some of you have done what I did in the early months of my Christian life. You have rewritten this passage of Scripture. Here is the way we have changed it. "These *feelings* I give you that you may know that you have eternal life." Instead of looking to what He has written, we look instead to our feelings. But we cannot depend on our feelings as to whether or not we have eternal life. Why? Our feelings are so prone to change. Emotionally, we're so constituted that we don't feel today like we did yesterday. Sometimes I feel like I could go down to the Forest Park Zoo in Fort Worth, get in the cage with a tiger, fight him and whip him in three rounds. The next day I wouldn't want to tangle with a little kitten that kept me awake by crying on my window sill. That's the way our feelings are. They're up; they're down; they vacillate; they fluctuate; they oscillate. For you to depend on your feelings as to whether or not you have eternal life would be closely akin to trying to anchor a boat by casting the anchor on the deck. We have to anchor to something that is fixed and firm, that does not waver, that does not change, and that something is the infallible, inspired, inerrant Word. His promise does not fluctuate; it does not change; it does not vacillate; it does not oscillate. God does not say, "I'm giving you certain feelings that you may know." He says, "I'm putting it down in black and white. I am going on record. I'm going to say to you in my Word that you may know that you have eternal life if you put your trust in the Lord Jesus Christ."

I was saved when I was 19 years of age. I trusted in Jesus, but I began to question, "Am I really saved? Do I really have eternal life?" That question plunged me into doubt, and I lived in a valley of doubt for a number of months. You could have seen me kneeling on the floor of my dormitory room in college, praying, "Oh, Lord Jesus, I pray that You will save me. I trust You as my Savior; please save me." If I could only have seen His hand writing my name in the Lamb's Book of Life, that probably might have satisfied me for a while, or a special delivery letter, postmarked heaven, saying: "Dear Roy, you're saved; signed, God," – that might have done it. But God wanted me to come to the place where I was willing to trust in His promise, plus nothing. Oh, I praise Him for leading me to this promise in 1 John 5:13: "I've written to you who believe, who trust Jesus, that you may know that you have eternal life."

I know if I died today that heaven would be my home. I know that I would go to be with Jesus. I know it because I have the Word of a God that cannot lie. He says, "I have written to tell you that you may have eternal life and know it, if your trust is in the One who died for you on the cross." When I die, I'm going to meet God, resting on the strength of His promise, saved by the blood of the One who died for me, assured by the Word of the God who did it all. If I should die before I wake...

As it is with you right now, if you should die before you wake, would it be eternal life or eternal death for you?

8

WHAT IS THE GOSPEL?

DR. JIMMY DRAPER

Former President

Lifeway Christian Resources

Nashville, Tennessee

IN THE UNITED STATES, MORE THAN FIVE MILLION SERMONS are preached each year. In a typical preaching ministry of 40 years, a minister will speak an astonishing 27,600,000 words. That much speaking would fill over 500 books!

We like to speak of preaching the gospel. All of these millions of words find their center and circumference in one categorizing word: *gospel*. Since that is the case, it is vital to clearly understand what the gospel means. Some may claim that is irrelevant because everyone knows what the gospel is.

Unfortunately, that is a naive assumption and is simply not true. Words do not mean the same thing to everyone.

On a bumper sticker you may read: "The most important things in life are not things." "Things" is used in two opposite ways in that sentence. The second use refers directly to material things. The first use does not mean that at all. It refers to spiritual values.

In 20th century Christianity, some preachers and theologians have had the attitude of Alice in Wonderland: a word can mean whatever they want it to mean. But *gospel* must mean something specific.

Some mean by "*gospel*" something that is less than the gospel. Others mean something that is more than the gospel. What indeed is the gospel?

Rudolph Bultmann towers over the mid-20th century as a theologian. A layman who faithfully ushered at his local church in Marburg, Germany, he believed that the gospel had a significance without any relationship to the historical facts of the death, burial and resurrection of Jesus Christ. He believed that those historical faces were without historical foundation. Indeed, he believed it was carnal to depend on historical facts. He believed that seeking the historical facts of the gospel diminishes our trust in God and is a form of works righteousness. He believed less than the gospel.

Others today believe that the form or method of worship and preaching/teaching are more important than the historical facts of the gospel. It may be in the form of reliance on change (innovative) or in resistance to change (traditional), but such an approach is to believe less than the gospel.

On the other hand, there are those who believe more than the gospel. Cults and sectarian movements require a belief in more than the gospel, not to mention some major Christian churches. Mormons add the *Pearl of Great Price* and *Doctrine of Covenants* to the Bible as the basis of their gospel. Charismatics add gifts, signs and wonders to the gospel. Christian Science adds the teachings of Mary Baker Glover Patterson Eddy to the gospel. Roman Catholicism has always added the teachings of the fathers to the gospel.

Others seek to obscure and intellectualize the gospel, beyond understanding. One seminary student depicted in a cartoon Jesus talking to Simon Peter at Caesarea Philippi. Peter is responding to the question, "But who do you say that the Son of Man is?"

Peter answers, "Thou art the paradoxical Kerygma, the epistological manifestation of the existential ground of ontological ultimacy."

To which Jesus responds, "Huh?"

What is the gospel?

I. The Definition

The gospel of Mark, believed by many to be the earliest gospel written, begins with the simple proclamation: "The beginning of the gospel of Jesus Christ, the Son of God." The gospel reveals the historic facts concerning Jesus Christ. The gospel is not myth or fiction. It is based upon eyewitness evidence of the words and deeds of Jesus Christ.

We must never surrender that the gospel is based upon the eyewitness accounts of those who actually saw the Lord Jesus Christ, heard His words, and witnessed His deeds.

The gospel reveals the significance of the historic facts about Jesus Christ. The gospel is fact plus significance. The people beneath the cross of Jesus saw the same events. Some Roman soldiers sat under the cross and did nothing more than gamble for Jesus' robe.

Another Roman centurion looked at the same events and said, "Truly this man was the Son of God" *(Mark 15:39)*.

The facts about Jesus alone are not the gospel. The gospel is facts concerning the interpretation of those facts in the Word of God. That interpretation rests first and finally on the inerrant Word of God, not the feeble attempts of men.

God's Word tells us that the significance of the Man dying on the cross is the payment of the ransom price for sin. His penal substitutionary death became the source of forgiveness and eternal life to those who believe.

What exactly is the gospel? It is a commonly used term and yet we frequently don't define it. "Preach the gospel," Jesus said, "in all the world to every creature." We are frequently told that we should join hands to preach the gospel. That is true, but what is the gospel?

Ask the average Christian what the gospel is, and he/she would probably reply that it is how a person gets saved. It is the good news of salvation. Of course, the word "gospel" means good news. The Greek word means to announce or proclaim something good. Well, what is the good news? What must a person do to become a Christian, to become saved?

Most would give the answer Paul gave in Acts 16:31, "Believe on the Lord Jesus Christ and you will be saved." That is correct, but let's go on one step further. What does it mean to believe on the Lord Jesus Christ? Believe what? Do we simply believe that there was a man named Jesus? That is not enough. Do we simply believe that He died on the cross? Even Hindus generally recognize that.

Well, you say, He not only died, but He rose from the dead. Yes, He did, and it is necessary to believe that to be saved, as Paul declares in *Romans 10:9-10*. But you can believe Jesus rose from the dead and still not be saved, because that is not the full extent or definition of the gospel.

Or, someone will say that the gospel really means that you need to have a personal relationship with Jesus Christ. That is true, but what does that mean? Many Christian Scientists think they have a personal relationship with Jesus Christ. Mormons and Jehovah's Witnesses think they do, too.

I am afraid we have obscured the meaning of the gospel until it means different things to different people. What has emerged is often not the gospel at all.

Probably the clearest and simplest definition of the gospel in Scripture is in *1 Corinthians 15:1-4*. Paul declares:

"Moreover, brethren, I declare to you the gospel which I preached to you, which also you received...For I delivered to you first of all that which I also received: that Christ died for our sins according to the Scriptures; and that He was buried, and that He rose again the third day according to the Scriptures…"

According to the Word of God, the gospel consists of these three statements: Christ died for our sins, He was buried (meaning He actually died), and He rose on the third day. To be even more precise, essentially the gospel means that Jesus Christ died for our sins, He was really dead, and He rose the third day.

II. THE DISTINCTION

We need to focus on the phrase, "died for our sins." It is not enough that Jesus died. Many non-Christians believe that. There are even some non-Christians who believe that He rose from the dead. But the question is, what does it mean that He died for our sins?

One Baptist theologian said some time ago that the gospel is that Jesus died and rose again. No! That is not the gospel. The gospel is that Christ died for our sins and then rose again the third day. What does it mean that He died for our sins? It means that the death of Jesus Christ was a penal substitutionary atonement for our sins. Substitutionary means that He died in our place. It means that someone does something on behalf of or in the place of someone else. He died in our place, as our substitute. But, the word "penal" is also very important. That suggests that when He died as our substitute, He died in a penal capacity. That is, He was accepting judgment in Himself. He was suffering punishment that was intended for us, that should have fallen upon us, but fell on Him instead. It means that when Jesus hung on the cross, and during that awful time when He cried out, "My God, My God, why hast Thou forsaken me?," He was actually bearing our sins and the sins of the whole world, and at that time the wrath of God against sin was poured out upon His only begotten Son. His death was penal substitutionary atonement.

In 1984, I proposed that Southern Baptists agree on some basic theological parameters that we could all rally around. I suggested that we could begin to work through the theological concerns that we were dealing with if we could agree on these four things:

1. The hypostatic union: the undiminished deity and genuine humanity of Jesus Christ.

2. The substitutionary atonement.

3. The literal, bodily resurrection of Jesus Christ from the grave, a literal bodily ascension into heaven, and a literal, bodily return of Jesus Christ to earth.

4. Justification by God's grace through faith.

I stated that it is assumed that we view the Bible as the unquestioned and infallible, inerrant Word of God to mankind. Yet, no one took me up on my proposal. At first, I wondered why. Then it dawned on me that the real problem is in the nature of the gospel and specifically the substitutionary atonement of Christ. Those who have moved away from historic Bible doctrine do not and will not accept this distinction, that the death of Jesus Christ carried a penal, substitutionary meaning.

The Word of God very clearly teaches that this is the meaning of the death of Christ. In 1 Corinthians 5:7, the apostle Paul declares that Jesus Christ is our "Passover lamb" who has been sacrificed for us.

Remember the Passover lamb during the tenth plague in Egypt in Exodus

12? God was about to bring the last extreme judgment upon the people of Egypt because Pharaoh refused to let His people go free. The firstborn son in each house of the Egyptians was to die that night. Even Pharaoh's son would die. But, to preserve God's people, Israel, from this judgment, God instructed the Israelites to slay a lamb and take its blood and sprinkle it on the doorposts. Then He said, "When I pass through Egypt and see the blood on the door, I will pass over you."

Symbolically, it meant that when the judgment of God falls on the households of Egypt, His judgment will fall upon the innocent substitute and not upon you. It was symbolized by the lamb. Centuries later, Paul said that Jesus Christ was our Passover lamb. In other words, the judgment of God fell upon Him, not upon us because we are protected from His judgment by His blood and by His death.

Perhaps the most extensive and most explicit passage in all of the Word of God on this distinction is *Isaiah 53:4-6*: "Surely He hath borne our griefs, and carried our sorrows: yet we did esteem him stricken, smitten of God, and afflicted..." Those words mean that we thought He was suffering at that time for His own sins/crimes, but He was not. "He was wounded for our transgressions, he was bruised for our iniquities: the chastisement of our peace was upon him..." That means that the punishment that produced our peace was upon Him. "And with his stripe [the word is singular, not plural; with this single wound] we are healed." With what wound? The wound that the soldiers put on Him with the scourge, or crown of thorns, or spear? No! "All we like sheep have gone astray; we have turned every one to his own way; and the Lord hath laid on him the iniquity of us all." It is the wound that the Father inflicted upon Him that produces our salvation, our peace. That is penal, substitutionary atonement, and it is the biblical teaching as to what was accomplished by the sacrificial death of Christ – and that is central to the nature of the gospel.

We are to recognize that atonement and to appropriate it by faith if we are to be saved. In other words, we are to say to God, "I understand that Jesus took my sin to the cross and that the judgment that was due me as a sinner was inflicted on Him instead, and I now accept, receive, and appropriate that substitution by faith." That is what it means scripturally to believe in the Lord Jesus Christ.

III. THE DEMAND

1. Response of Faith

The gospel acts, energizes, convicts, judges and saves. That is why Paul wrote, "...for it is the power of God unto salvation..." (Romans 1:16). The gospel message conveys and carries the power of God to save.

The gospel demands our response. The preaching of Jesus always creates a crisis that requires a response. The presentation of the gospel creates a sort of courtroom atmosphere in which the people who hear of Him are compelled to make some decision. The declaration of the gospel of Jesus Christ creates a crisis of a mandatory decision. Not to decide is to decide against.

The gospel cannot be separated from Him. When Mark uses the phrase, "the gospel of Jesus Christ," the Greek literally means "the gospel about Jesus Christ" (objective genitive) or "the gospel that has its source in the message originating in Jesus Christ" (subjective genitive). That is to say, the message cannot be separated from the Messenger. The gospel is about Jesus and finds its first announcement and source in the Person of Jesus Christ.

A world-changing event took place on that day an Augustinian monk, Martin Luther, nailed 95 propositions for debate onto the massive door of the church in the German city of Wittenberg. As a professor of theology, he had taught his students Galatians and Romans.

For him the gospel had not been good news. He was terrified of the justice and severity of God. He was so conscious of his own sins that he would spend hours with his confessor, von Staupitz, confessing the most minor failings. To mortify his flesh, he would sleep in the cold German nights without blankets.

But one day a truth broke in upon him more vividly than any truth he had ever known.

"But to him who does not work but believes on Him who justifies the ungodly, his faith is accounted for righteousness." *(Romans 4:5)*

The gospel is so rich that it has many ways of being stated. The gospel as a new creation emphasizes the temporal truth that God has created a new way of being and ushered in a new era of being with Him.

On the other hand, the gospel stated as justification by faith comes from the forensic, or judicial, arena of the Roman world. Because of faith, God pronounces the sinner to be justified, right with God. Then the very righteousness of God is imputed to – written down to the account of – the sinner.

Luther was terrified that he had not done enough to be right with God. He was liberated by the gospel of justification by faith – that by faith alone we are made right with God for the sake of Christ.

The gospel as justification by faith redefines the righteousness of God. In the Old Testament that righteousness is an attribute of God, a perfect holiness that is unapproachable. In the New Testament the righteousness of God becomes not a cold attribute but a wonderful activity of God by which He makes sinners right with Him. Because of the gospel in the cross, God can both be righteous and at the same time make us righteous. That is good news indeed!

As Paul triumphantly declared in *Galatians 3:11,* "But that no one is justified by the law in the sight of God is evident, for 'the just shall live by faith.'"

The gospel means that one time in history, one Man in history did indeed keep the law of God perfectly, our Lord Jesus Christ. Having kept that law perfectly, He went to the cross and fell under a judgment He did not deserve to pay a price we could not pay. All we must do in order to know the benefit of that death is believe. We must come like William Cowper:

"Nothing in my hand I bring, simply to thy cross I cling;
Naked flee to Thee for dress, helpless come to Thee for grace."

2. Response of Obedience

When Jesus chose the twelve disciples, Mark writes that Jesus chose them "that they should be with him, and that he might send them forth to preach" *(Mark 3:14).*

There are some things which, if you know them, you are compelled to tell. I may know that one road is a shorter route than another, but I am not compelled to stop traffic and announce that the road is shorter.

But, if I know that the next bridge on the road is washed out, I am compelled to stop traffic and warn other drivers. The gospel is a message that is so vital that when you know it, you are required to tell.

3. Response of Transformation

The power of the resurrection is tantamount to the power to create, and that power belongs to God alone, "who gives life to the dead and calls into being that which does not exist" *(Romans 4:17).*

Christ has brought into the world of the present the power of the age to come, the age of the new creation – transformed lives. His nail-pierced hand reached out into the end time and drew its power back into this present needy age. That is why Paul could write, "Therefore, if anyone is in Christ, he is a new creation. The old has passed away; behold, the new has come" (2 Corinthians 5:17).

This gospel of our Lord Jesus Christ demands and produces transformation. We are not talking about belief in facts, but faith in the interpretation of these facts, which alone can bring us into a relationship with God and bring about transformation.

9

THE CROSS AND THE LOVE OF GOD

DR. J. KIE BOWMAN

Senior Pastor

Hyde Park Baptist Church

Austin, Texas

WHY WOULD U.S. MILITARY INTELLIGENCE need to hire a seminary graduate? I am not sure, but that's where a friend of mine went after our graduation. When I ran into him a few years later, he wouldn't tell me exactly what he did for military intelligence, but he did tell me a story I will never forget.

He had been in East Berlin before the fall of the Berlin Wall in the late 1980s. A pastor and a group of evangelical Christians behind the Iron Curtain in East Berlin desperately wanted to build a new church.

The government of East Berlin said that if churches in the West sent the money, the Christians could build a church in the city. So, the word went out to Christians in the West and money came.

Unfortunately, the Communist government confiscated the money. Instead of letting the Christians build a church, the government built a huge globe in the center of the city, a telecommunications globe, that would allow them to listen in on the conversations of the people – especially the conversations of the churches and the Christians.

The huge globe was a perfect sphere placed high in the city where everybody could see it. It had a bronze metallic surface, a covering of something like shingles, surrounding the globe that the people of the city could see being added day after day. The hearts of those Christians sank as they saw this object being built with money that was supposed to build their church.

My friend shared with me that on the very first day after the globe was completed, as the sun came up, because of the configuration of those metal plates, the surface of the globe reflected the sun to look like a perfect cross of Jesus Christ! All the city saw it, and all the Christians realized that God loved them, seeing that cross as the symbol of the love of God.

Nothing proves the love of God like the cross. The cross says, "I love you." The Bible says, "But God demonstrates his own love for us in this: While we were still sinners, Christ died for us" (Romans 5:8 NIV). I heard about a man who spent his life teaching about love. He was a seminary professor. He taught about love. He preached about love. He conducted seminars about love. He wrote books about love. As a matter of fact, they started calling him "Dr. Love."

Before long, Dr. Love grew older and was able to retire. One day, he was helping around the house and decided to do a big project. For days, he worked on a brand new cement driveway. He used a big long trowel to smooth out the cement. He was feeling pretty good about himself when a neighbor's dog ran through the wet cement. Just behind that neighbor dog came the neighbor boy chasing the dog, running through that wet cement, totally destroying the driveway that Dr. Love had worked on.

Dr. Love went berserk. He picked up the long trowel that he had been working with and started chasing that little neighbor kid around the block, screaming "I'm going to get you! I'm going to get you!"

The neighbors were astonished! They couldn't believe it! Dr. Love's wife couldn't believe it! She had never seen him like this before. She went out and said, "Honey, you have preached about love. You have written about love. You have taught about love!" But she could hear him screaming in the background, "Woman, that was love in the abstract; this is love in the concrete!"

I want you to know that the cross is God's love, not in the abstract, but in the concrete. You can touch it. It can touch you, and you can feel it.

In Romans 5 there is, perhaps, one of the greatest descriptions you will ever find of love. The apostle Paul says,

"You see, at just the right time, when we were still powerless, Christ died for the ungodly." *(Romans 5:6 NIV)*

The timing of the cross was not love in the abstract. It was love in the concrete. F. F. Bruce said it well: "It was a time when nothing else would do."

"You see, at just the right time, when we were still powerless, Christ died for the ungodly. Very rarely will anyone die for a righteous man, though for a good man someone might possibly dare to die. But God demonstrates His own love for us in this: While we were still sinners, Christ died for us." (Romans 5:6-8 NIV)

The Book of Romans is a book of logic. It is Paul's great Christian argument for justification, sanctification and glorification. In chapters one, two and three, under the inspiration of the Holy Spirit, he showed us that man is a sinner, that he can not save himself, and that he is under the judgment of God.

In chapter four, he described the doctrine of justification by faith and used Abraham as the supreme example. But in chapter five, the greatest truth of all comes from the pen of the apostle Paul. He asks and answers the question, "How can God justify sinners and still be Himself – just?" And the answer is that He does it by the cross.

The cross is God's answer to man's greatest need and, therefore, has become for us the supreme symbol of God's love for man. John R. W. Stott, in his book *The Cross of Christ,* said, "The fact that a cross became the Christian symbol, and that Christians stubbornly refused in spite of the ridicule to discard it in favour of something less offensive, can have only one explanation. It means that the centrality of the cross originated in the mind of Jesus Himself." Reflecting on the importance of the cross, Samuel L. Zwimmer said it like this, "If the cross of Christ is anything, it is surely everything."

Just think about it. If someone who had never visited a church came to the church where I pastor, what would they see? First they would see our steeple from miles away and, at the top, they'd see a cross. Entering the building, they would notice magnificent stained glass windows. In one of the most prominent windows is a 20-foot tall depiction of Christ on the cross. In fact, in our worship center, of the 34 stained-glass windows with images in them, the cross is depicted 17 times. This first-time guest might sit down next to someone, a lady perhaps, and around her neck would be a piece of jewelry, a necklace in the shape of a cross. Before long, a great praise team gets up and starts to sing *Oh, the Wonderful Cross.* Again, the guest is reminded of the cross. The stranger notices a man nearby with a little gold cross on his lapel. The guest might come on any one of a number of Sundays and see a table with the elements that represent the body of Jesus Christ, and the preacher would have preached about the cross. Perhaps unconsciously, he might notice the Christian flag in the corner with its simple but obvious red rendering of the cross.

What would a person think who came into my church and everywhere saw the symbol of the cross? You may even ask me why the church is so obsessed with the cross. I'll tell you why. That is where my Savior died for me. That is why Christians love the cross. The symbol of His death is the symbol of our life!

There is an overriding and primary truth in Paul's message. It is this – the cross demonstrates the love of God! The love of God is good news! And our hearts need to know – and we want to believe – that God really loves us.

One day when my daughters were small they were wading in the shallow end of a motel pool in the spring of the year. It was too cold to swim, so I was sitting on a lawn chair beside the pool. Laura, who was two, jumped off the steps and into about three feet of water. That was over her head, so she was frightened. She was flailing in that cold water as if she were in the middle of the perfect storm! She was never in any real danger because I was right there, but I wasn't too happy about having to jump into that freezing pool of water. As I was carrying her back to the room, I sternly said, "Laura, what were you thinking?" This little two-year-old said, "I was thinking about God. I know He loves me." She was right. God does love her.

The Bible says that God loves us. And the cross proves it. The cross demonstrates the love of God. Romans 5 tells us that. It says,

"You see, at just the right time, when we were still powerless, Christ died for the ungodly. Very rarely will anyone die for a righteous man, though for a good man someone might possibly dare to die. But God demonstrates his own love for us in this: While we were still sinners, Christ died for us." *(Romans 5:6-8 NIV)*

God demonstrates His love. The word, "demonstrates" is the Greek word *sunistemi.* It comes from two words – *sun,* which means "with," and *histemi,* which means "to stand." *Sunistemi* means "to stand with." The word means, He stands with us. He stands by us. At the cross, God stands with sinful man. He proves His love. The cross says "God is with you."

Let me tell you why He does it. It's because He knows us. Even though He sent us the Bible, we still sinned. He sent the Ten Commandments, and we still sinned. He sent the prophets of God, and we still sinned. Selfishly, we kept asking, is there more?

Could there be a little more? What have you done for me lately, God? God said, "I will send my Son to extend His hands to the right and to the left. I will suspend Him between heaven and earth as a citizen of neither place, and I will allow Him to be crucified for the sins of the whole world. I will prove my love for sinful man." The cross proves the love of God. It demonstrates the love of God.

How does the cross demonstrate the love of God? First of all, the cross demonstrates that He loves us sympathetically. Notice the words that appear in verses six and eight. *"At just the right time, when we were still powerless, Christ died for the ungodly."* In verse eight we are told that *"God demonstrates His own love for us in this: While we were still sinners, Christ died for us."*

Do you see the sympathy at the cross? God cares for sinners. If ever anyone had the right to judge, God has the right to judge. If ever anyone had the right to criticize, God does. If ever anyone had the right to point the finger of condemnation, God's long finger could be pointed at every one of us. If ever anyone had the right to stand back and say, "I don't want to touch this mess," God had the right to do so because we are *powerless, ungodly, sinners.* In order to love us, God loves us in spite of what we are. He loves us as we are, but He loves us too much to leave us as we are.

In the Greek New Testament, these three words – *powerless, ungodly, sinner* – stand out like a beacon because all of these words begin with the same letter, *alpha*, and end with the same two letters, *omicron* and *nu*. These three words sound alike: *asthenon, asebon* and *'amartalon*. It is as if God were saying, "Can you see what you are?" Can I make it any more clear? Will it take a poetic description before you see that you are *powerless, ungodly, sinners?"*

The word *powerless* means that we are completely without ability to save ourselves. The word *ungodly* means that we are totally depraved. Depravity does not mean we always are as bad as we could be. It does mean that every aspect of our life has been affected by the fall. The Bible also says we are *sinners*. It is that famous Bible word that talks about "missing the mark." That is what we are. That is who we are, *powerless, ungodly, sinners*. The good news is that God has sympathy for sinners. God loves sinners. God loves us.

The Bishop of Paris told a story about some boys who decided on a bet that they were going to go and make an artificial confession to the priest at the cathedral. They agreed to pay the one who made the big confession. They wanted to go in and really raise the hair on the back of the neck of this old priest. They had to make sure he had never heard a confession like it.

The boys began to plot and scheme and got a little money together. They drew straws to see which one would tell a confession that would shock the old priest. Well, little did they know that the old priest was standing by the window listening to what those boys were saying.

So, the chosen boy went in and said, "Father, I have a confession to make." The priest told him to step into the confessional booth. The boy stepped in and began to make up sins he had only dreamed about. He began to tell things he had never done before. He lied to the old priest, and the priest knew exactly what he was doing. When the boy couldn't think of anything else, he repeated it all again!

When he was done, he went outside, laughed, and told his friends to give him the money. They said, "No, no, no, no. You didn't make penance. You've got to do whatever the old priest says you have to do for penance."

The impenitent boy didn't want to do that. It wasn't part of the deal. But his friends insisted. So he went in to see the priest, a little less confident this time, and he said, "Sir, I'm here to do my penance." The old priest, knowing exactly what had happened, said, "I want you to walk into the great cathedral out into the worship area. I want you to look up on the wall, and you will see engraved there, in stone, the body of a man nailed to a cross – the crucified Christ. I want you to get down on your knees in front of that man nailed to that cross, and I want you to look up at that man, nailed to the cross, and I want you to say, 'This thou has done for me, and I don't care.'"

The boy wasn't too happy, but he went into that great, magnificent cathedral, bowed down and looked up into the face of bleeding love and dying mercy. He said, "This thou has done for me, and I...This thou has done for me, and I..." He could not finish. The realization that Christ died for him convicted him of his real sins. The Bishop of Paris said, "I know that story is true because I was that boy."

There is something about the cross that says to the heart of sinners, "You are welcome at the foot of the cross." I've got good news for you. God loves sinners. He loves us sympathetically.

There is more. God shows His love for us sacrificially. Look again at Romans 5. This is perhaps one of my favorite verses in the New Testament. We should all memorize this verse:

"But God demonstrates His own love for us in this: While we were still sinners, Christ died for us." *(Romans 5:8 NIV)*

Do you see the sacrifice of the cross? *Christ died for us.* That is the language of sacrifice. He did more then preach, teach and heal. He died for us. That is a part of Christ's sacrifice – a painful death not for His sins, but for yours and for mine. The cross was an instrument of unusual torture even for the ancient world. The Romans imported it into their culture from the barbarians at the edge of civilization. There were other methods of execution for capital crimes – stoning, hanging, beheading – all horrible in their own way, but the cross was the worst. It was slow death. It was agony from beginning to end. It was designed not just to kill but to kill in the most painful way possible. Even in our language when we speak of pain beyond the threshold of toleration, we speak of excruciating pain. The word "excruciating" comes from two Latin words "ex" and "crux." The word for cross is "crux" – it is in the center of excruciating – pain like the cross. It is unbearable pain. His painful, willing sacrifice on the cross proves His love.

The apostle John, reflecting back on the cross many years later, wrote:

"This is love: not that we loved God, but that he loved us and sent his Son as an atoning sacrifice for our sins." *(I John 4:10 NIV)*

We see on the news every day young men and young women going to the battlefields willing to die on behalf of a great and noble cause. The apostle Paul even acknowledges that for a good man, or maybe for a good cause, someone might possibly dare to die. But he said God sent His Son to die, not when we were better…not when we were noble…God sent His Son to die *for us while we were still sinners.* The word "for" is an important word, even though it is a small word. It is the Greek word *huper.* It means "in behalf of." That word simply means "in my place." This points to the ancient doctrine of the substitutionary death of Jesus Christ. His sacrifice was not just the physical pain of the cross – it was also a spiritual sacrifice. Christ took our place – our sin, our judgment, our death on Himself at the cross.

In my study, I have a book with an English translation of the oldest sermon manuscript in existence. It dates back to about 150 A.D. In that early sermon, over and over the ancient homiletician discusses the cross of Jesus, how Jesus died on the cross for sinners like you and me. Repeatedly in that nearly 2000-year-old sermon, the preacher says Jesus died *for* sinners – he uses the language of substitution and sacrifice.

The church has from the beginning proclaimed, the church has from the beginning preached, that Jesus died *for* us — that He died in our place, that He took our place on the cross. The language of sacrifice and substitution is nothing new. It is the biblical and historical way to describe the cross. No wonder the beautiful old hymn says, "There is a fountain filled with blood, drawn from Emmanuel's veins. And sinners plunged beneath that flood lose all their guilty stains." Christ took our place on the cross.

On the day after Christmas one year, my family and I were headed to the mall, but on the way, we had to stop by the pediatrician. My oldest daughter, who is an adult now, was at that time five years old. She had a little infection — something minor that kids get.

My oldest daughter and my wife went into the doctor's office while my younger daughter and I waited. I wasn't paying any attention to the time because I was interested in my younger daughter playing with some blocks and toys.

Quite a bit of time passed when finally the nurse, a friend of the family, came out and said, "Kie, would you come back here for a moment?" I thought that was a little odd, but I said, "Sure." I told Laura, "Come with Daddy." But the nurse said, "I'll watch Laura." I began to think, this is not right, something's wrong here.

I walked back into the examining room where the doctor was standing. He looked concerned. Amanda, my little five-year-old with long blonde hair and big blue eyes, was looking up as if she didn't know what to think. My wife, who rarely sheds tears, was sitting in a chair sobbing. I asked, "What's wrong?"

The doctor, a young man whose bedside manner had not been developed yet, looked at me and said bluntly, "Amanda has juvenile sugar diabetes. Tomorrow morning, we are going to check her into Scottish Rite Hospital in

Atlanta so that we can teach her how to give herself two shots of insulin a day, which she will take for the rest of her life."

Every dad will understand when I say this. On that day when I heard those words, the earth opened up and swallowed me. I said, "This can't be right. It can't be true. It can't be correct!" My wife, who has worked in the medical profession and in hospitals all of our married life, said, "I saw them run the tests twice. It is right."

We gathered everything up to go. I went out to the car, my little family with me, with tears rolling down my cheeks. Our hearts were broken. My wife began to explain to me some of the things we might have to look forward to in the years to come having a little girl with juvenile sugar diabetes. She would have a shortened life span with numerous other health complications along the way. This little girl who never liked any kind of pain faced daily shots. Here was a little girl whom we didn't have to correct very often. If we merely looked at her, she would do the right thing. Now to think she would have to give herself shots for an incurable disease was almost more than we could bear.

My immediate thoughts that day focused on how sweet she was, how innocent she was, how tender she was. We loved our little girl more than life itself. We were young, too, and unaccustomed to tragedy, and our pain was almost unbearable. Our little girl with an incurable childhood disease which could threaten both the quality and length of her life did not seem possible. We went home that day. We didn't go to the mall. We just went home to settle down and face the reality that things would never be the same. We began to realize that all of our tomorrows would be different from all of our yesterdays.

That day, we tried our best to give our children the best day they could have. On and off, all day, my wife and I would look at one another, break down, weep and embrace. At the same time we tried to take good care of those little girls.

I had to put Amanda to bed, my little five-year-old girl with those big blue eyes and long blonde hair. I sat on the edge of her little bed, with pink and frill everywhere, and told her she was sick. She would not be exactly the same as she had always been. Things were going to be different, but we still loved her and we would always take care of her.

Can you imagine how I felt trying to tell my little girl she was going to get shots every day for the rest of her life, she wasn't going to feel good, and she was going to the hospital the next day? When my wife and I got our little girls to bed, and we had finally gone to bed ourselves, as the minutes ticked into hours throughout the night, the tears flowed.

Have you ever cried until you are numb inside? You know you hurt, but you can't cry any more – that's where I had gotten to. My wife, who was lying in bed next to me, gently rocked the bed every so often as she sobbed silently through the night.

I never will forget what happened at two o'clock in the morning. I knew what time it was because I could see the green lights of the digital clock beside our bed shining in the reflection of my wife's tears. At 2:00 a.m., she turned to me and said what I'd been thinking all day long, but I hadn't said. My wife turned to me and said what every parent can understand. She said, "I wish it could be me."

I knew exactly what she meant. I knew that in an instant, if it were possible, she would have taken that little girl's place. In an instant, I too would have taken my little girl's place so she wouldn't have to experience any pain, any harm, any danger. Either of us, if it had been possible, though it was not, would have immediately, without a thought, without praying about it, would have taken her place. Every parent understands what I am talking about.

Later that morning, I woke up early because I wanted to pray before we went to the hospital. We had to be there at 7:30 a.m. I hadn't slept much that night, but I awoke early. I slipped down beside the bed, but every time I tried to pray, the words made no sense at all. As I prayed, it seemed like my words got about as far as the ceiling and hit the floor with a thud. As I struggled with the desire to pray, for some reason the words "thank you" came from my lips. It was, finally, the only thing that seemed to make any sense at all.

I could not explain why it made sense. I didn't know why at the time, but as I knelt there for about 30 minutes, I continually prayed, "Thank you, thank you, thank you." I guess it was because God has never failed me. I wasn't about to turn my back on Him after all He had done for us.

At the hospital, once again, my wife had gone with Amanda to take one final test. I filled out some forms and then took Laura, our youngest girl, down to the cafeteria to get breakfast. No sooner had we stepped up to the checkout line, I felt a hand on my shoulder. I turned around, and it was our young pediatrician. He said, "Kie, go home. There is no sugar diabetes."

"Now wait a minute, wait a minute," I said. "What do you mean there is no sugar diabetes?" No one can understand this except to say that love is irrational sometimes. I had been up all night. I wanted something better than just to go home. We had just had the worst night of our lives! Don't merely pat me on the back and say, "Go home!"

I said, "What are you talking about?" He said, "We have run every test we can run. Yesterday, her blood sugar was out of sight. Today, it is down in a normal range." I said, "Well, is it going to come back?" The answer was simple – there is no sugar diabetes. He said that our prayers had been answered. "Go home."

Now you may ask me, did God heal her or was the doctor wrong the first time? I don't know. But either way, I praise the Lord for it. I give Him all the glory. But here is what I learned: When I was so desperate to see my little girl well, and when my wife said, as only a mother can say and mean it with all of her heart, "I wish it could be me," as we lay there through that empty night concerned about our little girl, there was one thing I knew for certain – even though I would be willing to take my little girl's place, I could not do it. But I know someone who can. And I know someone who did – His name is Jesus. He took our place. Beyond just the temporary need of healing the body, Jesus took our place in death, punishment and hell. He died on what should have been *my* cross. *While we were still sinners, Christ died for us.* He took our place.

That is why Dallas Holm used to sing:

"Calvary, Calvary, was it there for Him, or was it there for me?
Calvary, Calvary, is that my cross He's taking to Calvary?"

The question of that song is haunting, but the answer is clear – it *was* my cross He took to Calvary. It was *my* cross, and He took it up Calvary to bring me to God.

Recently, I toured England and Scotland tracing the steps of some of history's greatest preachers. While on The Strand in London, I noticed what looked to be a beautiful spire, like a cathedral spire, a cross, a steeple. It was not on top of a building but was raised up out of the ground not far from the historic Savoy Hotel in London. I asked my guide what it was. He said it was Charring Cross. It had been a gift to the nation of England. It stands near a station, near a depot today called Charring Cross Station.

Charring Cross is almost centrally located in a historic section of London. If I were standing on The Strand and looking at Charring Cross, I would see this cross rising up out of the concrete in the middle of this bustling city called London. If I were standing on The Strand looking at the cross, I would see behind it the Thames River. Over the river is London Bridge, and there is Big Ben. A little further is the House of Parliament. Then, if you swing in the other direction, you would see Buckingham Palace and Number Ten Downing Street, the home of the Prime Minister. You can see from Charring Cross the famous Trafalgar Square. In front of Charring Cross, a few blocks away, is Piccadilly Circus. From Charring Cross in another direction is the wonderful place called Hyde Park, where Princess Diana has been memorialized. The British Museum is also only a short distance from Charring Cross. You can see that somehow Charring Cross has become a center for a part of London.

I heard about a little boy who got lost on that side of London. An English police officer found the little boy. He was crying. The policeman said, "Son, would you like me to take you back to the station and call your mum?" The little boy said, "No, sir." The boy said, "Just take me to the Cross, and I'll find my way home from there."

This is what I want you to know. If you find your way to the cross, you can find your way home. You can find your way to God. You can find God's love. That's because God demonstrates His love for you at the cross.

10

THE CALL TO REPENTANCE

DR. MAC BRUNSON

Senior Pastor

First Baptist Church

Jacksonville, Florida

IN 1988, A BUSINESSMAN BY THE NAME OF BEN PATTERSON decided that he, along with three of his friends, was going to climb the highest peak in Yosemite National Park, which was Mount Lyell. And in order to do that, they had to climb and cross a huge glacier to get to the mountain, and it would take them an entire day to cross this glacier.

Now two of these men were professionals; the other two were not. Ben was not a professional climber, and he tells the story that as they made their way across this massive glacier for hours, the two experts opened up a big gap and went out ahead of the other two. Ben said, "Well, I'm naturally competitive, and I wanted to beat them to the top and show them that a rank amateur could be as good as a professional mountain climber." So, as he relates, "I found a direction to go off in, and for 30 minutes I moved in the opposite direction in order to come up around where these professional climbers were going, until I discovered that I was caught in a cul-de-sac." He said, "I was stuck just in this cul-de-sac of nothing but ice, ten feet away from the rock, but I couldn't move, and I was hanging at a 45-degree angle." He added, "If I made any step in any direction, my feet would have come out from under me, and I would have slid…tumbled…fallen…what looked like 50 miles down into this ravine.

ATT

I just stood there not knowing what to do."

Do you know how he got out? Ben said, "It took an hour for my experienced climbing friends to find me. One of them leaned out and used an ice pick to chip out two little footsteps in the glacier. Then he gave me the following instructions: 'Ben, you must step out from where you are and put your foot where the first foothold is and, without a moment's hesitation, swing your other foot across and land it in the second step. Then, at the same time, reach out, and I'll grab your hand and pull you up on the rock to safety. But listen carefully, as you step across, don't lean into the mountain, if anything, lean out a bit from it. Otherwise, your feet will fly out from under you and you will slide down into the ravine below.'"

Ben said, "When I am on the edge of a cliff, my instinct is to lie down and hug the mountain, to become one with it, not lean away from it; but that was what my good friend was telling me to do. As I stood trembling on that glacier, I looked at him very hard for a moment. Then based solely on what I believed to be true about the good will and good sense of my friend, I decided to say no to what I felt, to lean out, step out, traverse the ice into safety, and it took less than two seconds to learn that what he said was right."

Ben Patterson found himself in a situation in which a lot of Christians find themselves today. We have taken shortcuts spiritually in our lives. We have decided that we have a better plan and a better way than God and God's Word, and so we just strike out on our own and get ourselves into a slippery situation where if we take another step, we're going to lose it all. And there is no way out of these situations for the people of God except to step into repentance and reach up to God for Him to deliver us out of the situation we've gotten into.

I want you to take God's Word and look with me at Jeremiah, chapter 8. When you come to Jeremiah; chapter 8, let me explain something to you – Jeremiah, chapter 7, chapter 8, chapter 9, and chapter 10 are all sermons of

Jeremiah. You're going to hear how Jeremiah preached to his people, or the people of Jerusalem. These are called the Temple Gate Sermons. They were messages that God placed on Jeremiah's heart, and He said, "I want you to go down there to the temple, and as the people are going in and coming out, you stand out there and you preach these messages to them." So I am going to give you just a portion of a sermon that Jeremiah preached to the people as they came in and out of the temple.

Now you've got to understand a little bit of the background when you come to Jeremiah, chapter 8. Let me give you just a brief history; let me tell you something about them nationally. Jeremiah, chapter 8 is a message preached around 605 B.C., which is a very important date. Let me tell you what was happening to put this sermon into context. Assyria had been the dominant world empire for nearly 200 years, and it was unraveling. Over to the East in a place now called Iraq, but in that day called Babylon, there was a man named Nabopolassar who was beginning to build a military machine unlike anything the world had ever seen. He had a son that you know by the name of Nebuchadnezzar, and at this time, while the Assyrian empire was unraveling, Nabopolassar began to take his military machine to Assyria for a great battle.

Now Assyria had an alliance with Egypt, and there was a Pharaoh there by the name of Pharaoh Neko. Neko took all of the army of Egypt and he began to move up to intercept the armies of Nabopolassar and Babylon to come to the aid of Assyria. In order to get there, where did he have to go through? Israel. So he asked for permission, and King Josiah said, "No, you can't come through here to go and rescue Assyria." And the Pharaoh of Egypt said, "Well, forget that, I'm coming through there anyway," and Josiah raised this army up and they went out and met in a place that is called, in the Hebrew tongue, Harmegiddo, or Armageddon, the Valley of Jezreel or Megiddo. Kind of interesting isn't it?

These armies met and the Egyptians killed Judah's King Josiah, and defeated his army, and they went up to a battle called Charchemish, one of the greatest battles in ancient history; and there at the battle of Charchemish the Egyptians were defeated by Nabopolassar, and the armies of Babylon and the Assyrians were eventually done in, and that is the background of chapter 8 of Jeremiah.

Now you need to understand that they were in a national crisis. Their king had either just been killed or was about to be killed. They were going to see the demise, the unraveling of the nation of Judah. In just a few short years they were going to go through a succession of kings who were just terrible, and the nation was going to fall apart. In a few years Nebuchadnezzar was going to invade and destroy the city and take all of the best of the people off to captivity in Babylon. That is what was happening nationally; they were in the midst of a war.

We Americans can understand some of what they were going through economically, militarily and nationally. We ought to have a good understanding of what these people were experiencing. The reason they were having all this trouble nationally is because spiritually, they were in a mess. They were stuck in a situation and could not get out of it. They were free falling by the time you come to Jeremiah, chapter 8. Spiritually, they had said essentially, "We are not going to worship just Jehovah God; we're going to worship every other god as well." They had become enamored with the gods of the other nations. That had been a problem for Israel since the days they came up out of Egypt. They came out of Egypt and repeatedly fell into idolatry and worshipping these pagan gods of the nations they went through. They came into the land, they got their first king, which was Saul, and Saul, in the end, turned from praying to God to consulting a witch. Sounds like Nancy Reagan, doesn't it?

A necromancer says, let's talk to the dead about our future. We have one who was dead now alive who has a word about our future. Of course you know what happened to Saul. David came to the throne, and for the years that David was there, there was this great worship of God; even in the midst of David's sin, there was no question but that God was the God of Israel. And then Solomon came to the throne, and you know how the Bible says that his wives from these other nations began to turn his heart away from God and he built all of these centers of worship for those wives, so they could go and worship their gods all over the country, and the nation began to fall. The northern kingdom as it split from the southern kingdom of Judah began to fall into this idolatry; and God watched this very patiently, and as they went off into this idolatry, God said to them, "If you'll worship me, I will establish you in the land, but if you turn and worship other gods, I will scatter you to the nations." So Israel turned and worshipped the gods of these other nations. They didn't turn their backs on God, on Jehovah. They kept Jehovah. They went to the temple to worship Jehovah, but then they worshipped these other gods as well.

You remember what God commanded? "You shall have no other gods before me." Do you know what the Hebrew means right there? You shall have no other gods in my presence. In other words, God says you shall have no other gods where He can see. Now where can God see? Everywhere! And they brought them literally to the town of Manasseh; they brought them into the temple. It would be like bringing a Buddha and setting a Buddha up in the sanctuary of First Baptist Church that historically has stood on the Word of God. They brought them into the temple, and God said to the nation, "You have so longed to worship these other gods that I'm going to give you into the hands of the nations who dreamed up these gods," and they went into captivity for 70 years. And do you know what? They got so sick of those other nations and those other nations' gods that Israel, after the captivity, never had another problem with idolatry again. In South Carolina we would say, "God broke 'em from sucking eggs." (You've gotta be country to understand that.) That was the situation.

Now consider this – on the National Day of Prayer, after September 11th, in the National Cathedral, we had all those who were ministers of the gospel of Jesus Christ, but we also had representatives from every other religion in this country and around the world. We are there, friend.

In fact, we have so longed to live the lifestyle of those that we watch on the television and in the movies. Do you remember a time when the only people who got divorced were those people in Hollywood? Do you remember that? There was a time when the only time you ever heard of homosexuality was if you heard of Errol Flynn and then eventually Rock Hudson. But we have so longed for that lifestyle that God has said, "Fine, you want that lifestyle? You'll get what comes with that lifestyle." And now our homes are a mess, our children are growing up in alternate lifestyles, and homosexuality and divorce are as rampant in the church as they are in the nation.

God says, "You can have it, it can be yours. You've longed for these gods of these other nations, and then you can have not only their gods, but go and worship them where they are worshipped in their home temples. And the only way out of this is a step towards Me and repentance; and reach up so I can jerk you out of the mess you have gotten into."

I'm going to show you two things as I introduce this concept of repentance that's found all the way through the Word of God. When God's people are stuck in sin, God calls His people to repentance. Look at Jeremiah, chapter 1, verse 9: *"Then the Lord stretched out His hand and touched my mouth, and the Lord said to me, 'Behold, I have put My words in your mouth.'"* So when you come to Jeremiah, chapter 8 and verse 4, that is exactly what has happened here.

God has put His words in the mouth of the prophet and the prophet now is going to speak, and he is going to ask three questions. The first two questions really are questions that are rhetorical and the response is clear. Now look at this, *"Do men fall and not get up again?"* Well, the answer is, of course they don't. Men fall, and they get right back up. If somebody stumbles and falls, he gets up. In fact, what have we taught our children? You watch little toddlers. There's a mother or dad who's got the hand of a toddler, and that toddler will stumble and fall, and what does the parent do? He or she will pick him up. But we are taught from birth, from the time we can walk, that if we fall, get back up. We take our children and put them on a bicycle, and we are teaching them to ride. When they fall, we say, "Get back up – get up!"

I've been standing at the steps when some of our adults have fallen down steps, and it always terrifies me when somebody does that. What's the first thing somebody says? "Here, let's get you up." That's the first thing we want to do. Let's get them up, let's pick them up. I remember the first time I was thrown from a horse. I was about six or seven years of age; my sister who is twelve years older than I am was riding a horse in front of me, and she looked around and said, "Get up, just get up. Get back on the horse; if you don't get back on, then you'll never ride again."

Did you ever give that advice to somebody? I hope you were a little more compassionate. But God asked the question. He said, *"Do men fall and not get up again?"* Well, sure they do. It's a logical question. Then He comes to the second question, *"Does one turn away and not repent?"* That is, does one who turns aside, does he not turn back again and return?

You can look at it this way; before you left the house this morning, you got up, took a shower, dressed, then came down here to the church. You're going to go back. That's the question. It's logical; it makes sense. When you turn and go somewhere, do you not turn around and come back home? Well, the answer is yes. That's just logical.

Now look at verse 5, where God then asked this question, *"Why then has this people, Jerusalem, turned away in continual apostasy? They hold fast to deceit, they refuse to return."* Let me show you something here, congregation. There is a word in the Hebrew, and the word is *shuwb*, which means to repent. It means to return or to turn again. I want you to notice something: Look again at verse 5, "*Why then has this people, Jerusalem, turned away?*" That's one time it's used. "*In continual*" – the word there is *shuwb* in the Hebrew, we translate it *apostasy* – "*in continual turning.*" Then, "*they hold fast to deceit, they refuse to return.*" There's *shuwb* again – three times in one verse. Go back to verse 4, "*Do men fall and not get up again? Does one turn away* (shuwb) *and not repent?*" There's the word again; five times in two verses, this word that you can translate as turn or return or repent is used. It is as if God is trying to get a message across that His people need to turn. Jeremiah preaches on repentance more than any other person in all of Scripture. Henry Blackaby says that 90 to 95 percent of the time in Scripture, when repentance is talked about, it is a repentance of God's people.

Right here God is calling these people to repent. He is calling them to turn. Just look at verse 5 – turn away, repent, and turn away, from continual turning. They refuse to return. It is just used constantly. We can say, "Why? Why is God hammering this concept of repentance?" I want to tell you why; because to refuse to repent is to invite the judgment of God.

I want to show you something. Look with me at Isaiah, chapter 55, verses 6 and 7: "Seek the Lord while He may be found; call upon Him while He is near. Let the wicked forsake his ways and the unrighteous man his thoughts; and let him return [there it is] to the Lord..." Let him return, let him turn back, let him repent and come back to the Lord.

Look with me at Ezekiel, chapter 18, verses 31 and 32: "'Cast away from you all your transgressions which you have committed and make yourselves a new heart and a new spirit! For why will you die, O house of Israel? For I have no pleasure in the death of anyone who dies,' declares the Lord God. 'Therefore, repent and live.'" Do you see that? Look at 2 Chronicles, chapter 7, that very familiar passage that you probably can quote: "...If My people who are called by My name humble themselves and pray and seek My face and turn..." Turn from what? From their wicked ways. Over and over and over, why? Because, if we refuse to repent and turn, we have no other alternative but to slide and to fall.

Now let me show you something else. Look at Psalm 7, verses 11 and 12: "God is a righteous judge, and a God who has indignation every day. If a man does not repent..." Do you see that? "If a man does not repent, He [that is, God] will sharpen His sword; He has bent His bow and made it ready." Go to Jeremiah, chapter 15, and look at verse 6: "'You who have forsaken me,' declares the Lord, 'You keep going backward...'" Now look at that. He is talking about backsliding there. And what's the answer to that? The answer is turning around. We are going backward, therefore we need to turn around and move the opposite direction. "'So I will stretch out my hand against you and destroy you...'" In essence God said, "I am tired of putting up with this!"

Now this is the Word of God. That didn't come out of Nashville. That didn't come out of somebody's pamphlet. That comes right straight out of the Word of God. There are over 120 verses that deal with just this word that we translate as repent or turn or return, and so you've got to do something with the whole subject of repentance because it is practically on every single page of the Word of God. And the Bible says, "If you don't repent" – and He is speaking to His people – He says, "I will bring judgment on you."

That is what Jeremiah is saying in Jeremiah, chapter 8, in the year 605 B.C., right before the entire nation begins to unravel.. Well, I ought to tell you something, if there was ever a word for America, this is the word for America right here. Return, repent, God is calling; not the prophet, not a preacher, not an evangelist. God is continuously calling His people who are in sin, to repent and to return and to come back.

Let me tell you something, I'm sharing this with you out of a pastor's heart; we don't really live in a world of reality most of the time. We live in a make-believe world. We play at church, most of the time. Yes, we play at church. Most of the time, this isn't a world of reality at all. All you do when you turn on television now is see reality TV, which is not reality at all. Have you been fired by Donald Trump? Have you ever been in his board room? That's not reality, that's fantasy. Have you seen this Asian American by the name of William Hung, who sings? Have you heard him sing? If you've heard him sing, you can understand why they had every right to throw him off of the show. That guy's got a recording contract now. I'm waiting on mine to come any day. If they can put that guy on TV to sing, surely they can put me on TV to sing. That's not reality, that's fantasy TV. We don't live in a world of reality.

On November 22, 1963, in the city of London, there was a play that was going on that was written by David Lodge, the British novelist and playwright. In one scene, there was to be a young man who would walk into the scene carrying a transistor radio. He was to set the radio down, turn it on, and while they carried on this conversation – he was going in for a job interview – the radio was to be playing in the background, but you've already caught the date. David Lodge was there. He was at the theater there in London where the play was ongoing, and so he was sitting there; knowing everything that was going on. This young man walked in, had the transistor radio, set it down, turned it on, and it was supposed to be a comedy. It was supposed to be a funny scene, when suddenly, out of this transistor radio came a news broadcast that said, "The American President, John F. Kennedy, has just been assassinated in Dallas." Everybody stopped. Everybody was shocked. The entire audience gasped and the young actor reached back, turned the radio off, tried to go on with the play, but they realized it was impossible to go on with the play when a word of reality had entered into that theater. Here's a word of reality that enters into the church this morning, and the word of reality is from God, and the word is repent.

That's the word of reality. Repent. God's people are called to repentance.

Let me show you just one other simple thing right here. Look back in Jeremiah, chapter 8, verses 6 and 7, when God's people were stuck in sin. They were in penitence, which is a refusal to repent, which is a spiritual abnormality. It is abnormal for the people of God not to repent.

Now I want to tell you something, I say this as lovingly as I can; I have never seen a subject that I know will create more debate among wise theologians than repentance. There must be a reason. Whenever I preach on repentance, I guarantee you before the sun goes down on the City of Jacksonville, I'll have at least one email, and I will be chewed up one side and down the other for preaching on repentance.

Why doesn't Satan want us to preach it? Because he knows if we do it, something happens. It is abnormal for the people of God not to repent. Now let me just read this to you, "I have listened and heard..." God's speaking now, God says, "I've listened to everything they've said." Do you realize that God has heard everything you've said since you got up this morning? He's been listening. He is the unseen listener to every conversation. He's listening to your thoughts. "They have spoken what is not right." But look at this, God is just, and this is incredulous to God. God is almost in disbelief saying "I can't believe it. I've been listening, and I've heard, they've not spoken what is right. No man has repented of his wickedness." You say, "Well, now, preacher, this is all Old Testament." You hang on. Do you know what the first sermon of Jesus in the New Testament is? Repent and be saved.

It says, "I have listened and heard, they have spoken what is not right; no man repented of his wickedness, saying, 'What have I done?'" You watch these people, you've caught them in a lie saying, "Well, what did I do? "I didn't do anything." "Well, yeah, I slept with somebody else's wife, but yeah, what did I do?" "What's so bad about that?" "Everybody else does it." "I cheated on my income tax, I didn't do anything that is so bad." "I haven't done anything that is wrong." That's exactly what He is saying. God says that's what they are saying, "Well, what have I done?" Everyone turned to his own course. That is, they turned away from God's will, like a horse charging into battle.

Have you ever seen that John Wayne movie, *The Searchers*? That is one of the best movies ever made. When the Indians lead him out and away from the settlers, and they looked back and saw all of the smoke coming up, and they realized that the Indians had lead them out, the Indians had attacked the settlement, put everybody to death, and burned the 15 homes, he whipped that horse around and took off. That's exactly what He is saying here. He is saying, we are running off in every other direction except in the direction God is calling us to, like a horse that is running into battle.

He gives you an unbelievable illustration right here of the birds: "Even the stork in the sky knows her seasons…" He says the stork knows when she is supposed to return. "…And the turtledove and the swift and the thrush observe the time of their migration…" He says even these birds, with their little bird brains, know when they are suppose to turn and return. He says it is written into nature itself that you turn around and go back. He finishes that verse with these words: *"But My people do not know…"*

So now people do not know, but He says you can get down to the birds, and the birds know. Tierra del Fuego is at the very end of Argentina. There is a little bird there that they call the red knot. It's a sandpiper. If you are from the Carolinas like I am, you see them all over the beach. About mid-May they leave the very tip of Argentina, the southern tip, and they fly all the way up that spiny coast of Argentina, up over Brazil, by Guyana, all the way up Belize, all that way, and then they turn and head out over the Atlantic. They will fly for one solid week without landing, without eating. For one week, they will fly out over the Atlantic, and they will make their way on up to the Chesapeake Bay and the

Delaware Bay where the horseshoe crabs come about the middle of May and lay their eggs. It happens every year. It was happening before white Americans were ever on this soil called America. Those birds hit it just right when the horseshoe crabs lay their eggs, and every one of those little sandpipers will eat 135,000 horseshoe crab eggs. They will gain enough strength to continue flying all the way up to the northern regions of Canada, 9,000 miles one way from Argentina. Now listen to this. They will get there and they'll mate. The female will lay four speckled brown eggs. She and her mate will hatch those eggs, and by mid-July the female will fly by herself. Maybe she is sick of the husband and she is sick of the kids. She will fly by herself 9,000 miles back to Tierra del Fuego. One week later, the male has had all of the kids he can take, so he leaves, and flies 9,000 miles all the way back to the bottom tip of Argentina. By mid-August, without a college degree, without ever taking physics or geography, without a map and without a global positioning system, those little baby birds will fly the exact same route 9,000 miles to the tip of Argentina where they will meet back up with mom and dad. Eighteen-thousand miles a year, and the brightest scientific minds can't figure it out; but God says that a bird knows when to turn and come back, but My people don't know.

11

IS GOD A MAN OR WOMAN?

DR. ERGUN CANER

Dean

Liberty Baptist Theological Seminary

Lynchburg, Virginia

IN ROMANS 8:14-17, WE READ:

"For all who are being led by the Spirit of God, these are sons of God. For you have not received a spirit of slavery leading to fear again, but you have received a spirit of adoption as sons by which we cry out, 'Abba! Father!' The Spirit Himself testifies with our spirit that we are children of God, and if children, heirs also, heirs of God and fellow heirs with Christ, if indeed we suffer with Him so that we may also be glorified with Him." *(NASB)*

In January of 2002, a popular publisher, perhaps the most popular publisher in America, made an announcement that it was releasing the gender-neutral Bible. This Bible in America was a little different from when you normally hear of a gender-neutral Bible. Here in America, the gender-neutral Bible said anytime there was a reference to humanity and mankind, it turned it into humankind. For in Europe, the gender-neutral Bible is different. The gender-neutral Bible, for the majority of denominations and the majority of publishers, means that any reference to God as man, in masculine terminology with masculine pronouns and masculine descriptors, is to be excised from the text, removed from the Bible.

They think that we who are Bible-believing evangelicals actually believe that God is a man. Because when we reference God in the Bible, it is always "He" or "Father" or "Lord" or "His" or "Him." Even though this has happened in the recent past, this is not a new discussion. Back in the middle ages, Julian of Norwich wrote an entire treatise entitled "Christ our Mother." But the discussion has been increasing in our culture. Twenty years ago, the discussion was over who is God, the nature of God.

A very popular book called *Godtalk* came out with a chapter entitled, "Can A Male God Save Women?" One Jewish feminist scholar, Rita Goss, whenever she references God, says God-she. Are they right? Do we honestly believe in a "God with male genitalia?"

Is, in fact, God a man? Come on! You know the verse, you can cite it with me. John 4:24, "God is spirit, and those who worship Him must worship in spirit and in truth." Hosea 11:9 says, "...I am God and not man, the Holy One in your midst..." The Bible is clear that God is a spirit.

So, how in the world have we gotten in this position? How in the world has every mainline denomination save two given into politically correct, hierarchical, metaphysical liturgy? How have we gotten to this point? You know. We have reached the saturation point of the politically correct pulpits.

They miss the point. If we're not saying God is man, what are we saying? The most essential point: God is Father, He's not man, He is *Father*. In other words, God is not man in relation to His gender; He is Father in relation to His children.

When we reference God as Father, it is not a biological issue; it is a theological issue. You see, when you remove God as Father from the Bible, when you mess with this book, you are not touching God. You are not messing with His holiness; you are not messing with His glory one bit.

God is not disturbed by the silliness of man. But they are robbing you and me of our divine rights and our divine privileges and our divine standing in Him. His provision is invoked for His children. Why? Because He is Father! In this most familiar text by the apostle Paul, let us look precisely at those things that define God's relationship with His children.

I. THE FATHER BINDS US TOGETHER (ROMANS 8:14) - "SONS OF GOD"

Notice Paul's admonition: all who are saved by the blood of Christ are considered "sons." We are equal. We are family. The profundity of those words cannot be overstated. All of us — regardless of race, age, gender, or heritage — are family. Why? *Because we have a common Father.*

We all come from various and different backgrounds. I am a Turkish immigrant. I was raised as a Sunni Muslim, and when we came to America, we settled in the north. This makes me a Yankee. My wife is not just Southern, she is a Southern belle. She likes living on a farm, which makes no sense to me. We live five minutes from the grocery store! Why farm if the actual food is waiting five minutes away? If I'm hungry for hamburger I don't go build a cow, grow a cow, or whatever you do with a cow. I go to where the meat is already prepared.

But my wife will take the tomatoes, and she will place them on the window sill and let them ripen. And then at an appropriate moment, she will take two pieces of white bread, and she will take a special brand of mayonnaise. She is very brand specific. She will take a knife and slather the two pieces of bread with mayonnaise, put this huge chunk of tomato on the bread, salt and pepper it, and put it together.

As a Yankee, may I interject that if there is no meat on that bread, it is not a sandwich. I have very few rules by which I operate when I eat, but one rule is that whatever I eat must have had at one time a parent and a face. And yet we have been married for twelve years, happily. How? Because God has shaped me and broken me. He has united us. We are husband and wife, and in Christ, we are family.

You may not like me, but you have to love me. Isn't that right? Because we're family. We have virtually nothing in common. We eat different foods, we sing different songs, we speak differently, we have different languages, we read different things. We are different people. We have virtually nothing in common, except a Father who binds us together.

I usually preach in two or three different churches a week. I get to see various denominations, and various groups, various churches, even among Baptists. Christians are the most varied bunch in the world. We have absolutely nothing in common save the God we serve. I've been in every kind of worship service in the world. I cannot possibly imagine how we are united if it were not for the Father-heart of God.

I've been in high liturgical churches. It's the kind of church where if you sit down randomly in a pew, somebody's going to talk to you. "Excuse me, that's my pew." You know the kind of church I'm talking about. "My mama sat there, my grandmamma sat there, that fits our family posterior." The kind of church where if you say "amen" out loud, they're going to spin around to look and see who said that. "Excuse me, but that wasn't in the bulletin."

They sing different songs in high church, in Latin sometimes. I don't know what they are saying. You stand, you sit, you turn, you spin, it's like "Jazzercise." You may say, "I don't like that kind of worship." You may say, "It's too formal, it's too liturgical for me, I don't like that." That's fine. But in those churches, if they are born again children of God; guess what? You have to love them, because they're your family.

I've been to country churches. I've pastored country churches; most notably, the Wood Baptist Church in Franklin County, North Carolina. They sing a different kind of song out there. They sing the "sliding" hymns. In those churches if you can't find the note, *hunt* for it.

At the country church, I didn't need a clock. I knew exactly when 12:00 was, because sitting over in the left-hand pew was Nanny Belle Gupton. And at 12:00 noon, every Sunday, Nanny Belle would sit there, without taking her eyes off of me. She would open up her purse and reach into that purse and pull out something that looked like a toothbrush and a little vial. *Snuff.* I know, you're going to say, "That's wrong, that's evil, that's sinful." Hey, she's over 90 years old! She could have outlived every one of you. Sometimes if I was feeling ornery, I would just make up points in my sermon, just to watch her fill up. You say, "those backward, outhouse churches." Hey, guess what? That's fine, if it's not your cup of tea, that's great. But you know what? They're your family.

About a third of the time I get the pleasure of preaching in black churches. Different kind of singing going on there. Different kind of worship, you don't just walk in when you want. Ushers with white gloves meet you. Deacons begin the service. Gentlemen, if you have a green suit, you have green shoes. You match. And hats! I'm not talking pillbox hats. I'm talking satellite dish hats. Got a curtain rod on the front, it operates by remote so this veil pulls back. And the deacons begin the services singing something different. They don't begin with announcements; deacons line up in the front. The oldest deacon stands up in the middle and begins. It's not preaching that is monologue, either. We preach monologue, I speak, you sit, you listen. No, they talk back. It's preaching as dialogue. I was in the middle of preaching at a black church in Richardson, Texas, I was preaching about David and Goliath, and I said, "Let me show you what David said..."

A woman on the front row stood and said, "What'd he say?"

I lost my place in the middle of the sermon!

You know what, it's different, but they're your family. We don't have anything in common. We sing differently, act differently, look differently, worship differently, but you know what we've got in common? One Lord, one faith, one God, one baptism, one Lord all in all. We are family united together. We are bound together by a common Father.

II. THE FATHER BATHES US IN HIS LOVE (ROMANS 8:16) - "ABBA, FATHER"

Notice Paul says, "We cry out Abba! Father!" It is a term of intimacy. You know "Father" *(pater)*; "Abba" is the Aramaic term of intimacy that a child alone has for his or her parent. It is the equivalency in my language to *papa*. Please hear me. When you mess with the God of the Bible and the Bible of my God, you know what you're taking out? You're taking out one of the few distinct differences between Christianity and any other world system.

No other system believes in a personal, intimate relationship with the Father. You and I come close, we come boldly before the throne of grace to obtain mercy in a time of need. It is an intimate term. There is no such thing in Islam, no such thing as having a personal relationship with Allah. Allah is transcendent, he is removed, he is creator, he is judge, but he is not personal. You and I both know that God is transcendent and He is imminent, He is intimate, He is personal, He is there for you.

III. THE FATHER BEQUEATHS TO US AN INHERITANCE (ROMANS 8:17) - "HEIRS"

We are joined together as inheritors of the promise, inheritors of His prize. Do you know what that means? That means the moment you were saved, my brother, the moment you were saved, my sister, God took upon His shoulders every need of your provision. My God shall supply all my needs. Why? Because He's Father.

He has drawn me into His fold, and provides for me my deepest needs. You know what it also means? It means that you're no better than I am, and I'm no better than you. We're the same. You see, evolution is impenitently racist. In Christianity; we're all on level ground. Evolution says that you could have come from a better primordial ooze than I came from. The primordial ooze from which I came was genetically inferior, the primordial ooze from which you came may have been genetically superior, and thus, you are better than me.

But Jesus Christ says we have one Divine Parent. One God. We are all from Adam, we are all from Noah, we are all family. Nobody's better than anybody else. And everything you've got, and everything I've got, came from the same Father. Look at church parking lots. There are some fancy cars, I saw an Escalade pulling up here. I almost got hit by a Suburban coming up here. I'm driving a ratty old pickup truck with 200,000 miles on it. But you know what, that Escalade is from the Father. That ratty old truck gets me from A to B, and it's from the Father.

The Father bequeaths to us His inheritance. Do you know why my people (Muslims) always use the term "Sons of Abraham?" Because of inheritance. Do you know why Muslims always say they are sons of Ishmael? Because of inheritance. One of our celebrations was called Eid al-Fitr. We would celebrate Abrahim, Abraham. Taking his son to the top of Mt. Moriah to sacrifice his son, he brings up the knife, he brings it down, and at the last minute Allah prepares a ram in the thicket and he preserves the life of *Ishmael*.

Imagine my surprise when I got saved and saw the true story. Twenty-two hundred years after Moses wrote it down, 2,700 years after it actually happened,

Mohammed changed the book. Why? Because they believe that as sons and progeny of the older child, they deserve the inheritance and that is Israel.

Hear me very carefully: I was raised to hate the Jews. I was taught, we were taught, that the Jews drink the blood of our Palestinian brethren. I was raised to think that the Jews hated us, and then I got saved and I came to Romans 9-11, and you know what I discovered? The Jews are the children of God. Israel is the priest nation of God. You know what that means? If it were not for Jesus Christ, we'd be across the line from one another. But because of the shed blood of Jesus Christ, I don't have to shed my blood!

IV. THE FATHER BEARS OUR BURDENS (ROMANS 8: 17) "SUFFER WITH HIM"

You, my friend, you came here and you wondered who's going to be with me in the darkest hour? God will. If we suffer with Him. You know what that means? It doesn't just mean that you suffer like He suffered, or you suffer because He suffered, but you suffer and *He suffers alongside with you.*

I failed every test until Jesus saved me. And then I got saved, and I started going to ministerial training, and I passed everything except for one. I saw autopsies, I saw an embalming, and I thought all that stuff was fascinating. However, I passed out at age 18 – I passed out watching a birth.

In 1999, my wife was pregnant, and at first we had an agreement. Her mama was going to be in the delivery room with her, that was the agreement. Nevertheless, I put on the paper clothes and went into the delivery room, and when they wanted to put up the blue curtain, I said, "Take that curtain down!"

I didn't get sick; I didn't get dizzy; I didn't get woozy. Why? That's my wife. That's my child. You know what? My nausea was gone because of my intimacy with my wife and my intimacy with my child. How much more infinitely, exponentially greater is God's care for you? And do you know why?

Because He's Father.

I'll go back to the original question. Is God a man or a woman? Is God a man? Of course not. Is God a woman? Absolutely not. God is more than a man, and He's more than a woman. God is Father.

12

GAME OVER:

WHAT HAPPENS AFTER I DIE?

KERRY SHOOK

Senior Pastor

Fellowship Of The Woodlands

Houston, Texas

DO YOU REMEMBER THE BASKETBALL GAME that just wouldn't end? It was the 1972 men's basketball final between the former Soviet Union and the USA. The American team had never lost a basketball game in the Olympics, and when Doug Collins sank two free throws with three seconds left to put the Americans up by one point, it looked like our winning streak would stay intact. But, an Eastern Bloc referee just wouldn't let the game end until the Soviets had won.

After being cheated out of the gold medal, the American team didn't accept the silver medal, and those silver medals are still in a vault somewhere in Switzerland.

When it comes to the game of life, though, there will come a moment when the final buzzer sounds and it's game over. You can't avoid it; you can't cheat your way around it. There will come a moment at the end of life when the final buzzer will sound and no one can stop it. It's game over.

WHAT HAPPENS WHEN YOU DIE?

You are never really ready to live until you are ready to die.

A new poll just came out that shows that 81 percent of Americans believe in life after death. It used to be that nobody really wanted to talk about this subject, but I'm finding that more and more people want to talk about this. I think it's because millions of baby boomers are aging, and the closer you get to something, the more interested you are in it. Somebody sent me an article recently. It's a comedian's take on the phenomenon of aging:

"Do you realize that the only time in our lives when we like to get old is when we are kids? If you are less than ten years old you are so excited about aging that you think in fractions. 'How old are you?' 'Four and a half.' I mean, you are never 36 and a half. But when you are four, it's 'I'm four and a half going on five.' Then you get into your teens and now they can't hold you back. You jump to the next number or even a few ahead. 'How old are you?' 'I'm going to be sixteen.' You may be thirteen, but you are going to be sixteen. Then you become twenty-one. Even the words sound like a ceremony. You *become* 21. But then you turn 30. What happened there? It makes it sound like bad milk. He *turned.* We're going to have to throw him out. He *turned.* So you become 21. You turn 30. Then you are pushing 40. Whoa. Put on the brakes, it's all slipping away. Before you know it you reach 50 and your dreams are gone. But wait, you make it to 60. You didn't think you would, but you make it to 60. So, you become 21, turn 30, push 40, reach 50 and make it to 60 and by then you've built up so much speed that you hit 70. After that it's just a day-to-day thing. You hit Wednesday. Big deal. Then you get into your eighties and every day is just a complete cycle. You hit lunch. You turn 4:30. You reach bedtime. That's a big deal in your eighties. It doesn't end there. Into the nineties you start going backwards. 'Well, I was just 92.' Then a strange thing happens. If you make it over 100 you become a little kid again. 'I'm 100 and a half.'"

Well, I hope that you'll live to be 100 and a half, but no matter how old you live to be, there will come a time, a moment in your life, when the final buzzer sounds and it's game over. Look at Ecclesiastes 7:4, our first verse. "A wise person thinks much about death, while the fool thinks only about having a good time now." He's saying it's wise to prepare for the inevitable. It's not wise to ignore the inevitable. He's saying it's wise to think about what's going to happen when the final buzzer sounds because it brings a sharpness of focus to my life. It helps me live a more purposeful life and to make every moment of my life count. I want you to look at this next verse, Ecclesiastes 3:11. "...He (God) has planted eternity in the human heart..." God has placed deep in the hearts of every person the knowledge that there is something more to this life than just the here and now, because you are made for a purpose. The Amplified Bible puts it like this: "He (God) has made everything beautiful in its time. He also has planted eternity in men's hearts and mind [a divinely implanted sense of a purpose working through the ages which nothing under the sun but God alone can satisfy]..."

You were made for a reason. God put you on this earth for a reason, and God has a plan for your life. God, the Bible says, has placed eternity in every one of our hearts. The Bible is very clear about it, that death is not the end. One day your heart will stop beating, but you won't stop, you'll keep going on. You'll live forever in eternity. In fact, one moment after you die you'll either experience the greatest celebration ever or the greatest separation ever.

Some people will experience separation in eternity. A recent survey showed that more Americans believe in heaven and hell than ever before. Did you know that more Americans today believe in a real heaven and a real hell than back in the conservative 1950s? The vast majority of Americans believe in a real heaven and a real hell. Well, whether we believe it or not, it's real. Look at 2 Thessalonians 1:8-9. "He will punish those who do not know God and do not obey the gospel of our Lord Jesus. They will be punished with everlasting destruction and shut out from the presence of the Lord..." Hell is a real place. Jesus Christ believed in it. In fact, Jesus spoke more about hell than He even did about heaven. I'd rather just talk about heaven, the Good News, but I wouldn't be honest if I didn't tell you the whole picture. The truth is, hell is just as real as heaven.

The Bible says hell is a place of physical suffering. It's a place of fire and torment. It's a real place. But then it's also a place of emotional suffering. The Bible uses the phrase "weeping and gnashing of teeth" many times to describe hell. That's a picture of deep, emotional suffering. It's the picture of deep, emotional regret like you would have if you make a bad decision and you say to yourself, "Oh, what was I thinking? If I could just go back in time and correct that decision." In life here on this earth we make a bad decision and we usually get a chance to make up for it. But in hell it will be emotional regret for all eternity – deep, emotional regret. Then it will be a place of relational suffering, the Bible says. Every so often I have someone tell me, "Well, Pastor, I don't think I'll mind going to hell because heaven sounds so boring. All my buddies are going to be in hell anyway." It's as if hell is some big pool hall where all your drinking buddies gather to party for all eternity. Jesus said it's a place of total darkness, a place of absolute loneliness, relational darkness, and complete relational separation and isolation. C. S. Lewis said hell is nothing but yourself for all eternity. The relational suffering is enormous, but worst of all, it's a place of spiritual suffering. The Bible says in the last verse that they will be shut out from the Lord's presence. God's presence here on earth provides all the good things that we have. There is good and evil in the world, but everything that's good really comes from God's presence here – all the compassion, creativity, patience, love, and kindness, all that comes from God's presence. Hell is complete separation from God's presence. So, there will be no compassion, no creativity, no patience, no love, and no kindness, nothing good. Complete separation from the presence of God.

Then the question is, how can a loving God send someone to such an awful place? The answer is, He doesn't. People make the choice. He doesn't want anyone to go there. Look at this verse, 2 Peter 3:9. "...He is patient with you, not wanting anyone to perish, but everyone to come to repentance." Whenever I hear someone ask how a loving God can send someone to hell, I know that no one has ever explained that the only sending God has ever done is when He sent His own Son to this earth to die for us so we wouldn't have to go there. God doesn't send anyone there.

Why is hell there? Jesus said it was not made for people; it was made for Satan and his fallen angels, called demons. Well, why do people go there? People go there, basically, because they choose to go there. You don't make the decision about heaven and hell when you get there. You make that decision while you are on this earth. The decisions we make during this life on earth are magnified in eternity. For example, if I make the decision that I want to be close to God here on this earth, and I say, "Jesus, I need You – I need Your forgiveness, I can't make it in life without You – I need You in my life – I want to be close to You," then, when I get to heaven, when I get to eternity, that decision is magnified and I'll be in His presence forever. But, if I make the decision here on this earth that I'm going to call the shots in my life, and I say, "God, I know what's best for me – Jesus, I don't think I need Your forgiveness because I'm a pretty good person – I'm going to go it alone – I think I'll be okay – I think I can handle this thing – I don't need You in my life," if I make that decision here on this earth, in an eternity that decision is magnified, and I'll live separated from Him forever.

We have this powerful thing that God has given us. It's called free will. He gives us the choice. God could have created you as a puppet on a string with which He controls you. He could have created you as a robot, programmed with a computer chip to love Him back and to serve Him and follow Him and to want Him in your life, but He didn't do that. He took the greatest risk of all when He made us with this powerful thing called free will. So we have the actual power to reject Him. The God who made us could have just made us to love Him, to serve Him, to always do the right things that we should do, but He didn't want to do that. He took the risk because love is a risk, and He loves us so much. He made you to love you, but He gives you the choice as to whether or not you are going to love Him back. What an unbelievable risk He took! He risked loving me so much that He even gives me power to reject Him. You have to step out and you have to risk in loving. You have to step out and risk being rejected, and lovingly, God provided us that example. He risked being rejected completely. So, He wants you to love Him back, but He gives you that choice. We have to decide.

One moment after death you will either experience separation in eternity or you will enjoy celebration in eternity. Heaven is a place of great celebration. Heaven is where the party is going on. But, it's also a place of no more. It's a place of no more pain. Look at Revelation 21:4: "He will wipe every tear from their eyes. There will be no more death or mourning or crying or pain, for the old order of things has passed away." Folks, heaven is a real place. A lot of times we think of heaven as this mystical place where all these clouds are and we're sitting on a cloud and we're sort of a mist ourselves. No, heaven is just as real as this book.

I remember growing up in church and singing in the children's choir in my church. The children's choir in the church I grew up in was nothing like the children's choir here at Fellowship of The Woodlands. Here at Fellowship of The Woodlands, our children do these plays where they have these huge sets and props and sing these cool songs and do these dances and have so much fun. It's really a cool thing. Over 200 kids are in it. But, the children's choir that I was in growing up wasn't quite like that. We had to wear these little white robes and sing these really boring songs. The two elderly ladies who taught the children's choir would say things like, "Kids, isn't this wonderful? This is what heaven is going to be like – singing songs to God all day." I'm thinking, ooooh, oh, man, that sounds boring to me. That sounds awful. That doesn't sound like heaven to me. That sounds like the other place to me. But, you know, you grew up thinking, "Well, I guess that's what heaven's like. I'm just going to be there bored out of my gourd playing a harp with wings sitting on a cloud." The Bible says that heaven is a perfect place full of adventure and excitement. The Bible talks about heaven and uses human words to describe what is humanly indescribable along with some symbolism to try to help us understand it a little bit. We can't even fathom it. It says there will be streets of gold and gates of pearls. What it's saying is that heaven just drips of value and significance and meaning and purpose and ultimate fulfillment. We'll have jobs there that will bring us ultimate fulfillment. Christ is there, so we will have compassion and all the creativity and all the purpose and all the meaning that we could ever imagine. That's just a little glimpse of what heaven is like, but we can't even fathom it.

Sometimes I have people ask me, "Kerry, will I be able to recognize my loved ones in heaven?" Of course you will. We're not going to be angels. A lot of people think we are going to be angels when we get up there, but the Bible clearly says we're not. God already has enough angels. We won't have wings and sit on a cloud. We're not going to be angels. We'll be the same people, but yet it says we'll get a new, glorified body in heaven. So what that means is there is no need for health clubs in heaven. You get a new, perfect body. It also means that yes, you will be able to recognize your loved ones, but some of them it will take you a while because they'll have a perfect body and you'll say, "Oh, man, I didn't recognize you – 70 pounds lighter. Man, that's amazing." And, "Oh, that's you, Pastor Kerry, with hair! It took me a while." So, yes, you'll be able to recognize your loved ones. It just may take you a while. I say a little bit of what heaven is going to be like and what eternity is like because there is no way that you can really make every moment of your life count until you live your life in light of eternity. You must realize that eternity is long and life is short.

I saw something at the NBA All-Star Game a year or two ago that illustrates this. They had chosen a fan months before the All-Star Game, I guess people wrote in or they had some contest. They chose this fan to come and take a shot from half court at halftime of the All-Star Game. He had one shot, just one shot. If he made it, he would win a million bucks. Well, the fan was chosen early on, so he went down to his local gym, and he would shoot hundreds of half court shots each and every day for that one chance to win a million bucks. But, when the time came, it was one shot. One shot only. Win a million bucks or nothing.

In life you've got one shot here on this earth and that's it. One shot to make a difference in the lives of others. You've got one shot to really love the Lord. You have the choice down here to love Him or not. You've got one shot in this one and only life to make every moment count and then it's all of eternity. In life, if you take the ball and you hand it to Jesus Christ, He will slam dunk it each and every time. If you take your one shot and you place it in His hands, He will help you make the most of life.

I want to share with you two principles that will forever change your life, to help you live your life in light of eternity.

I. LIVE EACH MOMENT PREPARED FOR ETERNITY.

You're not really ready to live until you're ready to die. You don't have to be worried about it. You don't have to be worried about eternity because you can get it settled. The Bible says that these things are written that you may know you have eternal life. If you're not for sure that you have eternal life right now, if you're not for sure you'll be in heaven one day, then you can know for sure today. Look what it says in 1 John 5:11-12. "And this is what God has testified: He has given us eternal life, and this life is in his Son. So whoever has God's Son has life; whoever does not have His Son does not have life." He's basically saying that getting into heaven is all about who you know. If you know the Son, you get in. If you don't know the Son, you don't. Now, heaven is a perfect place for perfect people, and the problem is that we're not perfect. We've all sinned. But that's why Christ came to take our place, so that we could then have our place in heaven one day. Not that we could ever deserve it, not that we could ever earn it, but He's the one who made the way for us. Now I'm a friend of God, the Bible says, because of what Christ has done.

Richard Mouw, the president of Fuller Seminary, said that when he was in kindergarten they had a very special guest come to their kindergarten one day in December – Santa Claus. He said that Santa Claus walked in that door with a big red suit, with big black boots, with a white beard, and with a gruff voice saying "Ho, Ho, Ho, who's been naughty or nice? I know who's been naughty or nice, so kids, come forward and tell Santa what you want for Christmas!" He said that all the five-year-olds were terrified. Nobody moved, and the teacher was a little bit embarrassed that no kid wanted to walk up to the throne of judgment of Santa Claus. But, Santa looked right at Rich Mouw, and he said, "Son, you come up here first." Rich said, "I walked real slowly up to Santa Claus, not knowing why I had been chosen. But," he said, "what I didn't know was that the man in that Santa Claus suit was Mr. Cooper, a friend of mine from church who was friends with my family, who was always really nice to me. He was my friend. He sensed when I got close to him that I was afraid, because he leaned over and pulled down his beard and quietly, so no one else could hear, he said, 'Hey, Rich, don't be afraid, it's just me, Mr. Cooper, your friend.'" Rich said, "All my fears just melted. I felt so much better."

That's exactly what happens when we come to Christ. We become friends with Christ. He takes our place. Not that we could earn it. Not that we could deserve it. We ought to be afraid because we are imperfect and He's a perfect Holy God. We ought to be afraid, but yet He takes away all our fear because He says, "Hey, Kerry, you know Me, I'm your friend, Jesus. You know Me. You accepted Me. I'm your friend, Jesus. You don't have to be afraid of eternity. I'm your friend." It makes all the difference in the world. You can get your eternity settled so that you can know that Christ is in your life. You really can't live and make the most of every moment until you know your eternity is settled. Then it frees you up to enjoy life and to make a difference in others' lives when you know that, when you are prepared. Then the second thing I must do is:

II. LIVE EACH MOMENT INVESTING IN ETERNITY.

So often we live down here on this earth like we are going to be here forever. Let me illustrate it this way. Let's say you go on vacation, and you go to a hotel room, and you know you are going to be there a couple of weeks, but you don't like the interior decorating of the room. So you call in your own interior decorator. You put a lot of money into it and change the curtains and change the whole interior decor of the room. Then you want a bigger television. You don't like the little television there, so you get a big screen TV brought in. Then you go outside and you don't like the shrubs and the landscaping, so you hire a landscaper. You get out there and you work really hard as well, and you change all the landscaping at the hotel, and then you go home. That's exactly what many people do today on this earth. They think they are going to be here forever. All they concentrate on are things that are temporary, that just don't last – that won't make it past the test of time – that won't last for all eternity. They focus on accomplishments or achievements or material things, all of these things. God says there is nothing wrong with those things, it's just that they will not last for eternity. What lasts is our relationships. Our relationship with Him. Our relationship with others. So many times we focus on things that just don't last.

Look at Ecclesiastes 11:7-8, which essentially says, "It is a wonderful thing to be alive! If a person lives to be very old, let him rejoice in every day of life, but let him also remember that eternity is far longer, and that everything down here is futile in comparison." Just imagine I have a huge, black dot right here. And then attached to that black dot is a line that goes all the way around this building, all the way out the door, all the way out Highway 242, down 242 to I-45, all the way down I-45 to Dallas, all the way to Canada and just keeps going. The black dot up here would represent our time here on earth. That line would represent all of eternity. What we have here on this earth, 60, 70, 80 years, it's not anything compared to all of eternity. But the amazing thing is, what you do with that dot of time here on this earth determines everything about your eternity. What you do with Jesus Christ determines where you spend eternity. What you do with your time, talent and treasure determines what rewards you get in eternity. What I do with my one dot of time here on this earth determines everything about all of eternity because life is preparation for eternity. If you don't understand that, you'll never understand life. If you don't understand the fact that life is preparation for eternity, then you won't understand what's going on in your life right now. You will get discouraged, you'll be stressed out, you'll have a lot of anxiety, and you just won't get what life is. Life is preparation for eternity. The problems and the pressures and the stresses of life come into our lives to build our character, because it's our character we take into heaven with us. You get a new body when you get to heaven, so we don't take our bodies with us. We get a new body. But, we take our character. Whenever problems and pressures and stress come into my life, God uses that to build my character, to make me more like Jesus Christ. The problem is, we don't focus on our character very often. We focus on a lot of things that just won't last.

It reminds me of a story about a woman in her fifties who had a heart attack and was rushed to the hospital, where she died and went to meet God. She said, "God, I had so much more to accomplish on this earth. Can't You send me back?" God said, "Okay, I'll send you back for 30 more years." She woke up in the hospital bed and she thought, "Well, I've got 30 more years and since I'm already here in the hospital, I think I'll have some plastic surgery done." So she got a nose job, a face lift, a tummy tuck, she got the extreme makeover. The day she got out of the hospital, she walked out, crossed the street, got hit by a truck and killed. She went up to meet God and she said, "God, what's the deal? I thought You said I had 30 years left." God said, "Oh, I know, I'm sorry. I just didn't recognize you." There is nothing wrong with trying to look good, but we need to make sure we have that inner beauty, that character. That's what God wants to build in our lives. We spend so much of our time focused on things that won't last for one month, much less for all eternity. God wants us to spend our time focused on things that are going to last forever.

What will last forever? Two things: The first is God's Word. The Bible says that the grass withers and the flowers fade, but the Word of God stands forever. So, when I spend time in God's Word putting it into my life, building my character, becoming more like Christ, learning the values from God's Word, applying it in my life, that's going to last forever. I take that with me into eternity.

The second thing that lasts forever is people. People live forever in eternity. So anytime you do anything to make a difference in the lives of others, it's going to last forever because people last forever. We need to spend our time on the things that last forever. That's why relationships are the most important thing in your life.

We really ought to spend our time doing things that make a difference. I just believe with all my heart that you ought to ask yourself the question, if you knew you only had six months to live, what would you do? That's how you ought to live your life, because life is short and eternity is long, and we're all terminal. I really believe that if you knew you had six months left to live that you would live a lot differently. You would spend your time not so much on accomplishments, but on relationships. You would spend your time with the people that matter most, building their lives. I really believe you would give more of your talent and your treasure and your time to make a difference to your church for God's kingdom. I really believe that you would do some things that you've always wanted to do, but you put off and said one day, one day, one day. This is your moment. Until you understand that, you will never live the kind of life God has meant for you to live. Until you understand that this is your moment.

Why did God allow you to be born at this time in history? It is the most exciting time to be alive. Of all the moments of history, this is your one moment. This is your one shot. So, how are you living your life? You can spend your life, you can waste your life, or you can invest your life. Invest your life in eternity.

The great news is that for the believer, the end is really just the beginning.

That's why we can enjoy every day. Make the most of it and step out in faith and trust Him. This is just the beginning. The end here on earth is just the beginning, and we can't even imagine what heaven is going to be like. We can only imagine. But, until you begin to start imagining a little bit of what heaven is going to be like, you can never really live here on this earth. Make sure you know Christ. Make sure you are investing your life in things that matter.

13

PROOF OF LIFE

DR. FRANK HARBER

Senior Pastor

Champions Gate Church

Bedford, Texas

(with a special testimony from Russell Fisher, M.D.)

EACH YEAR ON THIS PLANET, over 25,000 people are kidnapped. We don't hear about a lot about these kidnappings in the United States because we are blessed to have very few. In many Third World countries, people are kidnapped and held for ransom. Columbia is the kidnapping capital of the world, followed by Mexico, Brazil, and Russia.

People are kidnapped and then held for ransom to such a degree that it makes international travel a very daunting task indeed in many countries. In fact, many travelers now have special insurance for such catastrophes. Entire companies have been formed to deal with these situations on behalf of the families. These institutions have been trained to deal with the kidnappers, in order to try to secure the release of the kidnapped person. When they are dealing with the kidnappers, there is one primary thing they are looking for each time. It is called "proof of life." In kidnapping, proof of life is everything. If the person is already deceased, then there is nothing to talk about. There is no reason even to speak to the kidnappers, except to try to hunt them down and prosecute them.

We need to try and understand exactly what happened to Jesus on the cross, why He had to die, and the manner of suffering that He went through,

♦ 161 ♦

because the story of Christianity is about the death and resurrection of Jesus Christ. Not only do we have proof of life concerning the resurrection, but there is also something very important that is often overlooked.

When it comes to the crucifixion, you need proof of death. If someone came up to you off the street and declared that they had recently been resurrected from the dead, you would have a hard time believing it – not from the standpoint that they would be standing in front of you alive, but you would have a hard time believing they were actually once dead. In fact, one thing that you would want from someone who said they had been resurrected would be proof of death. That's exactly what we find in the story of Christianity. We find the story of a man named Jesus who actually physically, medically, scientifically, and historically died. He then rose again from the dead, which is the proof of life.

The method by which Jesus died was crucifixion. Crucifixion was the most horrible death that a person could ever go through. Today we have different methods of capital punishment, such as lethal injection, the electric chair, and the gas chamber. In ancient times you could be stoned, you could be placed before a firing squad, and you could be fed to lions. All of those methods of capital punishment pale in comparison to the crucifixion. The crucifixion is the cruelest form of capital punishment ever devised in the history of mankind. I believe today as Christians we need to be educated about exactly what happened to Jesus Christ and the fact that He actually physically, medically, and historically died.

Dr. Russell Fisher is a cardiologist who specializes in invasive cardiology, heart catheterization, coronary heart disease, congestive heart failure, and heart rhythm abnormalities. His specialty is electrophysiology or heart rhythm problems. In the pages that follow, Dr. Fisher tells us what medically happened to Jesus at the crucifixion:

A Medical Doctor's Testimony

When you examine what Jesus had to go through, it's astonishing. First, understand that all of this began in the middle of the night – so for an extended period, at least six hours, He was under extreme stress – so extreme, the Scripture says, "his sweat was like drops of blood…"

Sweating blood is a clear medical condition. It is called hematidrosis. When the body is under extreme stress, hemorrhaging can occur within the sweat glands, and one can clearly see blood coming through the skin. It is a sign of extreme stress. Jesus had to walk two and one-half miles between midnight and six in the morning. He then underwent extreme physical abuse and blood loss in the form of beating.

Jesus was repeatedly beaten across the head. This is referred to as close head trauma, similar to what a boxer would experience. Multiple brain hemorrhages could have occurred. In this condition, Jesus had been without food or water, under extreme stress all night, and had fluid and blood loss from the beatings. All of this would put anyone in a much-weakened position.

After the extreme beating and physical abuse, He still had to carry the cross. The cross weighed approximately 85 pounds, and He would have had to carry it at least 600 yards in His terribly weakened condition. When the body is under that kind of stress, the muscles start to break down, and the acid in the system builds up. This condition is called metabolic acidosis. When metabolic acidosis reaches an extreme, the acid level goes extremely high, and the kidneys, liver, and brain all begin to fail.

Next, Jesus was placed on the cross. The Romans liked to take the nails and put them into the outstretched arms. The nails were placed between the bones right over a nerve called the median nerve. The nail would go through the median nerve on both sides, thus severing the median nerve and paralyzing the hands. Any subsequent movement would cause excruciating pain. Then they nailed the feet to the cross, adding more agony to the body.

At this point, Jesus was not only bearing the excruciating pain from the nails, but His body was also being pulled down by gravity. This dramatically impairs the function of breathing. To better understand the logistics of what took place, we must first understand what happens when the body functions normally. When we breathe and talk, we have what is called "passive respiration." We don't even have to think about breathing; the diaphragm moves, but the chest doesn't move up or down when we breathe or talk. Active respiration is when a person takes a deep breath and the lungs must expand with air before the active expiration will allow the air to be released. On the cross, the chest mechanics were dramatically altered, because Jesus would not have been able to breathe normally due to the force of gravity and the weight of His body. He would have been able to breathe in (passive respiration), but the only way He could have exhaled was by pushing Himself up. When the body cannot breathe out, the person begins to retain acid, which is called respiratory acidosis. When respiratory acidosis occurs on top of metabolic acidosis, the body shuts down. Not only that, but the serum potassium rises dramatically, causing irreversible heart rhythm abnormalities. Unless it is corrected immediately, death results.

The Bible also talks about the spear being pressed into Jesus' side, releasing water and blood. At this point, Jesus would have been in what is called "high-output cardiac failure." This is a condition where the fluid builds up in the lining around the lung and in the space around the heart. When His side was pierced with the sword, the fluid released would be clear and appear to be water. The sword most likely pierced the lung, the lining around the heart, the pericardium, the right atrium and the right ventricle.

At the end, something catastrophic occurred to cause Jesus' death, though we are unsure of exactly what that catastrophic event was. It could have been arrhythmia related to the high potassium. It could have been from bleeding in the brain. When bleeding occurs in the brain, there is a high-pressure build up, and the pressure causes part of the brain to herniate. When the brain herniates through part of the brain stem, there is instant death. Jesus could have died of liver failure, renal failure, rhythm failure, or cardiac arrest.

THE BIBLICAL PERSPECTIVE

Now we will walk through what Dr. Fisher just talked about from a biblical perspective by closely examining what happened to Jesus Christ. We begin in the Garden of Gethsemane in Luke 22:44, "And being in anguish, he prayed more earnestly, and his sweat was like drops of blood falling to the ground." Dr. Fisher has delineated this medical condition where one can literally sweat drops of blood. This condition, which has been medically documented, is associated with extreme stress and extreme shock.

This stress causes weakening of the skin and makes it very susceptible to injury. It was in this fragile state that Jesus Christ was scourged. The Bible tells us in Matthew 27:25 that Pilate handed Jesus over to be scourged and crucified. This scourging will prove to have profound implications for the cross.

The Romans had a practice of scourging people before crucifixion. The reason they did this was to speed up the process of death during the crucifixion. In the process of scourging, the victim would be tied to a post and the back would be exposed. The Romans would then take a whip, which was called the flagellum, and they would whip the back of the person. The whip was embedded with pieces of bones from sheep, metal fragments, and small iron balls that would literally strip the skin off the back. This process caused extreme blood loss, thus weakening the victim. Jewish law said that no one could receive more than 40 lashes with a whip. In fact, under Jewish law, a victim could only receive 39 lashes, and many people did not even survive that. The Romans had no such laws. They could literally scourge a person to death.

The Romans were also very meticulous about selecting people to perform the scourging. They only chose people who enjoyed doing it. These people took their job very seriously and saw this as an incredible deterrent to crime. Many times they would scourge people within inches of death. Immediately after Jesus was scourged, the Bible tells us that the soldiers then began to beat Him. Matthew 27:28-30 says that they stripped Him and put a scarlet robe on Him. (The scarlet robe has great significance concerning the blood of Jesus Christ.)

Next, they placed a crown of thorns on His brow. The thorns would have been one to two inches long and were compressed into His skull, causing extreme pain. The soldiers began to spit on Him and mock Him. They took a staff and beat Him on the head, driving these two-inch thorns into the head of Jesus Christ. They mocked him, saying, "Hail, King of the Jews."

This was only the beginning of the crucifixion process. From there, Jesus was forced to carry the 80 to 110-pound cross bar approximately 650 yards through the streets of Jerusalem. We call this path the "Via Dolorosa," which means the way of suffering. Jesus had been scourged so badly that He wasn't able to make it all of the way, so the soldiers grabbed a man, Simon of Cyrene, who carried Jesus' cross outside the city gates. The reason they went outside the city gates is that it was against the law to crucify someone within the city. The cross was carried to a place called Golgotha; which in Aramaic means "the place of the skull." It was there that they proceeded with the crucifixion.

Crucifixion originated with the Persians. Alexander the Great, when he discovered this method of execution, liked it very much and brought it back to the Mediterranean world. The Romans noticed it and enjoyed it because crucifixion could inflict the most pain and do so over a prolonged period. We know much about the process of Roman crucifixion, because many Roman and Greek historians such as Seneca, Live, Plutarch, and others chronicled it. In fact, the historian Josephus, who witnessed many crucifixions, said that a crucifixion was the most horrible of any death that you could ever die. The Romans used it as a deterrent for crime, because anyone who ever saw a crucifixion would never want it to happen to them.

During crucifixion, the cross would be placed on the ground, and then the Romans would lay the victim down on top of it. At that point, they would take seven-inch nails and nail them directly into the wrists of the victim. This nail would go between the radial and ulna bones, and just as Dr. Fisher said, it would go into the median nerve. Some people mistakenly think that these nails went through the palms of Jesus. Actually, in the ancient world, the wrist was considered part of the hands. When that spike went into that nerve, it sent searing pain through the body. Next they would nail the feet to the cross. It was critical as they nailed the feet to the cross that they made sure that the victim's knees were flexed. The reason they wanted the knees flexed is because they wanted to give the prisoner a fighting chance during crucifixion. The whole thrust of the execution by crucifixion is to bring about suffocation and difficulty in breathing. Therefore, they would flex the victim's knees so they could move up and down. If they couldn't go up and down, as Dr. Fisher explained, they weren't going to be able to breathe.

The biggest challenge from a crucifixion was not the pain from your hands, feet, or sliding up and down on the rough-hewn cross, which was very painful, the problem was breathing. As the victim hung there, he was only going to be able to take very shallow breaths. He had to move up and down in order to breathe. Because of this inability to breathe, the lungs would begin to collapse. It happened slowly at first. Small areas of the lungs would collapse, causing hypoxia. They then would begin to fill with carbon dioxide and fluid.

The next thing that happened to the victim was that waves of cramps would sweep through all over the muscles of the body. It caused relentless throbbing and searing pain. Eventually either the heart would fail or suffocation would occur.

With the challenge of breathing, think about Jesus trying to talk during His crucifixion. It is recorded when Jesus was on the cross that He uttered seven different sayings. These were difficult to say at the least. In the process of rising up, He could only speak as He exhaled. My brother, a licensed speech pathologist, was explaining to me exactly what would happen during the process of crucifixion. In order to talk, the victim would have to get into a position where he could exhale. As that was happening, he would put pressure on his hands and feet and his back would be sliding on the cross and he would only have time for a short gasp of air. In fact, in trying to talk, he would not be able to talk in a normal voice; it would be a very shrill sound. Anyone who heard Jesus talk while on the cross would have literally had the hair on his neck stand up. If someone who knew Him heard Him speak, it would have caused them to weep incredibly. It would be an unbelievable sound to hear Him speak on the cross.

The cross was a device of incredible suffering and was designed to crucify a person over a period of two to three days. Many times, the Romans shortened this time by scourging people. The more they scourged them, the less time they spent on the cross. It's estimated that Jesus was on the cross from three to six hours. This tells us that the scourging was very severe. You can read about it in Mark 15:34. Even Pilate was surprised about the short time that Jesus was on the cross.

Interestingly enough, the last words that Jesus uttered from the cross were these: "Into your hands I commend my spirit." I've always found that to be an interesting choice of last words because immediately after Jesus spoke those words, He died. I believe that the main reason Jesus died was not from one of the physical causes of death we have talked about, but because He gave up His spirit; He gave up His life. I believe this is consistent with John 10:17-18. Jesus said, "I lay down my life – only to take it up again." He said, "No one takes it from me, but I lay it down of my own accord." He said, "I have authority to lay it down and authority to take it up again. This command I received from my Father." Jesus spoke that seventh statement from the cross, and then He literally physically and medically died.

In fact, the soldiers decided to speed up the crucifixion by breaking the legs of the prisoners. In John 19:32-33, the Bible says, "The soldiers therefore came and broke the legs of the first man who had been crucified with Jesus, and then those of the other. But when they came to Jesus and found that he was already dead, they did not break his legs." They would break the legs of the prisoners so they would not have any ability to breathe. They would die within a matter of minutes after the legs were broken. When they came to Jesus they noticed that He was already dead. They verified His death. It was proof of death.

They went a step further. John 19:34 says, "Instead, one of the soldiers pierced Jesus' side with a spear, bringing a sudden flow of blood and water." The Romans were meticulous about how they did this. They would go to the right side, and they would thrust the spear between the ribs, through the pericardium, and right into the heart. Immediately they saw a flow of blood and water which indicated a certain medical death. From the account that we have, you can be sure that Jesus Christ died. He was medically, physically, and historically dead. Proof of death. We have massive amounts of writing that indicate Jesus Christ was definitely crucified on a cross and verifiably dead. These sources include the Bible, early church fathers, and the patristic fathers. We also have evidence from non-Christian historical sources. The great first century historian Josephus verified that Jesus died by crucifixion. Proof of death.

Dr. Harry Reimer was a scientist. He was born in 1890 and lived until 1952. He became the president of the Science Research Bureau, and he happened to be an outspoken Christian. One day he was lecturing at a college campus. There he allowed the students to ask him questions. One student responded with this question: "What did Jesus Christ do that no one else ever did?" Dr. Reimer, sensing that there was something behind the question, asked, "Young man, would you happen to be a Jew?" The young man said, "Yes." Dr. Reimer said, "If you are a Jew, I assume that you know the early history of your people and that the Roman Emperors, such as Titus, Pilate, and many other Roman emperors, crucified some 30,000 Jews." The student said, "That is correct. I am aware of the fact that there were some 30,000 Jews put to death under the Roman system of crucifixion." Dr. Reimer said, "Here's what I would like you to do. Young man, I'm going to name one of those 30,000 and I would like for you to name one of those 30,000. I name Jesus Christ, who do you name?" There was silence. The young man couldn't name even one of the other 30,000 Jewish people who was crucified. I doubt anyone can. Why? Because there was something about Jesus' death that was different from anyone who ever lived. Not only with Jesus was there proof of death, but then He rose again from the dead. Now there is proof of life.

The story of Christianity is different from any other story that you will ever hear. It's a story about a person who was dead and who was resurrected from the grave. The message of the cross is so powerful. With the story of the cross, God took a great instrument of shame, perhaps the greatest instrument of shame and execution ever known, and turned it into a symbol of glory. The cross represents man's worst, but it also represents "God's best." Through the cross, God was able to turn something tragic into something wonderful.

The cross is the death certificate. It's only through the cross that the resurrection is given significance. You can't have a resurrection without a cross. The cross has no significance without the resurrection. The cross has such great meaning, because of what it means for our lives. The Bible says that we are all held hostage by sin. Sin's ransom is death. Because of sin, you and I will physically die, and if you die in your sins, the Bible says, "You will be eternally separated from God." But God sent His Son to pay the ransom. It was a very high ransom indeed. Jesus Christ, 2,000 years ago, came and died on a cross and paid the penalty for your sin so that you could be set free. That's the good news today! When it comes to Jesus Christ, you have proof of death and proof of life. What does that mean? That means the ransom is paid.

14

THE ROAD IS RED

DR. ED YOUNG

Senior Pastor

Fellowship Church

Grapevine, Texas

A FRIEND OF MINE INVITED MY SON EJ AND ME to his place in Meridian, Texas. Now for most people that's an easy trip. But for me, it's pretty tough because I'm directionally-challenged. I've got to have the worst sense of direction of anybody you've ever met. So my wife, Lisa, who has a built-in GPS system in her brain, was kind enough to write down the directions to Meridian for me, and my son and I set off on this trip.

We'd been gone for about an hour. I was supposed to turn left, which was south toward Meridian. You guessed it – I turned right, which was north, and I was lost. But I didn't really realize I was lost. I thought I was making good time. After about twenty miles or so down this road, going the opposite direction, I looked at EJ and said, "Man, we're making great time, aren't we? This is really coming together. This is incredible!"

I drove longer and longer and longer, and then I began to have that sick, sinking feeling in the pit of my stomach, like "Ed, you're an idiot. You're lost again. This is pitiful." Yet, my pride did not really want me to admit it to myself, especially to, you know, my twelve-year-old son. So I continued to drive, and I knew I was lost.

Finally, I did what is very difficult for guys to do. I stopped the car, picked up my cell phone – thank God they invented cell phones for me because I get lost so much – and I called Lisa. Lisa said, "Ed, you are lost. Let me redirect you." So she gave me the right directions to get back on the right road. Then she said, "Honey, you have a GPS system in your car. Why don't you use it?"

Eventually I did make it to Meridian. And later on I found a map, and I saw where I had messed up. It was pretty sad. And I discovered something about being lost, because I'm lost a lot of the time when I'm driving around.

There are three stages of lostness. The first stage is when you're lost, but you don't know it. You're simply clueless about your condition. The second stage is when you're lost, and you know it, but pride will not really let you admit it to yourself or others. And the third stage is when you're lost, and you finally come clean and say, "You know, I'm lost and I'm going to ask for directions." Women will do that quickly. Guys, we have a hard time asking for directions, don't we? I don't know what it is, but we just don't do it.

These days, I think there are a lot of people who are lost. Not in a physical sense, but in a much deeper sense — a more comprehensive sense. A lot of people are lost in the spiritual sense. Some of you are lost and don't really know you're lost. Others here are lost, and you're telling yourself, "Well, I don't want to admit it." And some are lost and you're here for direction. You're here for meaning. You're saying, "God, is there a destination? Is there a focus for my life?"

God has placed in all of our lives a GPS system. We all know when we're lost, and there's something down deep that tells us we're lost.

Today I want to unpack this whole issue, this whole subject called lostness. And I want to relate lostness to a seemingly disconnected subject. I want to relate lostness to justice.

On the surface, justice and lostness don't seem like they gel. There doesn't seem to be a real vibe between the two. But if you really examine them, if you go a little bit deeper, you'll see how connective they are, how strongly they are held together.

We're lost. And because of our lostness, God did something. And the something that God did was all about justice. And this whole justice thing culminates with the feature presentation, if you will, known as Easter.

Think about this for a second. When the jets tore through the World Trade Towers, what did you say? You said, like I said, "Somebody's got to pay!" When Americans were killed, and their bodies were drug through the streets of Iraq, what did we say? "Somebody's got to pay!" When a child is abducted and murdered, we say, "Somebody's got to pay!"

Why do we have this atonement awareness in our minds and in our hearts? Why do we have this somebody's-got-to-pay mentality? Animals don't have it. I have three dogs that weigh about 160 pounds each. They're like cattle. When one of them gets out of our yard and lumbers down our street, the other dogs and cats in the neighborhood don't say, "Ah, he's out! The big dog is out, Ed! I'm going to call the cops. He's broken the law. You need to put the dog away five to ten years."

Animals don't have it. Only human beings have this somebody's-got-to-pay attitude. Only human beings have this justice thing going on. And what's so funny is to talk to an evolutionist, because evolutionists cannot come up with a plausible explanation regarding why we have this somebody's-got-to-pay mentality.

It's not just a 21st century thing. You study every tribe, every culture, every people group, and all of them have devised some sort of a system to pay for wrongdoings. You commit a crime in some cultures and you're thrown in prison. In other cultures you pay a fine. In other cultures you have the ultimate penalty – death.

God, on one hand, is loving. He's full of grace and mercy and forgiveness. On the other hand, though, God is a God of justice. He's holy. He's pure.

The Last Sermon I Would Preach

God can't wink at sin. God can't say, "Boys will be boys, girls will be girls. No big deal. No problem." God is a loving God, but because He is a holy God, sin must have a payment. And that brings us to the book of Genesis, the first book of the Bible.

About a week ago I took my family to see a movie, and we were on time. That's a huge thing, because Lisa and I have four kids. To get four kids into a theater on time for a movie?! You know, movies these days ... let's say this one started at 5:30. Really it doesn't start at 5:30, it starts at 5:45 because there are fifteen minutes of previews.

I like previews. Previews are kind of like teasers of the coming, future feature films, you know? They show us the highlights and stuff like that. And women kind of watch and go, "Oh, girl, I'm going to go see that one. Brad Pitt! That's coming this summer. I'll be there for that." Or guys, you know, we see some kind of chase scene and say, "Hey, dude, I'll be there when that film comes out, man. That's going to be awesome! You know? Look at Arnold. Yeah, man, that's great!"

God is all about sneak previews. Because of our lostness and because of His justice, because of His love and because of His holiness. Throughout the pages of Scripture, He gives us sneak preview after sneak preview pointing to the ultimate feature film, pointing to the ultimate feature attraction. It's almost like you're looking at a road, a red road, that points you to the ultimate destination.

In the book of Genesis, specifically *Genesis 2:17*, God is talking to Adam and Eve. He says this, "You must not eat from the tree of the knowledge of good and evil, for when you eat of it you will surely die."

God made Adam and Eve in His image. They were in a perfect place. But check this out: with the high-risk gift of the freedom of choice comes the high-risk principle of atonement.

We have the gift, the high-risk gift, from God of the freedom of choice. I can't make you do something. You can't make me choose something. I have that gift. Along with that gift is the high-cost principle of atonement. And that's what God was telling Adam and Eve.

"Adam and Eve, I love you. I know you love me, and you're free to either express your love to me or not. If you rebel, though," God says, "You are going to have to pay the piper. You are going to have to pay for your own sins in a place called hell — forever." That's what this verse means. If you sin, you're going to die. You have to pay for your own sins. You'll have to atone for your own sins in hell forever. Ugh!

What did Adam and Eve do? You know the story. They sinned. They rebelled. God is a holy God. Sin must have punishment. As I said earlier, He can't say, "Boys will be boys, girls will be girls. No problem. No big deal." Sin must have a payment.

Well, here the plot clots. In Genesis 3:7, "Then the eyes of both of them…" (this is after they sinned) "…were opened, and they realized they were naked; so they sewed fig leaves together and made coverings for themselves." This word "coverings" in the Hebrew is pronounced "he-doe." We get the word "Speedo" from it! I hope you know that was a little bit of humor. Some are going, "Oh, really? I'm going to write that down. He-doe." No, I'm kidding.

God did, though, say something very important to Adam and Eve. He said, "You know, because of your sin, there are going to be some consequences. I'm a holy God. I'm a just God. I made you in my image. You blew your opportunity. And because of that, sin is going to make everything sideways on the earth. There is going to be sickness and disease. Childbirth is going to be painful. The ground is not going to be as fertile."

All creation, though, was sitting on the edge of their courtside seats waiting to see what God would do. They were just waiting to see what God would do.

"What's God going to do? I don't know. I mean God said He's going to take them out. This is going to be cool. He's just going to wipe them out. Watch this, Adam and Eve. It's going to be...oh, man, this is going to be incredible! What do you think? What do you think?"

Well, you know what God does? God does something unique. One would think, because of His holiness and justness, He would just nuke 'em, He would wipe them out, call down lightning from the sky. That's what you would think. You know what God does? He provides another way for sin to be dealt with. He provides an alternative route, another path.

Well, let's see. Because this verse, Genesis 3:21, is a verse that a lot of people have read before, most of you skipped the significance. This verse is so rich.

> "The LORD God made garments of skin for Adam and his wife and clothed them" (Genesis 3:21).

You say, "Ed, that's it? God's a seamstress? That's what you want me to know?" No, no, no. It's much deeper than that.

Adam and Eve had never seen death before. Put yourself in their sandals for a second. They'd never seen the unnatural movements of a dying animal. They had never heard the shrills. They had never seen blood soak into the soil of the garden. God skinned the animal and covered their nakedness. God is introducing the essence of our faith – substitutionary atonement.

The word "atone" means "to cover." The word "atonement" means an innocent third party must shed its blood to cover for the sins of the guilty party, thereby allowing the guilty party to go free. That's what happened.

God could've said, "Adam and Eve, you pay for your own sins in a place called hell." He didn't. God said, "I'm going to provide another way –

atonement. And this shedding of blood will cover your sins."

Now, go to the book of Exodus. You remember the book of Exodus? It's all about Moses and the children of Israel. Well, there was a problem. The Israelites were in bondage under Egyptian slavery. The Egyptians were sinning all over the place. God's people, the Israelites, were sinning all over the place. It was one big honkin' sinful mess.

God said in no uncertain terms, "It's atonement time. Somebody's got to pay." So He told Moses, "Tell your people to go out, and I want every household to kill an unblemished lamb. Take the blood of the lamb and put it on the doorpost. Because on a certain night," God said, "I'm sending a death angel around. And if the death angel sees the blood applied to the doorpost of your home, he'll pass over the house. If he does not see the blood applied, if people ignore my directive, the death angel will take the life of the firstborn male child of every family."

A lot of people obeyed God's directive. A lot of people didn't. Those who didn't suffered death. Those who did were passed over.

Dads, for a second, picture yourself in this situation. Here it is: you walk in your backyard, look around your herd of lambs, and you pick the best one. And your son, your oldest son is right there with you. So you pick up maybe his pet, and you take a knife out of the sheath. And as you get ready to stab it, your son goes, "Dad, what are you doing? What are you thinking? That's my pet!" As the father, you'd have to say, "Son, it's atonement time. It's either your life or the life of the lamb." And many scholars believe that when the blood was applied to the doorpost, it was applied in the shape of a cross.

Go to the book of Leviticus. Leviticus talks all about the Day of Atonement and all about the sacrificial system. In every town and every village with a sacrificial system going on, tens of thousands of animals were dying, because remember, the shed blood of these animals could not take away sin, but they could cover sin. The blood of animals could cover sin, but it could not make someone righteous. So they had to do it over and over and over again.

Well, this high priest on the Day of Atonement would go to the holy of holies, and he would kill a goat, and the goat would symbolize the forgiveness of the nation's sins. Then he would take another goat, give it to this real buff guy, this tri-athlete type of guy, and he would run out into the wilderness, and at the twelve-mile marker he would stop and let the scapegoat go. And this scapegoat represented that the guilt from the sins was lost.

See the foreshadowing? See the red road paved in blood? See the destination? See where this feature film is going?

Press the fast-forward button about, I don't know, several hundred years and think about Isaiah. Isaiah. This guy was a wild guy. Man! He started talking about some unusual things and holding all these conferences and things like that. And he was talking about stuff that made people's heads spin, because Isaiah was insinuating that God was going to send a human being to atone for the sins of the world, and that this human being was going to do it one time, once and for all. This human being was going to be so powerful, so amazing, that His sacrifice would reach all the way back to the beginning of time, the present and ahead to the future.

Well, let me have Isaiah tell you. Here's what he said in *Isaiah 53:5*, "He was pierced for our transgressions..." What?! He? His audience probably said, "You mean a person?"

[The verse continues] "He was crushed for our iniquities; the punishment that brought us peace was upon Him, and by His wounds we are healed."

Once again, the animal sacrifices could not make the people righteous. They could just cover the sin. That's why they had to do it over and over again. Well, Isaiah says, "This someone's going to come, and He's going to do it once for all time."

Enter Jesus. He walks up to John the Baptist, over in the New Testament. John the Baptist had this unique wardrobe. He preached a lot out in the desert and all that stuff. And here's what John said about Jesus in John 1:29, "Look, the Lamb of God who…" What? Say it with me, "…takes away the sin of the world."

See, atonement until this time had to do with "to cover, to atone, to cover." Now it means "to take away." Jesus will not only cover our sins, He's going to take them away.

Well, let's continue reading about when Christ kick-started His ministry. In Mark 10:45, Jesus said, "For even the Son of Man did not come to be served, but to serve, and to give His life as a ransom for many."

What did Jesus do? The second person of the Trinity lived a sinless life, He died a sacrificial death and He rose again. He conquered the grave.

When Adam and Eve saw God kill that animal right in front of their faces, they freaked out. When that Hebrew boy watched his father take the life of the lamb, I'm sure he lost it. What do you think heaven did when they saw Jesus dying on the cross for the world's sins? They wigged out!

On the cross, God treated Jesus like He was you and me so that He could turn around and treat you and me like we are Jesus. I hope you didn't miss that. On the cross, God treated Jesus like He was you and me so that He could turn around and treat you and me like we are Jesus.

"Ed, what are you implying?" Well, the Bible says that when a person makes the arrangement for Christ to come into his or her life, then the sins of that person are forgiven because the work has already been done. Christ has already paid the price. He said, "It is finished." He died on the cross for our sins – past, present and future – and He conquered the grave by rising again. Our sins are forgiven.

And a lot of Christians are running around going, "Man, my sins are forgiven. I'm a forgiven person. Isn't that amazing? Isn't that awesome?" It is. It really is.

I've talked to a lot of people who have seen this great movie *The Passion Of The Christ* by Mel Gibson. "Isn't this something, Ed? The suffering and the pain that Jesus went through for my sins?" And that's right. I highly recommend the movie. I think it's great.

But forgiveness of sin is only one-half of the deal. It's only one-half of the gospel. If that's all you know, you're missing the second half. As a believer, you don't really know who you are in Christ, because there's another half that most people don't talk about.

For example, if sinlessness was all that God needed for Christ to die on the cross for our sins, then Christ could've died when He was two. He didn't. Yes, He was sinless, but there's something else.

Remember, God is a God of justice. God has to have perfection. He can't wink at wrongdoing. He can't say, "Boys will be boys, girls will be girls." Sin must have a punishment. We can't fulfill the law. We're not perfect. What did Jesus do? Here's the second half of the gospel: Jesus perfectly obeyed the will of the Father. He was 100 percent righteous.

So as believers, when we receive Christ, we've got the forgiveness thing going on and ... check this out ... the righteousness of Christ is wired into our account.

When you face God, do you want to stand on your record of obedience or Christ's? I know which one I'm going to choose! I can't stand on my own. I mean, if I had to pay for my own sins, I would go straight to hell because I'm not perfect. I'm a moral foul-up. I'm a sinner. And so are you.

God, though, in His love and grace, provided another way, an alternative, another route. It's the red road — the red road of redemption and atonement paid ultimately by the blood of Jesus. And the reason we have the resurrection is because the resurrection is the evidence. It is the declaration of the perfect sacrifice of Jesus Christ. It's because of His sinlessness and also His righteousness. And when I receive that, when God looks at me, He doesn't see Ed Young, moral foul-up. He doesn't see Ed Young, supersonic sinner. He sees the forgiveness of Christ, and He sees the righteousness of His Son. Look how rich I am! Look how rich you are in Christ!

I checked the stats on death again, right before this service. They still are hovering around 100 percent. We're all going to die. We're all going to clock out. I'm going to ask you, "When you die, if you were to die right now, have you made the proper arrangements for your sins? Are you planning on paying for your own sins? Are you planning on standing on your own obedience, your own track record? Or have you made arrangements to receive what Christ did for you? Are you going to stand on Christ's record of obedience?"

You answer, "Well, Ed, dude, listen man. I, like, work with Meals on Wheels during Thanksgiving. And I serve the soup kitchen. And I give to United Way. And sometimes at church I'll even throw a bone in the offering plate, and I'm a lot better than most people. I really am. I'm a good guy, you know? I keep my nose clean, pay my taxes, and I'm honest. You know, I grew up Baptist...Catholic...Lutheran...."

That's not going to get you where you want to go. It's not going to happen. If that is what you're counting on to get you to heaven, you will have to pay for your own sins in a place of condemnation forever.

God's standards are perfect! I'm not perfect, you're not perfect. Christ *was* perfect. He has given us the perfect sacrifice, and He offers it to us.

But again, I can't do the deal for you. You can't do it for me. I can just tell you what the Bible says. Because with this high-risk — see how risky God is? — freedom of choice comes the high-cost principle of atonement.

Some of you right now are realizing you're lost. You know it. You're acting like you don't know it, but the Holy Spirit is all over you right now.

You're trying to think about what you're going to have for lunch. You're trying to think about everything else other than the deal. That's God. You better listen to Him and follow what He has for your life.

Well, I finally made it to Meridian, Texas, as I told you. And when I got to Meridian, I found a map and I said, "EJ, look where we messed up, man." See, I tried to bring him into it. I said, "See? We should've gone left here..." And as I looked at the map, you know, the road to Meridian that we should've gone on and turned on was in red ink! And the road that God wants you on is paved in red. So for eternal life, for peace, for freedom, the road is red.

15

WHO DO YOU SAY THAT I AM?

DR. O.S. HAWKINS

President – Chief Executive Officer

GuideStone Financial Resources of the Southern Baptist Convention

Dallas, Texas

IT SEEMS THAT EVERY EPOCH of Christian church history has a question from the lips of our Lord for which it could be particularly intended. For example, of the scores of questions asked in the gospels by our Lord, the first generational church was faced with the question of John 13:38 – "Will you lay down your life for My sake?" How many of our spiritual forefathers went to their martyr's deaths after facing that question from Christ? The apostolic fathers dealt personally with this...James, Peter, Paul...these were followed by the likes of Ignatius of Antioch and Polycarp of Smyrna.

Then came the Nicene fathers and another question emerged. For them it was the question of Matthew 22:42 – "What do you think about the Christ, whose son is He?" It was this question that brought them to Nicea in 325 A.D. Arius of Alexandria was preaching that the Son was not eternal with the Father but was created by the Father. Out of this Council of Nicea came the Nicene Creed which settled and affirmed for the church that the Son was of the same nature as the Father. In those days with this question on his heart, Athanasius stood tall as a defender of the faith.

As the church entered its dark period, being held in the clutches of the Roman popes, the Reformers broke through to the dawn of a new day when they were confronted with the question of John 11:40 – "Did I not say to you that if you would believe you would see the glory of God?" And so, armed with the truth of Romans, Martin Luther nailed his theses to the door of the church at Wittenburg and the glory of God filled Europe working through the likes of Calvin, Zwingli, Hubmaier, Manz, Knox, and all the others.

As the years of church history continued to unfold, and the great missionary movement advanced, they did so with the question of Luke 18:8 on their hearts and minds – "...when the Son of Man comes, will He find faith on the earth?" And so, William Carey and Hudson Taylor and David Livingstone and so many others left the confines and comforts of their homes for places like India and China and Africa with the question of their time burning in their hearts.

Then came the 20th century and prosperity filled the western church. The church gained influence and buildings and very subtly the emphasis of godly power changed to worldly influence. And consequently, there came the question of John 21:15 – "Do you love Me more than these?" Next, liberalism with its twin children of pluralism and inclusivism infiltrated the church, and from the lips of our Lord came the question of John 6:67 – "Will you also go away?" And unfortunately, many denominations and churches that once had evangelism and missions at their forefront and held to a high view of Scripture went away from the doctrinal truth their forefathers had held for generations.

And now, we find ourselves ministering in the 21st century. These are days of unbelievable challenge and opportunity. But Christ has a question for His church today. I believe it is the issue Southern Baptists and all true evangelicals must face for the next generation. It is the question of our time. It is the question of Matthew 16:15 – "Who do you say that I am?" This is the question for us! When so many other denominations have gone the way of pluralism and inclusivism, God is asking Southern Baptists – "Who do you say that I am?"

It is becoming more apparent that God is raising up Southern Baptists in the 21st century as a voice for righteousness in a culture that is filled with anti-Christian bigotry. While the American president and people are presently engaged in a war on terrorism, our pastors and pews are engaged in a war on truth. There are those among us in our culture today, just as in the Book of Jude, who seem to be bent on bringing down our twin towers of the truth and trustworthiness of the gospel. Perhaps no other single topic will be under attack during our remaining days of ministry as much as the issue of the exclusivity of the gospel. The next generation of Southern Baptist pastors must be prepared to answer the question of our time — "Who do you say that I am?"

There are two distinct styles of leadership prevalent today. There are those who lead by public consensus, and there are those who lead by personal conviction. This is particularly true in American political culture and, unfortunately, it has spilled into our church culture as well. We have seen professional politicians who lead by public consensus. It seems a stand is not taken on any issue until a poll is taken to see what the consensus of the people is on a particular subject, and then action is taken in accordance with public consensus. And then there are those politicians who lead by personal conviction. These individuals strive to make their decisions based on a conviction of what is right and wrong and then stand upon that personal conviction. Look at many of the major denominations today. They once made decisions on the basis of personal conviction. But now, in our sophisticated 21st century world, many find it more expedient to make decisions on the basis of public consensus. Is it any wonder that such things as political correctness and pluralistic compromise are the result? Those who lead by public consensus lead people where they "want" to go. Those who lead by personal conviction lead people where they "need" to go.

This is exactly the point the Lord Jesus was seeking to make when He took the disciples away from the Galilean crowds and moved them 25 miles to the north, to the headwaters of the Jordan River, near to the city Philip built in honor of the Caesar which became known as Caesarea Philippi. Our Lord knew the tendency we have to leave personal conviction for public consensus, and thus he framed two very important questions for our consideration. First, the question of public consensus – "Who do men say that I am?" (Matthew 16:13) Then, the question of personal conviction – "Who do you say that I am?" (Matthew 16:15) This is the question of our time. Southern Baptists, who do you say that He is? The next generation of Southern Baptists must be prepared to answer the question of our time. Who do you say that I am? The issue of the exclusivity of the gospel will be the single most important issue we will face in the next decade! And, if Southern Baptists do not give a certain sound – who will?

A QUESTION OF PUBLIC CONSENSUS (MATTHEW 16:13)

Note what happened around the fire at Caesarea Philippi. Jesus asked, "Who do men say that I am?" The disciples answered, "Some say you are John the Baptist. Some say you are Elijah. Some say you are Jeremiah. Some say you are one of the prophets." Here is a classic case of public consensus. They were giving their own polling results. They were aware that popular opinion, public consensus, was divided among four different opinions. Things have not changed much. There is still a lot of divided opinion today, and the words "some say" are present in our own modern vernacular.

"Some say you are John the Baptist." John the Baptist came preaching a message of repentance. These people sensed Jesus was a man of righteousness, and perhaps they thought of John the Baptist because of his preaching of repentance.

"Some say you are Elijah." These people must have sensed His greatness.

To the Jew, Elijah was one of the greatest prophets and teachers of all times. To this day, at the Seder meal, Elijah's chair is left vacant. Elijah was a man of prayer. The people of Palestine had watched our Lord Jesus calm storms with a prayer and multiply the loaves and fishes with a prayer. No wonder "some say" He is Elijah.

"Some say you are Jeremiah." These were obviously those who were aware of His tears, His passion, His burden for His people. They had seen the heart of Jesus. They had watched Him as He wept over the city of Jerusalem and as He wept at the grave of Lazarus. No wonder "some say" He is Jeremiah.

"Some say you are one of the prophets." Here is the very essence of public consensus. He was one of the prophets. These were those who did not know what to believe but could not discount His miracles and godly life. Some still say today that He is one of the prophets. Ask our Islamic friends. They will tell you that He is a prophet, but not as great as Mohammed. They will tell you He did not rise from the dead. Ask our Jewish friends and they will tell you He was a godly man and a prophet. Ask the "scholars" of the Jesus Seminar and they will have their own opinion as they seek to strip away His deity. Ask those who are advocates of the fad theology of "openness" today and they will tell you He had His own shortcomings on the side of omniscience. The question of public consensus still reveals that most think He was a great teacher or a prophet, but not God come in the flesh. The question of public consensus speaks of two things – it speaks of pluralistic compromise and political correctness.

The question of public consensus speaks of *pluralistic compromise.* We have a word for this – pluralism! Those who hold to this view believe that there are many paths to salvation, and the Lord Jesus is only one of them. They tell us that non-Christian religions are equally legitimate vehicles for salvation. Just like at Caesarea Philippi, "some say" that the Lord Jesus is "just one of the prophets." Thus the pluralist believes there is not just one way but a plurality of ways of salvation.

Some mainline denominations have taken their theological remote controls and pushed the mute button when it comes to topics such as the wrath and judgment of God, the sole authority of Scripture, and the insistence upon salvation through Christ alone. There are a lot of prominent liberal theologians who have crossed the theological Rubicon and embraced religious pluralism. We were seeing the beginning of this infiltration in the Southern Baptist Convention before the conservative resurgence. One former professor at one of our seminaries is in print as suggesting that there are other ways of salvation than belief in the Lord Jesus Christ alone. A former professor at another of our seminaries once castigated a former editor of a state Baptist paper for saying that those on the mission field who had never come to faith in Christ were "lost" and in danger of hell. When church leaders begin to question the validity of the exclusivity of the gospel and begin to believe that religious truth is not all important, it is only a matter of time until long held religious confessions and doctrines lose their relevance, resulting in a theological wandering. There is nothing that gives rise to pluralistic compromise any more than biblical illiteracy.

There is something that should amaze us all about these individuals who wave their flags of tolerance and pluralism. One seldom finds them criticizing other faiths for their own exclusivity. Have you ever heard of one of these liberal pluralists coming against Islam for its claims of exclusivity? Talk about exclusivity. I don't think anyone has been put to death in Phoenix or Dallas for converting to Christianity or converting to Judaism or Islam for that matter. Some seem to be more anti-Christian than anti-exclusivist. I'm amazed at how some Baptists have been characterized as purveyors of hate for their insistence upon the exclusivity of the gospel. And yet, in the name of their god, a Muslim extremist can fly an airplane into American buildings and murder thousands of innocent men, women, and children, and we are the purveyors of hate?

Theological liberals have a creed today. No, it is not the *Baptist Faith and Message* statement. It is the creed of pluralism. There is a concentrated effort to ensure that the next generations in America will be ignorant of the most elementary references to the foundations of our Judeo-Christian heritage. All one has to do is see how many elementary school textbooks are a part of the revisionist agenda. All one must do is see how many elementary schools no longer sing Christmas carols heralding and hailing the "Incarnate Deity," as we did at D. McRae Elementary School in East Fort Worth when I was a boy. Yes, there is the question of public consensus. It speaks of pluralistic compromise. Southern Baptists must avoid the temptation to deal with public consensus and the pluralism that results.

The question of public consensus – "Who do men say that I am?" – also speaks of *political correctness*. We have a word for political correctness – inclusivism! Those holding to this view are the people who believe that the scope and span of God's salvation is wide enough to encompass men and women who have not explicitly believed in the Lord Jesus Christ. That is, general revelation is adequate to bring all men to salvation even in the total absence of information about the gospel. While inclusivism differs from pluralism in believing that the Lord Jesus Christ is the only way to heaven, they both differ from exclusivity in the fact that they give no sense of necessity of the new birth. They say it is not necessary to know about the Lord Jesus or even believe in Him to receive salvation. For them, the requirement for salvation is simply to trust God under whatever form God is known to them, and perhaps some will receive knowledge of the Lord Jesus only after their death.

The most pointed question in the Bible is found in Acts 16 with the story of the Philippian jailer. He falls upon his knees before the apostle Paul and asks, "What must I do to be saved?" Had Paul been an inclusivist he would have replied, "Just calm down, you're already saved." But believing in an exclusive gospel as he did, and for which he would later give his life, Paul answered, "Believe on the Lord Jesus Christ and thou shalt be saved!"

Perhaps you say, "Well, all Baptists believe in the exclusivity of the gospel. Baptists do not adhere to pluralistic compromise or political correctness." Really? I came across an interesting book which I purchased from a bookstore at a Baptist divinity school on a campus of a Baptist university (formerly Southern Baptist) on the East Coast, written by a gentleman who was formerly a professor at a Baptist university in the South. The book has a fascinating title – *Ten Things I Learned Wrong from a Conservative Church.* Chapter 3 is entitled, "Third Wrong Teaching: Jesus is the Only Way to God." The following is a direct quote from this chapter: "Baptists and other dyed-in-the-wool conservatives have this thing about Jesus, that since the incarnation 2,000 years ago He is the only way to God." He does not put much stock in John's gospel. In fact, he insinuates that the Jesus of the fourth gospel was "arrogant" by stating that He was "The Way, The Truth, and The Life." He implies that Jesus was simply speaking metaphorically here. That is, since Jesus was not really "bread," as He said He was, then neither was He "The Way" as He said He was. This former professor goes on to say, "I don't think it is necessary for people to have an experience with Christ in order to enter the Kingdom of Heaven." Does anyone really wonder about the necessity of a conservative resurgence in the Southern Baptist Convention and the need of a confessional faith statement relating to who we are and what we believe?

Why should we as Southern Baptists be concerned about pluralistic compromise and political correctness? It is because they dramatically alter the very nature of our faith. There are two things at play here. The debate Southern Baptists have had over the last two decades is momentous. The future of world missions is at stake. Why? Pluralism affects our doctrine as believers, that is, what we believe, our message. When a man holds to pluralism, he is then forced to abandon virtually every core doctrine of the historic Christian faith. This involves such things as the Trinity, the deity of Christ, the incarnation, the virgin birth, the sinless life, the atonement, the resurrection, and the glorious return. To be a pluralist is impossible without a dedicated repudiation of the heart of the gospel of historic Christianity. The pluralism that has invaded many churches has been watering down the gospel message in the name of the Lord Jesus Christ for some time.

While pluralism affects our doctrine, inclusivism affects our duty as believers. That is, how we behave, our mission. When a man holds to inclusivistic thought, then he must abandon the duty of such Christian activities as evangelism and missions. He loses any sense of urgency and passion. This is why liberal churches and denominations have little if any emphasis on evangelism and missions. Doctrine affects duty...always!

Note what has happened to Southern Baptist missions in the past few years. Record numbers are going to the foreign fields. One thousand last year and one thousand the year before. Why? There is a renewed emphasis on the doctrine of the exclusivity of the gospel which brings a renewed sense of passion and urgency to take the gospel to the ends of the earth. The conservative resurgence is all-encompassing. Those early architects knew that doctrine always determines duty. Yes, "...for there is no other name under heaven given among men whereby we must be saved" (Acts 4:12).

As we hear continuing reports of deep declines in the mainline denominations in sending missionaries to the foreign fields, we see just the opposite with Southern Baptists. Why? We have thrown off the shabby coats of pluralism and inclusivism, of political correctness and pluralistic compromise. We have made a strong stand on the solid ground that Jesus Christ is the one and only way to heaven! This is not a theology that has "made in America" stamped on it. It is a theology made in heaven and delivered to a Palestinian world 2,000 years ago. It has not changed. It got to us across the centuries by the personal sacrifice of millions of believers. It came to us through their courage, commitment and conviction, their faith, fearlessness and fortitude. And now, we are stewards of this glorious gospel. This very fact moves us from the question of public consensus to the most important question – the question of personal conviction.

A QUESTION OF PERSONAL CONVICTION (MATTHEW 16:15)

There is an alternative to pluralism and its belief that God reveals Himself in all religious traditions, that many paths lead to the same place. There is also an alternative to inclusivism and its belief that salvation is through Jesus Christ but is not necessary to have an explicit knowledge or even faith in Him in order to obtain it. The alternative is exclusivity which says the central claims of our faith are absolute truth and thus claims to the contrary are to be rejected as false. It was this that brought about the question of personal conviction at Caesarea Philippi. What is really important to the Lord Jesus Christ is the question of personal conviction – "Who do you say that I am?" By the way, we're not the only exclusivists in the religious world. Do you think Orthodox Judaism is not exclusive? A reformed rabbi cannot even perform a wedding or *bar mitzvah* in Israel. Do you think Orthodox Islam is not exclusive? In some Islamic countries it is not a crime if you are a Christian, but it certainly is if you become one!

Our historic Christian faith is characterized by the exclusivity of the gospel. Jesus said, "I am the Way, the Truth, and the Life. No one comes to the Father except through me" (John 14:6). These are not our words, but His. If they were ours, it would be nothing less than arrogant bigotry. These are the words of the Lord Jesus Christ Himself. He doesn't simply say that He shows us the way, He says that He *is* the way. He does not say it is hard to come by another way, He says no one comes to the Father but through Him. The definite article is emphatic and repeated – "I am THE Way, THE Truth, and THE Life." It is no wonder that Jesus asks us the question of our time, the question of personal conviction – "Southern Baptists – Who do you say that I am?"

To say in our pluralistic culture that Christ is the only way to heaven is like waving a red cape in front of a raging bull. We saw this illustrated in the aftermath of the Iraqi war. Southern Baptists were a major part in the follow-up efforts of sending in food and relief supplies to the people of Iraq. Liberals screamed for fear that we might put a gospel tract in a box of food. These same people remained silent when the regime of Saddam Hussein was cutting out the tongues of multitudes of civilians who dared to speak against the atrocities of this cruel dictator. They never raised their voices as the ears of many were cut off for listening to any negative talk about their dictator. Liberals looked the other way when the regime fed dissidents into plastic shredders alive and feet first to accentuate the pain and agony. But now, they are on their soapboxes against any evangelistic witness in Iraq. I suppose they are convinced that the Iraqis who withstood 30 years of Saddam Hussein's tyranny could not stand a godly, spirit-filled Southern Baptist missionary with his or her message of hope and love. The 21st century has opened the door to a new world of opposition for those of us who hold to the exclusivity of the gospel. Yes, it is the question of our time – "Who do you say that I am?"

Now back to Caesarea Philippi. Having asked the question of public consensus, the Lord Jesus now looks at His disciples, and us, and asks the question of personal conviction, "Who do you say that I am?" When we read this question in our Greek New Testament, we immediately see that the "you" is emphatic. That is, it is placed in the sentence first for strong emphasis. "You, who do you say that I am? What about you?" It is interesting to know the opinions of others, but what really is important to our Lord is, "Who do YOU say that I am?" This is the question of our time, the question of personal conviction. The deity of Christ is still the foundation of Christian doctrine.

Not only is the language of the New Testament emphatic, it is plural. It was addressed to the disciples as a group, and it is addressed to Southern Baptists today. Who do you say that I am? Note the Lord Jesus is not asking what they thought or what they believed but what they "said." That is, He wanted to know if they were ready to verbally confess to His unique deity. The world is not interested in our opinion, but there is power in our confession. Southern Baptists, if no one else says to our world what Simon Peter said across the fire, may we be that still "certain sound."

Peter answered, "You are the Christ, the Son of the living God." Again, the "you" is emphatic, but it is singular here. In other words, Peter said, "You and You alone are the (definite article) Christ, the anointed one, the Messiah!" There is no one else and no other way home. Just as the emphatic "You" describes one person and one only, the definite article describes one and only one Messiah, and His sweet name is the Lord Jesus. Peter was saying that night, "Lord, You and You alone are the one the Bible reveals. You are the ram at Abraham's altar – You are the Passover Lamb, You are the blood of the everlasting covenant. You and You alone are the one and only Savior."

Christianity was birthed in a religiously pluralistic world. There are today the remains of a building in Rome called the Pantheon. It was the temple to all the gods. It was there that conquered people of the Roman Empire could go and worship the god they served whether he be Jupiter or Juno or whomever. However, throughout history the church has insisted that the Lord Jesus Christ is the only Savior and there is salvation in no one else. Our western culture is becoming more and more like the culture of the first century world where political correctness is the order of the day and where religious beliefs amount to little more than our personal taste, as if we were journeying down a cafeteria line choosing our personal food preferences. We have our own Pantheons in every city in America today. And, like those first generation followers of Christ, we are now faced with the question for our time – "Who do you say that I am?"

In a world where public consensus, with its pluralism and inclusivism, is the call of the day, Southern Baptists are making a bold statement that we are unashamedly exclusivists. We join Simon Peter in telling our world, "You and You alone are the Christ." What moved and motivated Simon Peter, as tradition tells us, to be crucified upside down? Did he give his life for pluralistic thought? Did Simon Peter believe in political correctness and pluralistic compromise? Call him to the witness stand and hear him say, "Nor is there salvation in any other, for there is no other name under heaven given among men whereby we must be saved" (Acts 4:12).

Put Paul on the witness stand to give testimony of the exclusivity of the gospel. Hear him say, "Even if we, or an angel from heaven, should preach a gospel other than the one we preached to you, let him be accursed" *(Galatians 1:8)*. What moved and motivated Paul to meet his martyr's death? It was his firm belief that Christ was the only way to heaven. Call John to the stand and listen to his testimony about the exclusivity of the gospel. Hear him say, "He who has the Son has life; he who does not have the Son of God does not have life" (1 John 5:12).

Call to the stand Stephen or Polycarp or Ignatius or Perpetua, who met her martyr's death as a young woman on the floor of the coliseum in Carthage, or any of these others who met their martyrs' deaths looking unto Jesus with a question of personal conviction upon their hearts. All those martyrs believed in the exclusivity of the gospel.

What motivated William Carey or our own Rebekah Naylor to go to India? What motivated Hudson Taylor or our own Lottie Moon to go to China? What motivated David Livingstone to go to Africa, or Bill Wallace or Bertha Smith to Shantung Province, or Bill Koehn to Yemen? Was it pluralism with its many roads to the same place? Was it inclusivism? No. It was the exclusivity of the gospel. It was the fact that there is "none other name under heaven given among men whereby you must be saved."

Southern Baptists, who do YOU say that He is? In a world of pluralistic compromise and political correctness, who do YOU say that He is? If He is *"ho Cristos"* ("the Christ"), then we need to take the cross off the steeple and put it back in the heart of the Sunday School. Sunday Schools in many churches have turned into nothing more than social hours and discussion groups for felt needs accompanied by coffee and doughnuts. If He is *"ho Cristos,"* we need to take the cross off the communion table and put it back in the middle of the sermon. Many modern sermons are void of the gospel and void of the cross. If He is *"ho Cristos,"* we need to take the crosses off our necklaces and put them back in the middle of the social ministries. If He is *"ho Cristos,"* we need to take the cross off our lapels and put it back in our music.

Jude warned about the day when the church would "go the way of Cain." What did he mean? Cain brought the offering of the best his human hands could bring. He had toiled in his field. He had worked hard and brought the best of human efforts as an offering to the Lord. But God did not accept it. He accepted Abel's offering, the lamb, the sacrifice. Cain had set aside the substitutionary sacrifice and the blood atonement. We are living in a day when many are "going the way of Cain." The question of our time, Southern Baptists, is the one of Matthew 16:15 – "Who do you say that I am?" It is a question of personal conviction, not a question of public consensus.

Southern Baptists, who do you SAY that He is? This speaks of our verbal witness. In all the discussions related to the changes in the *Baptist Faith and Message 2000*, the conversation seemed to have been centered on the addition of words related to either the Word or to women. However, it might be that the most significant change was the addition of two words we've seldom talked about that are related to our witness. The *Baptist Faith and Message 2000* says, "It is the duty of every child of God to win the lost by verbal witness undergirded by a Christian lifestyle." We added those words, "verbal witness." That is an important addition. "Who do you SAY I am?" He was not asking who do you think He is or who do you feel He is. What is important is who we SAY He is to a lost world.

We once had a country which shared our personal convictions. There are a lot of liberal legislators who might find it interesting to read the charters of their respective states and colonies. I wonder if the good Senator from Massachusetts has read the Charter of 1620 which says that Massachusetts was formed "to advance the enlargement of the Christian religion." I wonder if the Senator from Rhode Island knows that in 1683 his state was founded with these charter words, "We submit ourselves, our lives, our estates unto the Lord Jesus Christ, the King of Kings and the Lord of Lords, and to all those perfect and most absolute laws written in His holy Word." That is not too pluralistic nor inclusive! Perhaps the Senator from Connecticut would be surprised that the charter of his state says that Connecticut was founded "to preserve the purity of the gospel of the Lord Jesus Christ." And what about the great state of Maryland, next door to our nation's capitol? Her charter says that she was "formed by a pious zeal to extend the Christian gospel." The Senator from Delaware who is so interested in church/state issues might be surprised to learn that his charter reads that Delaware was "formed for the further propagation of the holy gospel."

When I was in the pastorate, I received a letter from the head of the Americans United for the Separation of Church and State. This letter was bemoaning the fact that there were church leaders in America who were trying to "Christianize America." I am unapologetically trying to Christianize America...and the world for that matter! This is the commission and calling of every follower of Christ.

There has been so much assault on Baptist beliefs today. Some of us are accused of being arrogant by holding to absolute truth. Are we surprised that we who are stewards of the gospel and hold to the truth of the gospel are called narrow? Truth is always narrow. Mathematical truth is narrow – two plus two equals four. There is no other option. That's pretty narrow. Scientific truth is narrow. Water freezes at 32 degrees Fahrenheit. It does not freeze at 33 or 34 degrees. That's pretty narrow. Historical truth is narrow. John Wilkes Booth shot Abraham Lincoln at the Ford Theater in Washington, D.C. He did not stab him in the Bowery in New York City. Geographical truth is narrow. Oklahoma and Texas are bordered by the Red River, not the Mississippi River. And, theological truth is narrow. The Lord Jesus said, "Enter through the narrow gate..." (Luke 13:24). Yes, "there is none other name under heaven whereby we must be saved."

Southern Baptists are leading the evangelical world today and not by public consensus but by personal conviction. This is the question for our time – "Who do you say that I am?" And we are answering with a certain sound. Thank God our missionaries are focused on winning men and women to Christ and planting churches. Thank God our seminaries are so structured today that all of them are teaching our young men and women to rightly divide the Word of Truth. While others are hung up with the question of public consensus, debating among themselves what "some say," we are facing the question of our time. And our answer? "You and You alone are the Christ!" There is no other way.

If it is true that Christ is the only Savior and the only way to heaven, then all other alternatives are false. Universalism is false. Pluralism is false.

Inclusivism is false. Non-Christian religions are false as they relate to eternal salvation. If this is all true, then we must join the songwriter of old in singing, *"I must needs go home by the way of the cross, there's no other way but this; I shall ne'er get sight of the gates of light, if the way of the cross I miss. The way of the cross leads home, the way of the cross leads home, it is sweet to know as I onward go, the way of the cross leads home."*

Yes, every epoch of church history has been faced with a question from the lips of our Lord. For us it is the question of our time — it is not the question of public consensus. Let others talk about what "some say." The question for us from the lips of our Lord Himself is this one — "Who do you say that I am?"

The last time I took W.A. Criswell to Israel, he wanted to drive all the way north to Caesarea Philippi. He knew this would most likely be his last visit to the Holy Land which he loved so passionately. I sought to talk him out of it because of the difficulty of the journey driving all that way from Jerusalem. But he was undeterred. Thus we drove north, up beyond the Galilee, all the way to the foothills of Mt. Hermon, to the very headwaters of the Jordan, to the spot where the Lord Jesus took His own disciples in Matthew 16 and where He asked the question of our time.

Upon arriving, we walked over and sat together on a rock under a tree. In a moment that old white-haired pulpit warrior stood up. Without saying a word, he reached down and picked up a small stone. He studied it carefully in his hand and said, "You are *petros*," a small pebble. Then, he turned and looked across the river and pointed to the big rock ledge and said, "And upon this *petra* (large solid rock), I will build my church." He proclaimed the message, "You are the Christ!"

Allow me to take the liberty of paraphrasing the way Dr. Criswell once put it. I think of that ultimate day when God says it is enough and calls me to appear before the judgment seat of Christ. Where is my hope? The speculation of modem theology and secularism, the speculation of pluralism with its pluralistic compromise, and inclusivism with its political correctness will not do. Let me hear again the old text, "Neither is there salvation in any other, for there is no other name under heaven given among men whereby you must be saved" (Acts 4:12). Let me sing again the old song, the lyric and melody are from God – What can wash away my sin? Nothing but the blood of Jesus.

And when that day comes, and we enter into His presence, the trumpet sounds and there go the patriarchs of the Old Testament. I see Noah and Abraham and Isaac and Jacob. But I'm not one of them. There are the prophets of the Old Testament, Isaiah and Jeremiah and Ezekiel. But I'm not one of them. There are the sweet Psalmists of Israel, David and Asaph and the sons of Korah. But I'm not one of them. And there go the glorious apostles of the New Testament, Peter, James and John, but I'm not one of them. And there, there are the martyrs of the church. There are Stephen and James and Polycarp and Ignatius and Savonarola and Tyndale and Huss and Koehn. But I'm not one of them.

And then, a great multitude which no one can number. And who are these? These are they who washed their robes white in the blood of the Lamb. They are before the throne and worship and serve Him day and night. I belong to that glorious throng of the redeemed. Who are these? The pluralists who live by pluralistic compromise would have you believe these are they who are devout men and women of religions around the world. These are Muslims and Buddhists and Hindus. These are they who just came a different path than we. Who are these? The inclusivists who live by political correctness would have you believe since Christ died for all men, these are they who are covered no matter what they believed or did not believe. These are they who are agnostics and even some who are atheists but for whom Christ died.

Who are these? Southern Baptists choose to answer with the Revelator of the Apocalypse. These are they whose robes have been washed white in the blood of the Lamb. These are they who have put their trust in Christ who said, "I am The Way, The Truth, and The Life. No one comes to the Father but by Me." These are they who say along with Peter, "There is none other name under heaven given among men whereby we must be saved."

Are these the ones who answer the question of public consensus with some vague reply, "Some say?" No, a thousand times no. These are they who answer the question of personal conviction with the words, "You and You alone are the one and only Christ, the Son of the living God!" Wash and be clean. Look and live. *"There is a fountain filled with blood drawn from Emmanuel's veins; and sinners plunged beneath that flood lose all their guilty stains."* Southern Baptists, here is the question of our time – "Who do you say that I am?" God has raised us up to answer boldly, "You and You alone are the Christ, the Son of the living God!" *"Dear dying Lamb, Thy precious blood shall never lose its power till all the ransomed church of God be saved to sin no more."*

WHAT NOW?

It may be that in reading this God's Spirit is leading you to put your faith and trust in Jesus Christ alone for eternal life. Heaven is God's free gift to you and cannot be earned or deserved. Yet, we are sinners and have all fallen short of God's perfect standard for our lives. He is a God of love and does not want to punish us for our sins, but He is also a God of justice and must punish sin. This is where the Lord Jesus steps in. He is the infinite God-man who came to take our sins in His own body on the cross. He "became sin for us that we might become the righteousness of God in Him." However, it is not enough to simply know all these facts; we must individually transfer our trust from ourselves and our own human effort to Christ alone and put our faith in Him for our own personal salvation.

The Lord Jesus said, "Behold, I stand at the door and knock. If anyone hears My voice and opens the door, I will come in to him..." *(Revelation 3:20).* If you would like to receive the free gift of eternal life through Jesus Christ, call on Him, right now. He has promised that "whoever calls on His name can be saved." The following is a suggested prayer:

Dear Lord Jesus:

I know I have sinned and do not deserve eternal life in and of myself. Thank you for dying on the cross for me. Please forgive me of my sin and come into my life right now. I turn to you and place all my trust in you for my eternal salvation. I accept your free gift of eternal life and forgiveness right now. Thank you for coming into my life.

If this prayer is the desire of your heart, you can claim the promise Jesus made to those who believe in Him — "Most assuredly, I say to you, he who believes in Me has everlasting life" (John 6:47).

Now, you can truly answer the question of our time — "Who do YOU say that I am?" You can now join millions of Christ's followers in saying, "You and you alone are the one and only Christ, the Savior of the world and the lover of my soul." Remember, Jesus asked, "Who do you SAY that I am?" Tell someone what you have just done in receiving Christ as your own personal Savior!

16

WHAT IS A GUY LIKE ME
DOING IN A PLACE LIKE THIS?

DR. HAYES WICKER

Senior Pastor

First Baptist Church

Naples, Florida

WHEN DR. JESS MOODY WAS PASTOR of the First Baptist Church of West Palm Beach, Florida, he was standing one night on his church property next to the Intercoastal Waterway. Suddenly, a sports car crashed into a wall. A young man had tried to commit suicide in the crash. Being unsuccessful, he jumped into the water and began swimming away from the shore, somehow hoping to drown. Jess called out, "Come back! God loves you, and I love you!" The student stopped and responded, "If you really mean that, I'll come back." Jess replied, "I really mean it; God loves you, and I love you." Fortunately, the young man turned around and was physically and eventually spiritually saved.

Luke 15 is God's "lost and found department" with the account of the lost sheep, the lost coin, and the lost son. The "prodigal son" was lost from home and the fellowship of the earthly father and the heavenly Father. His older brother was so cynical that he would have said that Humpty Dumpty was pushed! He was lost even while living on the farm and being daily in the house of his father. But, the lost can be found! The dead can live!

This story is the pearl of all parables. I never cease to be convicted by the beauty of grace and the urgency of repentance. If I had one message to preach before Christ comes again or before I die physically, I would share this message.

I. AT FIRST, I ASK: "WHAT IS A GUY LIKE ME DOING IN A PLACE LIKE THIS?" WHEN I REBEL AGAINST THE FATHER'S HOLINESS.

The rebellious younger son came to his father and asked for his share of the property. In village society, this request can only mean that he is impatient for the father's death when the division of wealth would naturally occur. A Middle Eastern father might grant legal possession but rarely the right of disposition. The son carefully avoided use of the word "inheritance" – that would have implied responsibility. He only wanted the cash for one-third of the property and the quick fix of pleasure.

There was not only a generation gap but a gorge between his parents and him. He had inherited a religious faith that was perhaps two sizes too big. Most significantly, he was rebelling against God. He thought the universe orbited around the tiny moon of his desires. In essence, sin longs for the death of God and wants its own way.

Though the sheep wandered away in dumbness, and the coin was inanimate, the son chose to deliberately break his father's heart, not caring how much others in the family will have to suffer when they sell off assets at any price in order to give him his money.

The young man "squandered his estate with loose living" in a "distant country." Growing up in Arizona, California was the "far country" to my generation of kids who longed for change. That is where you awaken to the sound of little birds choking every morning. It could be that the Southern California version of the Bible does not read, "verily, verily" but "for sure, for sure."

A terrible famine arose in the prodigal's playground. He had blown all of his money on big parties and temporary friends. He would not go home because of his pride but rather chose to "hire himself out to one of the citizens," who put him to work slopping the hogs. That was as low as a Jewish boy could go.

At any point in the journey, the boy could have turned around and gone home. God whispered through the emptiness of pleasure and then hunger. Finally, He shouted in the pigpen of disgust and despair. Perhaps you have scrounged in the garbage cans of the world's pleasures. You may be far away from God even now inwardly, yet staying outwardly in the church.

Someone is praying for you. Even as the dad allowed his son the freedom to leave, tears chased each other down weatherbeaten cheeks. However, he took the lasso of prayer and threw one end around the boy's heart and tied the other to his knees. Whenever he knelt in prayer, he pulled the prodigal a little closer to home.

Soon the young man realized that a lot of water had gone under the bridge, and a lot of bridges had gone under the water. As my old English friend, Roy Hession, said to me once, "Hayes, it's a long way out, but it's a short way back."

II. ALONG THE WAY, I ASK: "WHAT'S A GUY LIKE ME DOING IN A PLACE LIKE THIS?" WHEN I REPENT OF SIN'S WICKEDNESS.

We get excited about so many things, yet when was the last time you heard someone say, "I can't wait to repent!"? Jesus said, "...Be zealous and repent."

A. There is realization in this repentance.

He "came to his senses" means to recover from a coma. "Come back to your senses and stop sinning..." (1 Corinthians 15:34). If revival is "the beginning of a new obedience," as Charles Finney said, it is also the renewal of the realization that you don't have to be in a place like this or go to a place like hell. Wake up! Also, many Christians must change their minds about sin. The word repentance comes from two words, after and thought. Repentance is not really an afterthought but to change your mind on the basis of new evidence. A guy or a gal like you deserves better than the pigpen. The only answer is to "turn to God from idols" (1 Thessalonians 1:9).

B. There is contrition in this repentance.

Tears drip from every word of this confession. When the prodigal said first to God and then to his dad, "Father, I have sinned against heaven and in your sight," he was truly "sorrowful to the point of repentance" (2 Corinthians 7:9).

He was not like the guy who wrote to the Internal Revenue Service: "Enclosed is $150. I can't sleep. If I still can't sleep, I'll send the rest of it later." How do you know that you are truly sorry? There must be "earnestness" to change, "indignation" at sin, the "fear" of the Lord, "longing" for God's restoration," "zeal" "and avenging of wrong" (2 Corinthians 7:11). Whenever we are seeking to restore someone in church discipline and bring them to repentance, we apply the 2 Corinthians 7:11 test. It is not enough just to say like my young children who would flippantly whine, "Sorry!"

C. There is action in this repentance.

He did something about his feelings and failures. He said, "I will get up and go to my father." He left the pigpen. You must leave that harmful habit, those degrading friends, that wrong thinking, and go to the Father. Every failure is fresh incentive to seek the Lord. Every awareness of guilt is also incentive to repent and run to the Father. Most people run away from God when they "feel guilty." But this action must be accompanied by another key ingredient…

D. There is confession in this repentance.

He verbally admitted his wrong to his dad. "Take words with you and return to the Lord…" (Hosea 14:2). Our confession must be vertical to God and horizontal to others whom we have wronged. We say that we have sinned both "against heaven" and "in the sight" of others.

When I graduated from college, I had been blessed by a successful college pastorate just a few blocks from my school. Finishing in four years while pastoring your first church is not easy. However, I had a simple summer class to take in order to get the diploma. I still was allowed to go through the line at spring graduation. All those who were graduating were allowed to skip their finals – which I did. It was not until a few months later in a seminary missions class that God convicted me of my deceit. I determined to confess, to repent, and to get right no matter what the cost. I went immediately to my room and in faith called each professor. It is a miracle that college professors are even in the office during the late afternoon. I found one right after the other and confessed my sin, offering to take an F in their classes, drop out of seminary and return home. One professor indicated that he knew what I had done, but all forgave and encouraged me. However, if repentance is done in word by confession and in deed by restitution, we must be willing to do whatever is necessary, even if it means being less than a full-fledged son – "I am no longer worthy to be called your son."

What is keeping you from repentance? Is it your stubborn pride? Do you doubt the goodness of God? Wake up before it is too late. Realize that "because of your stubbornness and unrepentant heart you are storing up wrath for yourself in the day of wrath and revelation of the righteous judgment of God" (Romans 2:5), at the coming of the Lord Jesus to judge and to rule. It is not too late...there is still time.

III. FINALLY, I ASK: "WHAT IS A GUY LIKE ME DOING IN A PLACE LIKE THIS?" WHEN I RECOGNIZE THE FATHER'S GOODNESS.

A. This goodness is seen in the provision of His inheritance.

The son remembered the father's abundance and that even his hired servants were better off than he was. He used the term for "hired men" or "day laborers." They were lower on the social scale than slaves. A hired servant was not guaranteed a set wage, continued employment, or even that he would get paid at the end of the day. He was not allowed into the house. But even these people were better off than the prodigal amidst the famine and his desperation that would cause him to even eat the bean pods of the pigs.

Ben Hooper grew up some years ago in an eastern Tennessee town in a day when most boys knew their biological dads. However, he was called "an illegitimate child." He could hear the gossiping and whispering. A new preacher came to town and asked, "Whose boy are you? I know. The resemblance is unmistakable. You're a child of the heavenly Father! That's quite a responsibility. Now, go and live up to your inheritance." Ben Hooper was so motivated that he ultimately became governor of Tennessee. We have a far greater calling.

Jesus said to His disciples and to us, "No longer do I call you slaves...but I have called you friends..." (John 15:15). We have the commitment of the servant but also the companionship of a son. We are complete in Christ as His inheritors.

A southern preacher once expounded on God's Old Testament name of "I Am" like this: "He am that He am. He am always been and He am always gonna be. He Am." Jesus is everything we need. This is why Jesus said repeatedly in divine identification, "I am the Way...I am the Truth...I am the Life...I am the Light...I am the Bread...I am the Good Shepherd." He is the Way to those who are lost, the Truth to those in error, the Life to those who are dead, the Light to those in darkness, the Bread to those who are hungry, the Good Shepherd to those who are lost. To those in fear in the boat during a storm, the Wave-Walker said, "It is I [literally, I Am]; do not be afraid" (John 6:20).

Jesus is the Great Ocean ever seeking to fill the depths. This is not the outcast seeking the party, but the Party seeking the outcast. It is not the patient seeking the doctor, but the Great Physician seeking the patient. It is not the hungry seeking the bread, but the Bread seeking the hungry.

When my son, Evan, was five, he and I were praying during the first Persian Gulf War. He said, "Lord, help President Bush to....help President Bush to...what does he do, anyway?" We know what Jesus does. Where there is sin, He is drawn to it as the Need-Meter, the Sin-Cleanser, and the Life-Changer.

B. This goodness is seen in the compassion of His heart.

He feels with us. The Word speaks of the father's "compassion for him." When Jesus' good friend Lazarus died, we read about the God Man's "sweat of soul." He was "deeply moved in spirit," from a Greek word that speaks of the snorting of a horse. The classical Greeks saw their gods as being strong because they did not feel emotions. This was described as *apatheia* — we get our word "apathy" from this. Yet, *"Jesus wept"* (John 11:35). This was not some sympathy card in gold letters with rhyming words. It was not the fake wail of professional mourners, but a great groan from *"the God of all comfort"* (2 Corinthians 1:3).

He runs to us. The father in our story did not wait for the son to come all the way home, but he ran to him. God made the first move toward us. Villagers would often stone such rebels, but the dad wanted them to know that once a son, always a son. We didn't love God first, but He first loved us and ran all the way from heaven to a cross.

He also welcomes us. The father hugged and kissed him repeatedly, according to the tense of the Greek verb. We may not be acceptable but we are accepted. This truth forever answers the Pharisees' criticism of Jesus, which prompted the parable in Luke 15: "...*This man receives sinners...*" (Luke 15:2). How do you see the Father in your mind's eye? Is He smiling or frowning? Are His arms folded or opened wide? While there is still time, He welcomes you! For hands that had held the wine glasses, for feet that had strayed from home, for a back that had laid with harlots, the father gave a ring, sandals and the best robe. He would hear nothing of talk about being a hired man. God doesn't want you to grovel but to reign. When you truly repent, He warmly welcomes you.

He sacrifices for us. In killing the grain-fed beef, which was only reserved for special guests, the head of the household would spear the blood over the threshold of the door. We come back to God through the blood of the Lord Jesus Christ. Truly, "the way of the cross leads home." As the old Ira Sankey hymn sang, "You're only a step away from sin to grace." It's a long way out but a short way back and is only as far as a trip to the cross and a bath in the blood. You may have taken months or years to get this far away from the Father, but you can repent and come home to His open arms. Then you no longer will be "dead" but "come to life again." Literally, this word means to be "up and alive." You have been knocked down, but you can get up through the power of the resurrection and be alive.

C. This goodness is seen in the expression of his humiliation.

In order for the father to run to his son, he had to pick up his cloak exposing his undergarments for all to see. No one over 30 ever ran. He was willing to risk embarrassment to embrace his lost son. Thank God that Jesus was willing to die naked on the cross for us. But there was more humiliation for this loving dad.

The older brother came in from the fields and heard the joy cry, the rhythmic clapping, and the beating of the drums. He saw the circular dance. When he heard that his kid brother had returned, he exploded in legalistic and jealous rage. He had blown all that money on "steamy one-night-stands."

Normally at such banquets the older brother would be the headwaiter, shaking the hands of the guests. It was the father's way of saying, "You, our guests, are so great that even our sons are your servants." The older son would offer meat: "Eat this for my sake." Yet, he would have none of this.

He humiliated the loving father in front of all of his guests. He would not go in, but the dad did the unthinkable and went outside and began "pleading with him." This word means to call alongside and to see from the perspective of the dad. God pleads with us to be reconciled, to be repentant, to return. What grace!

Though the son did not use the customary term, "Oh, my father," yet the loving dad said, "Son." All of his goodness and inheritance was the older brother's to enjoy and even one-third more than the younger received. You may be inwardly resentful of "the fun" of the world's people. You've got it made! Jesus died for Pharisees, too. We too must "celebrate and rejoice." What a great Father we have!

Jesus leaves the account in mid-air. We could finish it by writing, "And the older brother went out and scourged the Father and nailed Him to a cross." He prayed continuously, "Forgive them" from the cross. As they threw Him onto the ground, He prayed, "Forgive them, for they do not know what they are doing…" (Luke 23:34). As they cast lots, as they nailed His hands, as they raised the crossbeam, as He hung for six hours, He prayed, "Forgive them…forgive them…forgive them." His humiliation became our redemption.

One day I will walk the streets of gold in heaven with far greater than a ring, shoes, or a robe. I will ask in amazement, "What is a guy like me doing in a place like this?" A voice like the sound of many waters will thunder from the throne of grace, "This son of mine was dead and has come to life; he was lost and has been found!" You also can hear that Voice, but you must come to Him now…before it is too late.

17

Jesus Christ Is Lord!

Dr. David Uth

Senior Pastor

First Baptist Church

Orlando, Florida

On October 19, 1856, a 22-year-old pastor in England started his message and announced to his congregation that they would meet again that evening in the Royal Surrey Gardens, a place reserved for concerts and special community events in London, England. This young man was Charles Spurgeon, who had already become a very popular preacher. People were flocking to church to hear the young eloquent preacher. God's anointing was on him, and each time he proclaimed God's Word, there was a special awe and power that was present.

That night a century and a half ago, when the young pastor arrived, there were 12,000 people gathered inside the auditorium, with another 10,000 outside who wanted to get in but found the auditorium full! Why did so many people come to hear a message from such a young man as Charles Spurgeon?

God's anointing on him was obvious, so that what happened next was a tragedy neither he nor the crowd expected would come to pass. Just as Spurgeon began to preach, somebody yelled, "Fire! Fire! The balcony is giving way!"

Although this was a prank inspired by an enemy of the gospel and there was no fire, the people stampeded to the exit doors. One can only imagine the stampede as people pushed and shoved their way to the exits, hardly concerned about anyone but themselves. There was pandemonium – seven people were trampled to death, and 28 others were injured badly enough to be hospitalized.

This event was an awful tragedy that devastated the young pastor. He had to be carried from the pulpit and did not open his mouth for several days. A friend took him to his home and cared for him, but the pastor was in such a confused state that he could not and would not speak to anybody. Finally, he regained his composure, and on Sunday, November 4th of that year, he walked into the church building, opened his Bible to Philippians 2, verse 9, and read these words of the apostle Paul: "Wherefore God also hath highly exalted him, and given him a name which is above every name" (KJV).

This young man became a prince among preachers and made an incredible impact on people who came to hear him proclaim the kingdom and kingship of God. That first Sunday after the awful fire, Spurgeon said, "I don't understand what's happened, but there is one thing I do understand – Jesus Christ is Lord." Then he read his text from Philippians 2:9, a verse in the famous passage where Paul declared the exaltation of Jesus Christ, who had been crucified on the cross for the salvation of the world (see Philippians 2:6-11). Spurgeon then said, "It is this text which has gotten me through the past days, and it is this truth upon which I have built my life."

Today, I want to reiterate that truth. There is no taller truth than this passage; it is like a mountain peak among Paul's letters to the Christians at Philippi just northwest of Galilee, where Jesus had lived and called His earliest followers. There is also no more solid foundation than that which Paul declared in this precious letter to that church.

Philippians is a letter Paul wrote from prison, urging the church at Philippi to have the mindset of Christ and to look out for each other, esteeming each other more highly than themselves. After this exhortation, Paul said they should carefully consider Christ Jesus, who though He was equal with God the Father in heaven, "emptied" Himself and assumed His role as a servant. His equality with God was not preserved for our salvation; He was made in our likeness, humbled Himself and became obedient to His Father in heaven unto death – yes, even the awful death on the cross!

This "self-emptying" of Christ qualified Him to be highly exalted and to receive the name which is above all others. Jesus Christ is *Lord,* and the day is coming when every knee will bow to Him and confess that He is Lord, to the glory of God the Father (see Philippians 2:9-11). Christ poured His life out and "emptied" Himself, taking the form of a servant to live among us and becoming like us in all respects except for sin. He is the Agent of Creation, the Word of God in human form (see John 1:1-18), and the Word by which God the Father created all things!

Yes, the divine Son of God became incarnate (in human flesh!) and was born of the virgin peasant girl named Mary. He came into our world to live and walk among us, helping the helpless, the poor, the crippled and discouraged by declaring God's good news to those most in need. That is the point of Paul's hymn to Christ and His humbling of Himself, being fully obedient to His Father – even though it meant the awful suffering of the cross, the most horrible execution adopted by the Romans to put fear in all those who would challenge the newly established empire. It was the most awful form of execution any major government had ever devised. That is also why Paul declared that God has "highly exalted Him and given Him a name above every name." Christ came at this period of history when virtually all those around the Mediterranean had been subdued by the Roman armies and brought within their governing power through promises of food and prosperity for those who would cooperate – and warnings to those who dared oppose the emperor.

The Romans had adopted a new designation for their highest office. Julius Caesar made a bold claim of being the one and only "Lord" – a title some Romans did not accept and which resulted in his assassination. However, when the young "adopted" son of Julius, Augustus Caesar, became the emperor, his personality and the people's cooperation resulted in the greatest cohesion of any empire in the ancient world. Right up to the time of the first *Christian* emperor 300 years later, this name "Lord" was supreme in the empire of Rome.

Saul of Tarsus, who took the name Paul and was a citizen of that empire, suffered death for claiming that Jesus Christ alone is the "Lord," the name which God the Father in heaven had given Him! Whereas the other apostles preached to Jews; Paul was called to declare the gospel to the Gentiles throughout the empire.

Ever since September 11, 2001, many have been shaken by the dangers of our world and the awful tragedy of those killed on that day. Paul's words concerning Jesus Christ as "Lord" have caused others to share with me as a pastor their faith and their concern for the future. It has also been my adequacy in the days since September 11th. It can be yours also. I have found consolation and divine truth in this passage of Scripture.

This passage has continued to amaze me through the years. Many scholars and other pastors have shared their testimony of this outstanding passage in Paul's letter to the Philippians. Scholars have noted that the confession of Paul is in the form of a hymn and one that the people probably sang to confess their faith in Jesus Christ as Lord. Just as we sing today, "He is Lord, He is Lord! He has risen from the dead, and He is Lord!" It is the oldest and deepest confession of our faith which you or I can make.

What else does this passage mean for us today? We need to scale the mighty peak and see what God is saying through the inspired apostle. When the Pope of the largest church in the world lands in a plane, he bows and kisses the ground. Why he does so was a mystery to a little grandmother who once witnessed his kissing the ground, and she said, "Oh, look at him! I know exactly how he feels. *I also hate to fly!*" I'm not sure the Pope would agree with her about his reason, and I wonder if we really understand what the Lordship of Christ is all about, even though we may sing or say these words so easily. Do we fully comprehend them?

What was it about these words that meant so much to Spurgeon and gave him hope in that horrible time as a young pastor whose "world" was shaken in that tragedy? How is it that this one truth rises above them all when you don't understand all the many circumstances around you? In Philippians 2:9, Paul declared that God the Father has highly exalted Christ and given Him the name or title above all others. What name? Jesus. Jesus Christ is *Lord.* Not Caesar or any other ruler of any empire; *Jesus Christ is Lord!* We must remember that all citizens of the Roman Empire were to confess the emperor as Lord as a test of their loyalty. Paul's preaching landed him in jail more than once, and yet his message has endured because it is the truth of God the Father in heaven. Jesus Christ is Lord! How may we better understand this truth today in our modern world?

What do you think when you hear the name of Judas, who betrayed Jesus for 30 pieces of silver? What about when you hear the name "Hitler," murderer of millions and deceiver of a great nation that brought on the greatest war in history? Contrast these names with the lowly Jesus, who laid aside His divinity in order to save humanity, but regained that divinity when His mission was accomplished. He is now and forever "Lord!" Yes, Jesus Christ is Lord, and both the Romans then and all nations now need to hear it again: Jesus Christ is Lord, to the glory of God the Father!

According to legend, when 70 Greek scholars were called upon to translate what Christians call the "Old Testament" from its Hebrew original to the Greek equivalent, they met on an island in the Mediterranean and worked separately, but (according to the legend), they came out with the same exact translation, known now as the *Septuagint* – the first translation of the Jewish Scriptures into Greek. These scholars knew that Greek had become the universal language of the

Roman Empire, and they wanted their translation to be available to all people of the empire (however, I can only say that they were not Baptists – 70 Baptist scholars could never have agreed on any one matter)!

This *Septuagint* translation of the Hebrew Scriptures into Greek rendered the divine name of God (Yahweh) as "Lord" – spelled the same as "Lord" in the sense of a ruler of a nation or empire, which the Romans had adopted. Although most of the passages where the word "Lord" (Greek: *kyrios*) is used refer clearly to God the Father, there are some passages (such as our text in Philippians 2) which refer to Jesus Christ the Son as Lord. This raises the eyebrows of some religious leaders who refer to Jesus as simply another outstanding preacher/teacher, but hardly the one true Lord of all.

To complicate matters further, in the Judaism at the time of Jesus, the ineffable name of Yahweh (which is often written as consonants YHWH) was considered to be too holy and majestic to be spoken, so they substituted the term *"Kyrios,"* or "Lord." Hence, the doctrine of the Trinity was developed partly because of this practice. God the Father, God the Son, God the Holy Spirit – the three are one God existing in three "persons" (or "faces" – another meaning of the word *persona*, from which we get our modern word for "person"). As God's human face, Jesus Christ has revealed God the Father's love!

You can see from this the way the divine "man" Jesus Christ became the "exact image of the Father" – the one and only true "Son of God" from eternity, the Second Person of the Trinity. Paul could therefore declare that Jesus Christ is Lord and shares with the Father in heaven a place at His right hand, for Christ is also "Lord" and in perfect unity with God the Father. This mystery of the Trinity includes the "Spirit" in the gospel of John – the *"Paraclete"* who will reveal Christ to each true believer. Thus, the Father "sends" the Son, and the Son dies on the cross and is raised from the dead, and the Spirit confirms the proclamation to each believing person!

What shall we say about this truth concerning Jesus Christ our "Lord?" We must love and obey Him who gave His life for us. We may hear someone say, "Come, and make Jesus the Lord of your life!" But we do not really "make" Him Lord; He *is* Lord! We must have enough sense to know that He is Lord and acknowledge His Lordship. We don't "make" Him Lord; He *is* Lord! You may say, "I don't believe He is Lord." That does not change the fact that it is God's own divine truth: Jesus is Lord, and we cannot cancel God's choice of Jesus as our Lord, although we may choose not to believe or trust in Him. Since He is Lord, all will one day bow to Him whom God the Father has designated as Lord. His "Lordship" is not open to us for a vote! His title as Lord is a divine truth. This is the apostle Paul's "gospel" – good news that God is the Father of amazing grace and love. He invites you to come to Christ and know and love both the Father and the Son in the power and conviction of the Holy Spirit.

Those terrorists at our public schools who scorned God will bow. Those at the school who have laughed at you because you are a Christian, or those in the places of business – anywhere and everywhere – all those that have scorned Christ and the cross of our Lord, they will all confess that He is Lord! "Today is the day of salvation," but tomorrow will be too late!

When Jesus encountered the demons and their leader, Satan, they knew Him. He spoke with authority and refused to allow them their freedom to rule over God's creation. Yes, even Satan – the arch enemy of Christ – is also going to bow at the feet of Jesus Christ the Lord! There was a song that referred to "the devil in a blue dress." That was a modern picture of how he may appear to some. But I don't think he will have horns, nor will he be able to masquerade as an angel of light again, nor will he be able to destroy one's marriage or take the life of a youth with drugs, liquor, etc.

This truth of the ultimate Lordship of Jesus Christ our Savior is what keeps us going day by day. It makes me glad to know that when I am on His side, I am on the winning side. Now I understand why Spurgeon chose this text and came out of that darkness that muted his tongue.

The last word is that all history will conclude at the feet of Jesus. I'm not looking forward to occupying a casket in a grave – I won't be there anyway! That is not the end of true life for the Christian.

Frankly, I don't want to be among people who deny the One who loved us and gave Himself for us. I don't plan to witness the punishments against demons, God-denying atheistic and unbelieving people who will not trust in the Lord. Surely, one of the torments of hell is knowing that those could have been saved who chose instead to be their own boss and do their own thing rather than surrender to Jesus Christ as Lord.

One day we shall all declare that Jesus Christ is Lord, whether for salvation or eternal damnation. If you are agnostic and want to know the truth, give your life to Christ. If you truly believe He is Lord, then confess Him now while you still have life and breath.

We have been looking at what the title "Lord" means in reference to the Lord Jesus Christ. God's raising of Jesus Christ from the dead was a unique act of God the Father – the Almighty God! "Jesus Christ is Lord" means that He lives; He is alive forevermore, for He is truly Lord just like His heavenly Father. The crucified Jesus is also the risen and living, eternal Lord, God's only (unique) Son, and our only true Savior!

Paul proclaims in Philippians 2:10-11 that God has exalted Him to the highest place. He has given Him a name that is above every name, that at the name of Jesus Christ, the Lord, every knee will bow – the tense is future – every knee shall bow in heaven and on earth and under the earth, and every tongue will confess that Jesus Christ is Lord, to the glory of God the Father!

What does it mean to declare that every tongue "will confess?" The prefix "con" means "with," then "fess," like "fess up." That means that one must confess the truth and agree with God's declaration. That is what "confess that Jesus is Lord" declares. One day every knee will hit the dirt at the feet of Jesus and every tongue will agree with the truth of His divinely appointed and deserved Lordship!

Paul continues by observing that three realms will confess the truth: 1) all those in heaven, and 2) all those on earth, and 3) all those under the earth. I have little hesitation about all angels in heaven confessing His divine Lordship, but what about "all those on earth?" Doesn't this include terrorists like Osama bin Laden and others like him? Yes, he, too, will one day fall at the feet of Jesus, and so will Mohammed, the founder of Islam, and every other religious and political leader who ever lived!

There is nothing that encourages me more than to know that one day, the enemy that has fought us all our lives, will get on his knees and say, "Jesus, You are Lord." Every demon in hell will say, "Jesus, You are Lord."

When there was a baby's cry in Bethlehem, there was trembling in hell, because from the very start they knew who He was. In fact, if you want to know something kind of fun, read in the New Testament who the first group was that recognized Jesus as the Son of God. It wasn't the disciples, nor His family, and it surely wasn't the Pharisees: it was the demons.

The first time they met Him, they were backing up. They were saying, "Uh, uh, uh, Jesus, please don't destroy us yet!" Even the demons know that Jesus Christ is Lord: but they just won't bow down and say it until one day when every knee bows and every tongue confesses.

There will be one last thing that will happen before we spend an eternity, either with Him or apart from Him. What you do with Jesus, the choice you make with Jesus really is a choice you will either live by or die by. For those who choose Jesus will live eternally; but those who say no will die eternally.

What will it take for us today to say, "You know what, for the rest of my life, I am going to make this decision, and I am going to make this choice. Then, all the other choices will come naturally, because, Jesus today I want to say something to you from my heart and with my lips, 'You are the Lord of my life.'"

The following letter is from a Marine who died during Desert Storm. Perhaps others may be like him, for many hundreds have died since that time. The Marine had a letter on him which he had written the night before he died:

"Look, God, I've never spoken to you before. You see, God, they told me you didn't exist, and like a fool, I believed them. Last night, in this sandbox, I saw you, and I figured right then that they lied to me…I had to come to this big old sandbox before I took the time to see the beauty of your face…but I'm glad I've come to know you and I'm sure glad I met you. I reckon the zero hour will be here any day now, but I'm not afraid since I know you are near me. God, I really like you a lot and I want you to know this. This fight that's coming will be terrible, I know, but I'm not afraid. I may come home tonight! …God, will you wait for me at the gate? P. S. It seems strange, but since I've met you, I'm not afraid to die."

God is waiting for you to make a genuine turn toward Him and Christ. The soldier realized the truth that night, and now I ask, how long will it take before you see and acknowledge that Jesus Christ is Lord? How many days do you have before a catastrophe of your own, an automobile accident, or a disease like cancer which takes the gift of life away? Yes, Jesus Christ is Lord! Will you receive Him today? Why not do it now? He will receive you.

18

THE ATTITUDE OF PHINEHAS

DR. TED TRAYLOR

Senior Pastor

Olive Baptist Church

Pensacola, Florida

As you study Psalm 105, you find it to be all about the faithfulness of our God, everything He's done for us. Psalm 105, those 45 verses, share with us over and over the faithfulness of God, the faithfulness of God, the faithfulness of God. When you come to Psalm 106 you find the unfaithfulness of mankind. In Psalm 105, God is faithful. In Psalm 106, Israel and mankind are unfaithful. But right in the midst of our unfaithfulness, Phinehas stands up to stand out. We find him in Psalm 106:28-31:

> *"They* [that is, Israel] *joined themselves also to Baal-peor* [Baal is the false god; peor is the place. And they're worshipping a false god. They've joined themselves to a false god in Peor], *and ate sacrifices offered to the dead. Thus they provoked Him* [that is, they provoked God] *to anger with their deeds, and the plague broke out among them. Then Phinehas stood up and interposed, and so the plague was stayed. And it was reckoned to him for righteousness, to all generations forever [NAS]."*

Verse 30 says, "Then Phinehas stood up." Here's my challenge to you today: In a dark and a wicked culture, will you stand up? When everybody else is bowing down to the false gods, will you stand up? When people are eating and drinking unto those that are dead, will you stand up? When a world says that Jesus is not God, will you stand up? Old Phinehas did. You ought to read the story, which is found in Numbers 25.

Let me tell you where old Phinehas was when he stood up. He was in Shittim. I shared that story one time and a little three-year-old told her momma, "He's going to have to clean his mouth out when he gets home." Well, they got to the city of Shittim. It's the last stop before they go across the Jordan into the Promised Land. And when they got to that city, the Bible says in Numbers 25 that the people of God joined themselves to the false god of Baal. When they joined themselves to the false god of Baal, the people of the region of Moab invited these people to come and give sacrifice and worship their god, and they bowed down to the false god. Israel joined themselves, and God got mad. The Bible says He sent a plague among the people. Then God said to Moses – you won't believe this – God said, "Moses, I want you to find every leader of every tribe and every man who bowed down to the false god. I want them killed today. I want them killed."

You have to understand what they did at church with Baal worship. Prostitutes were kept at the Temple of Baal. And when you worshiped Baal, the men came in and had sexual intercourse with the temple prostitutes. That's what the men of Israel were doing. God said to Moses, "Everybody who has entered into this worship, I want them dead before dark." And the people wept when they went to the tent of meeting. They wept and they cried out, "O, God, be merciful!" While they were crying out, one of the sons of Israel came and brought a Midianite prostitute with him. They were crying out to God and he walked in and said, "Look here, boys. Look at this lady. Don't you want to come over here and leave that house of worship? Come with me." He brought this Midianite woman right into the midst of the weeping and wailing and repentance. That's when Phinehas stood up.

Now Phinehas was a priest. As a matter of fact, he was the nephew of Moses, the son of Eleazar. His hands were accustomed to taking the utensils of worship in the Old Testament and dealing with them. He'd light the candle of the lamp. But, also, he was accustomed to taking a small dagger and taking those animals that they brought for sacrifice and cutting their throats and bleeding them and slicing them and preparing them for the altar. The Bible says that Phinehas that day laid aside the dagger, and he picked up a sword.

Tradition says that this man's name was Zimri, and Phinehas went after Zimri and the Midianite woman, and he ran them into a tent. When he found them in the tent, the Bible says that he took a sword and he ran it through both of them and killed them both. God said in effect, "Blessed be the name of Phinehas, for he will be and his family in perpetual priesthood 'til the end of time." Phinehas stood up.

I'm here to tell you, friend, anytime darkness comes, God always has a champion. That's what God's looking for in America today. He's looking for some champions with righteous indignation. He's looking for champions to have an honest spirit. He's looking for a champion who has a holy passion.

Now Phinehas was no palliator of sin. He did not say to make sin palatable. That's what is happening in the churches today. Phinehas said sin is sin is sin. His heart was sound in God's statutes. His whole nature was ablaze for the glory of God. I want you to look at it with me right here in Numbers 25. The Bible says in verses 10-12, "Then the Lord spoke to Moses saying, 'Phinehas the son of Eleazar, the son of Aaron the priest, has turned away My wrath from the sons of Israel in that he was jealous with My jealousy among them, so that I did not destroy the sons of Israel in my jealousy. Therefore, say, 'Behold, I give him my covenant of peace...'" Then verse 13 says, "'and it shall be for him and his descendants after him, a covenant of a perpetual priesthood...'"

THE LAST SERMON I WOULD PREACH

Why? Because he was jealous for the Lord our God.

Why was Phinehas blessed? Phinehas was blessed because he was jealous for one thing. He was jealous for the Lord our God. Now here is what God is calling us out for today. He is calling us to stand up in a culture that is crooked and dark and He is asking us to stand and be jealous for God and God alone. Oh, if we ever learn to just stand up, stand up, stand up for the jealousness of Holy God. You ask, "How do we do that, Pastor?" Well, there are four things I want to share with you that I glean from the life of Phinehas. I believe these four things should be in your life and they should be in mine. If we find these four things in our life we will be blessed as a royal priesthood as Phinehas was.

Number one, I share with you that if you're going to stand up as Phinehas stood up, and do it in our culture, you must have no other God but Jehovah. Jehovah rules! Jehovah is sufficient. No other God, no other name. You don't bow down to anything, save Jehovah God. You say, "Pastor, I'm not an idolater." Do you want to stand by that statement? Idolatry rules in America today. We have set aside the true God. We've picked up many others. Certainly the god that rules in our land is materialism. Oh, we bow down to anything that blesses us financially, even sexual immorality. What they did with Baal, that's nothing new in our culture today.

God is calling out people to say, "I've got no God but Jehovah. Jehovah is my God." We've got a little song we sing about that in the choir. There's no God like Jehovah. You know how that goes? There's no God like Jehovah. He's coming on the clouds. I like that song. That's good. There's no God but Jehovah. There's no other God. Hey, I want to let you in on a little secret: When you go down to the plurality rally, and they have all of these different religious speakers talking, and you've got a Mormon talking and you've got a rabbi talking and you've got a Buddhist monk talking, let me tell you, friend, all of that's idolatry. There is but one God, and Jehovah is His name. If you've bought into this idea that there's a plurality of gods in America and that you can stand and pledge allegiance to one nation, it doesn't say "under gods," it says "under God," and there is but one – and Jehovah is His name.

Now you can say that in church and people will applaud, but you begin to live that out there on the street, and let me tell you, there's a killing coming. Dear friends, if you're going to be a Phinehas, you've got to stand and say there is but one God and Jehovah is His name. And the only way He has revealed Himself is in His Son, and Jesus is His name. Oh, now, friend, the rubber will hit the road. You'll get traction when you begin to say Jesus is the only way.

I heard my buddy, Bill Anderson, down in Clearwater, Florida, once. He said this: "I pray in Jesus' name at a public function and somebody will walk up to me and say, 'Well, I liked everything you did until you got to the end of your prayer, and then you offended me when you prayed in Jesus' name.'" And Bill Anderson said, "Dear friend, you offend me when you don't pray in Jesus' name." I like that. You see, it's an affront to God to think you can walk in under any other name. And if we're going to play the feeling card, I'm going to start playing the "feeling" card. It's an offense unto God to think you can walk in under any other name other than the name that's above every name, a name whereby you must be saved. Let me tell you, if you're going to take a stand, number one, you will have no other God but Jehovah.

The second thing I glean from the life of Phinehas is that unchecked sinfulness will bring God's judgment. Friend, if we don't stand for righteousness and we do not check sin in our culture, God's judgment and His wrath will fall. I have no doubt in my mind that the judgment of God waits in the wings of our culture if it's not already among us. There's sin running rampant, unchecked. Where are the righteous pulpits today? Where are the godly and righteous lay people standing to say sin is sin is sin? We must deal with that. That's exactly what Phinehas did. He saw that sin was abounding, and it had to be dealt with. Phinehas dealt with it.

Now some people would say, "Well, Pastor, if Phinehas could take a sword and run through Zimri and that prostitute, then it will be okay for us to take a gun and go to the abortion clinic and kill somebody when she is going in to have an abortion." Now I want you to hear this. Phinehas was a priest. The law rested in the religious leader of Israel's day. The law of America does not rest with the evangelical church. The law of the land does not rest in your hands. And to go to an abortion clinic and take a gun and shoot a doctor or somebody else is sin against God, you ought to go to jail for it, and in my opinion, I think they ought to kill you if you do that. That makes me pro-capital punishment. I believe that from Romans 13 that the sword is not in my hand, it is not in your hand. The sword is placed in the hand of the governing officials as a minister of Holy God. But understand when I say to take a stand that you take a stand for holiness, and vengeance is not ours. Vengeance is the Lord's. We leave vengeance unto Him.

We stand for truth, and if the world kills us for standing for truth, so be it. We just get a promotion and go to heaven. Hallelujah! But you cannot sit idly by with sin going unchecked in our culture and say that you're standing for the lordship of Christ. You must take a stand and decide who is on the Lord's side, but you dare not take judgment into your own hands to think that you are God's implement of judgment.

Number three, Phinehas teaches that we must take full responsibility in standing up. Friend, nobody's responsible for you standing in your culture but you. I'm responsible for me, and you're responsible for you. Phinehas looked around, and you can imagine that they're in this prayer meeting, people are wailing, crying out to God, and Phinehas says, "Surely, surely somebody's going to do something about this. This guy is bringing a prostitute right in here." And it's as if God says, "Phinehas, thou art the man." There are some places in the Bible where I'd like to have been a fly on the wall. This is one of them. I wonder what Phinehas said when he jumped up with that sword. You know, if a guy jumps up with a sword he doesn't have to say anything if he points the right end at you. And he put them on the run.

Phinehas understood his responsibility. Dear friend, you are responsible as a Christian. If I were to ask you today, have you trusted Jesus Christ as your Lord and Savior, you'd say yes. Are you going to heaven when you die? Yes. That makes you a candidate to be salt and light. And dear friend, we can no longer sit idly by without being in the fullness of the Spirit of God, those people who will stand up in our culture and be counted with love and mercy and grace and truth. We must be. And nobody is going to be responsible for your home but you. Nobody's responsible for your workplace but you. Nobody's responsible for your circle of influence but you. Phinehas had to stand and you can't just point fingers at others and say, "Well, if he would or he would or he would..." No, no, no. It's you. You're responsible for your circle of influence.

Not only must we have no other God but Jehovah, realize unchecked sinfulness will bring God's judgment, and take full responsibility and stand up, but we must also believe one person can make a difference. Phinehas did. In the whole of the 106th Psalm, Phinehas is the only name mentioned for righteousness. Do you know you can make a difference? Did you know how True Love Waits got started? One kid wrote a paper. One person can make a difference. You just stand. I'm telling you, it would be amazing what God would do with you, if you'd just stand where you are. God can use one to make a difference. Do you think He did anything with Martin Luther during the Reformation? One man can make a difference.

You know, if there are enough of us who will stand one by one by one, we don't have to be a majority to change the culture. A majority of America was against kicking the Bible out of public schools, but a minority got it done. The majority of people would be for having prayer before a ballgame in America, but a minority got it stopped. You understand today, friend, it does not take a majority, it only takes a minority full of the Holy Ghost. These people have changed our culture as a minority full of the devil. Do you understand what one can do?

Look what one did in a negative way with Madalyn Murray O'Hair. I mean, if the devil can use one woman to do that, what could God do with one of you? With a tenacious love, look what God did with Mother Teresa. One woman in a godless culture filled with lepers. What a story. The power of one, one. Will you be one? Would you stand for Christ in our culture? You'll never stand until you're settled on who your God is.

I want to give you a test to find out who your God is today, and then I want us to do business with the Lord. I want to give you the "T" test. These are four questions that will help you understand who your God is.

Number one, what do you think about most? What occupies your mind? "As a man thinketh in his heart so he is." I want to ask you, "Who is your God?"

Number two, what do you talk about most? Do you ever go to these message boards on the Internet? That's an amazing thing to me. People will just say anything as long as they don't have to sign their name. They make up some moniker. I read them every now and then on the sports pages. They get these teams arguing against each other. It's an amazing thing what people will say. Now folks who sit around and type those messages have way too much time on their hands. And most of them, it seems to me, have less than one brain cell. They sure don't have another one to rub it against, I guarantee you. What do you talk about? What do you talk about?

Number three, where do you invest your treasure? You won't find your God far from there. Where do you invest your treasure?

And certainly number four, the last one that you would guess would be very easily discerned is, where do you spend your time? Your thoughts, your talk, your treasure, your time. Dear friend, if you come to the Lord Jesus, He ought to get your time, He ought to get your thoughts, He ought to get your tongue, He ought to get your treasure.

Love the Lord your God with all your heart, with all your soul, with all your mind. Now it's interesting what the Bible says about Phinehas. Here was God's blessing to Phinehas. Here's what He did to him. Phinehas is the priest and God says about Phinehas, "I'm going to bless Phinehas and give him and his family perpetual priesthood." If you go out to the cemetery, you'll see perpetual care. That means all the time. Somebody's supposed to take care of your grave until Jesus comes. Here, He says, "I'm going to give him perpetual priesthood."

Now watch this: Phinehas and his family were priests until the time of the Babylonian captivity when the priesthood ceased. Then when they came out of the Babylonian captivity the priesthood started over and Phinehas' name went on through a gentleman by the name of Ezra. And Ezra's time went on until the dark period of the Intertestamental Period between Malachi and the time when we saw this old nasty-looking fellow come walking eating honey and wild locusts and saying, "Behold the Lamb of God who comes to take away the sin of the world." John the Baptist said, "Here He comes." And here came Jesus after the order of Melchizadek the great high priest. Jesus was going to lay down his life. What I want you to see is Phinehas was preaching Jesus when he stood up. His perpetual priesthood ran all the way to Christ. And do you know what Peter now says about you and about me? He says you are a royal priesthood. Do you know that you've got Phinehas' spirit in you if you're naming the name of the Lord Jesus?

What I want to ask you today is, will you honor the name of your great, great, great, great, great, great, great cousin, Phinehas, and stand up? You say,

"Preacher, how do I stand?" Let me give you two or three things, and then I want us to do business with the Lord today. First, you've got to take the step to do it. If you're going to stand, you must trust Jesus Christ as your Lord and Savior. Jesus came and died for you as a sinner, and you say, "Preacher, I don't want to stand for Him." Well, He stood for you and He died. Perhaps you need to give your heart and life to Christ. That's the way you need to stand. Some of you have been saved, but never baptized. You've never walked into those waters.

I talked to a gentleman just this week. He said, "Preacher, I've been saved but I've never been baptized." I said, "What are you waiting on?" He said, "I don't know. I'm just kind of…." I said, "Scared?" He said, "No, I'm not scared." I said, "Ashamed?" "No, not ashamed." I said, "Embarrassed?" He said, "No." I said, "Well, what is it?" He said, "I don't know." I said, "Well, get on with it. Let's go. Do you know it to be the will of God?" "Yeah, I know. I hear you preach. I read the Bible. I know I ought to." He'd rather sit than stand. Some of you would rather sit than stand. Friend, our culture will not allow us to sit any longer. The kingdom calls for us to stand like Phinehas. For some of you, it's taking a stand for Christ by coming to be saved, for some of you, it is to take a stand and be baptized.

The Word of God says in Ecclesiastes 5:5: "*It is better that you should not vow than that you should vow and not pay.*" Here's my question to you today: If you are not a Christian, would you be willing to get saved and be baptized and join a local church? If everybody took this seriously, I'm here to tell you, America won't be the same. Now standing doesn't mean you take your big King James Version and hit somebody in the head with it. It means you're salt and light, and you begin to speak up and stand up and speak out and name the name.

Oh, my. If we really mean this, look out! Phinehas is coming. Draw swords! You need to unsheath your sword this week. Have you got it in your hand? I want you to take it. I want you to unsheath it this week and let loose the truth of God and see what the Lord might do.

19

THE POWER OF THE CROSS

DR. CURT DODD

Senior Pastor

Westside Church

Omaha, Nebraska

I BELIEVE THAT THE POWER OF THE CROSS is one of the most disregarded doctrines of the Christian faith today. We in church leadership have become very pragmatic in our teaching in recent years. We are concerned about the application of God's Word in the practical aspects of our lives, but we are often guilty of not laying a proper foundation of our faith at the foot of the cross. When people leave our gatherings and are enamored with the personality of the preacher, professionalism of the music, or the simplistic substance of the sermon, we have failed as ambassadors of Christ. Now, don't get me wrong. The application of God's Word to everyday life is essential for dynamic living, but the preaching of the cross of Christ must have preeminence! Let's examine the power of the cross.

"For Christ did not send me to baptize, but to preach the gospel — not with words of human wisdom, lest the cross of Christ be emptied of its power. For the message of the cross is foolishness to those who are perishing, but to us who are being saved, it is the power of God" (1 Corinthians 1:17-18 NIV).

What an awesome statement! But somehow, in our culture, we have lost the significance of what Paul has written. We focus on trying to be crafty with our words and powerful with our programs, as if the cross of Christ was not powerful enough to draw men's hearts and change men's lives.

"May I never boast except in the cross of our Lord Jesus Christ, through which the world has been crucified to me, and I to the world" (Galatians 6:14 NIV).

Paul was saying, "The cross is all that counts for me. Nothing the world holds enamors me any longer. I have died to what this world can offer. All I want to see is the cross – the cross of Christ. I am sold out to the preaching of that one thing – the power of the cross."

If believers fully understood and were experiencing the power of the cross, there would be little coercion or encouragement necessary for people to fully engage their lives, their resources, and their efforts for the kingdom of God. Could it be that the difference between New Testament Christianity and today's faith-walk is found?

To preach or teach anything less than the power of the cross is to build a theology upon a fault line. Though the structure may be wonderful, beautiful and ornate, and usable for a season, it will not stand the test of stress. Nothing but the cross will support the center of who we are as believers.

THE POWER TO MAKE US RIGHT

Now, I do not want to make a presupposition that everyone understands what I am saying, because we come from various backgrounds and experiences. When I say the cross of Christ, all of us conjure up different thoughts. Some may see a priest carrying an object with a cross on top. Some may have a picture of an altar boy, or a table with the sign of a cross, or different ornate objects. Or maybe our minds take us back some 2000 years ago to just outside Jerusalem where Jesus was crucified between two thieves. Regardless of what you visualize, I want to draw your focus in upon the cross of Christ – the cross where He shed His blood for you and for me – and to why this is so very, very important.

The cross has the power to make you right with God. Many of us have a mentality that we are right with God when we live right. Some of us feel that we are right with God because we show up for church. Others of us may feel like we are right with God because we give a large sum of money as an offering to God, while still others feel a greater closeness when they give spiritual counsel. Our "rightness" is not dependent upon actions that can be manufactured by our flesh. Our standing with God is based solely upon the finished work of Christ upon the cross.

Martin Lloyd Jones once wrote, "Superficial views of the work of Christ produce superficial human lives." Surface Christianity is social conformity to the expectations of others, whereas, true faith has its roots deeply planted in the work of Christ on our behalf. It is from this posture that we both ebb and flow as believers. To exist from any other position is to live unplugged from God's power source for our lives.

God knew the condition of mankind. He knew that the only way that a holy and perfect God could have a relationship with finite, physical, sinful men and women was for Him to pay the price of your sin and my sin. That is why He sent Jesus to the cross to shed His perfect blood, and by that sacrifice we are made right with Him. Simply put, He sees us as holy, perfect and acceptable of His fellowship through what Jesus has done for us. But how does this happen?

As you investigate the Old Testament, you find a system of laws, rules and regulations. We quickly find ourselves at the Ten Commandments and wince sharply when we examine the blackness of our hearts. It is our sin that cries out, "I want my way, God, and I'll do whatever I've got to do to get my way, even if it is to use Your Word and Your things to accomplish what I want." Our desperate condition of rebellion can only be remedied by a loving God! Thus, the need of the cross!

> "When you were dead in your sins and in the uncircumcision of your sinful nature, God made you alive with Christ. He forgave us all our sins, having canceled the written code, with its regulations that was against us and that stood opposed to us; he took it away, nailing it to the cross. And having disarmed the powers and authorities, he made a public spectacle of them, triumphing over them by the cross" (Colossians 2:13-15 NIV).

The Roman government used crucifixion to humiliate and punish criminals publicly. The convicted criminal was not only nailed to a cross, but his atrocities against society were often written on a plank above the head of the dying individual. All who passed by would see the laws that had been broken deserving death. Capture that picture in your mind and then travel to the Ten Commandments again and think of how you have been personally responsible for breaking many, if not all, of them.

What God is saying to us in Colossians 2:13-15 is that all of the rules and all of the regulations that you have personally broken that deserve death – every sin you have committed or will ever commit in the future – is nailed to the cross. It is there on the cross. When Jesus shed His blood, it covered all of your sin! God cancelled your sin, He forgave your sin, and He says to you now, "You are right with me because of what my Son has done for you! You are now my child! Forever!" That is why we celebrate Jesus! When we sing and say that He is the One and Only, and is worthy of our worship, it is because of what He has done.

The problem is that many of us don't bask long enough in what He has done for us. We still try to add things to the finished work of Christ. You cannot add a thing to the finished work of Christ. It is all done! It is all finished! Don't dare put yourself in the position, even mentally, of being special to God because of some effort on your part! Cower from even the slightest inclination to offer your performance to God as a reason for you to be heard in His courts! Instead, cry out with a grateful, thankful heart, "Oh, Jesus! You are my Savior, my Lord, my everything!" No wonder the apostle Paul wrote what he did!

Only the Spirit of God can speak to your heart and reveal to you the full implication of what you have just read. Being a child of God, having been forgiven by what Jesus has done for us, is what empowers us.

The cross has the power to make you right with your family. The Scripture says that you are to work out your salvation with fear and trembling. In other words, what God has worked in your heart because of your relationship with Jesus, He now wants to flow through your life and affect all of your relationships. You see, no longer is God an external force to you. No longer are you waiting for an anointing from the outside to fall on you. The wait is over for God to show up, as if He would come through the back door or the front door. He now lives inside of you – inside your heart. That is why the Bible says that our bodies are the temple of the Holy Spirit. God dwells inside the lives of those people who have turned from their sin and placed their faith in Jesus, and have thrown themselves hopelessly, helplessly upon Christ and Christ alone. Therefore, He desires to work out His life through their lives.

Knowing Jesus does not mean you will never have a harsh word with your wife or your husband. It does not guarantee your kids are always going to obey or that your parents are always going to do exactly what they ought to do. Many of us think that is what should happen, and that if there are problems in relationships, it means that somebody is out of fellowship with God. Sometimes God allows those problems in our lives to reveal to us how desperately we need Jesus and that there is no good thing that dwells in any of us. We want our agenda, our way, and that is often why we have conflict in our relationships.

The greatest thing you could ever do for your family is to fall in love with Jesus. We need to align ourselves with Jesus and say to him, "Jesus, I need You. My flesh is despicable! I need for You to love my wife, or love my husband, or love my kids, or love my parents through me." As you fall in love with Him, He will give you the power to love. Having Jesus in your heart will not allow you to be content when you are out of sorts with family members. Jesus who lives inside of you will give you the desire to have conflict reconciled and be made right.

The cross has the power to make you right with other believers. That same heartbeat of the cross will make itself known in the melodies of relationships with those outside your home. Those who know Christ, who love Him solely, now are your brothers and sisters. Eternity for them is the same as for you. You will be with them forever. They are partners in the faith. Though denominational lines may momentarily separate the opportunities for intimate fellowship, there will be a love and honest appreciation for those who love Christ in their heart.

That is why I love the mission field. Our culture of denominational structure and power is often erased in the third world. There, true believers in Christ are quick to cross predefined denominational lines for the advancement of the gospel. What makes that fellowship flow? Nothing but the cross! It has been said that the ground is level at the cross, and we often see that as a statement that puts all of us on a level playing field as to our standing with the Lord. It is also true that as believers in Christ, we all stand there at His cross together, eye to eye, shoulder to shoulder, heart to heart. Anyone who loves Jesus is one in whom I can't help but sense a kindred spirit!

Possibly you have seen a drawing of a chasm spanned with the cross. On one side is God, on the other man, and the gulf between is sin. That same pathway is traveled into relationships with other believers in Christ. He is the only one who can truly make brothers out of previous warriors.

The cross has the power to make you right with yourself. Here is where it gets personal. Possibly, you have been beating yourself up emotionally for a long time. Some of us feel more condemnation from within than we could ever feel from without. God doesn't want you to live in this wasteland of self-inflicted spiritual abuse.

What I am about to share with you is different from anything that you would ever hear on any of the talk shows or could read in any self-help books that speak of embracing the real you. Let me say this: you don't want to embrace the real you! You don't want to be right with the real you...the real you is full of a sin nature. You want to be lined up with the Spirit of God who lives inside of you, who makes you the new you. You want to embrace the new you!

God wants you to feel good about who you are in Christ, and to think like He thinks about you. Therefore, if you want to feel good, clean and forgiven, you must align yourself with what God sees and what He says about you. Only the cross has the power to make you right with yourself.

"How much more, then, will the blood of Christ, who through the eternal Spirit, offered himself unblemished to God, cleanse our consciences from acts that lead to death, so that we may serve the living God" *(Hebrews 9:14 NIV)!*

Read this passage again. Listen to it as you read it aloud. Meditate upon it. Let it sink in deep and then pray, "Oh, God, don't turn me loose from this verse until I understand it and I accept it and I am embraced by it."

Do you know what God says? He cleanses our consciences from acts that lead to death. When you give your life to Christ, God says, "I forgive you of all of your past sin, all of your present sin, and all of your future sin." The problem is that many of us have not accepted that, and we are allowing past sin to discount us. We condemn ourselves and we no longer feel worthy because of something we said or something we did in the past. We don't even have to let the evil one condemn us – we condemn ourselves! We don't see that we have been forgiven and our consciences are clean. To have a clean conscience does not mean that you don't acknowledge something that you did, but that you know that it is forgiven. Often, service to Christ is pre-empted by a guilty conscience.

Once you sin, your naivety can never be reclaimed, but your innocence can be restored. Your naivety cannot be reclaimed because you have crossed over, but your innocence can be reclaimed and restored because God says, "You're cleansed. You're forgiven. And you must not condemn yourself, because you are forgiven."

When you come to Christ, you allow Him to wash your sins away — past, present, and future. He cleanses your conscience so that you no longer carry the guilt of what you have done. Though you will never forget what you have done, you now know that you have been forgiven and you are no longer discounted by Him. Therefore, you are not to beat yourself up or to beat anyone else up, because forgiven people are free people.

Individuals who would condemn you and tell you that you don't measure up are the very people who don't understand the power of the cross. It is at the cross that we are embraced by God's love. It is at the cross that we are fitted with the power of God. This power takes us into a different dimension in which we can live this life for His glory with great freedom and great joy. You will never again be content to live any other way, because you are under the banner of the cross. No longer can you withhold honoring Him, praising Him and adoring Him, because He has set you free – really free – from the inside out.

The Power to Keep You Straight

"If we have been united with him like this in his death, we will certainly also be united with him in his resurrection. For we know that our old self was crucified with him so that the body of sin might be done away with, that we should no longer be slaves to sin – because anyone who has died has been freed from sin. Now if we died with Christ, we believe that we will also live with him. For we know that since Christ was raised from the dead, he cannot die again; death no longer has mastery over him. The death he died, he died to sin once for all, but the life he lives, he lives to God. In the same way, count yourselves dead to sin but alive to God in Christ Jesus. Therefore do not let sin reign in your mortal body so that you obey its evil desires. Do not offer the parts of your body to sin, as instruments of wickedness, but rather offer yourselves to God, as those who have been brought from death to life; and offer the parts of your body to him as instruments of righteousness. For sin shall not be your master, because you are not under law, but under grace" (Romans 6:5-14 NIV).

Do you know why lost people sin? Because they are connected! Imagine in your mind a huge chain, a big black chain, spanning from sin, coming all the way through your arms, through a black heart, and out the other side, connected to sin. When you are without Christ, you are connected to the sin nature and are bound to the control of that nature. The reason people sin who do not know Christ, and don't have any problem with it, is that they are connected. I mean, they have to sin! If sin pulls them this way, they go this way. If it pulls them that way, they go that way. They are connected to the sin nature and have only personal willpower to assist them toward right living and thinking.

That is why Paul would write, "Sometimes the good I want to do, I don't do, and the bad I do, I don't want to do." That is when you chose to hook up to that sin nature. But something happens when we turn our lives over to Christ. He breaks the master link to the sin nature chain within. He literally shatters one of the links inside of me, and no longer is sin my master. But just like a chain, it still clangs for my attention. I can choose to hook back up. I don't have to. But when I choose to, I get hooked back up. That's how believers can act like non-believers, because they choose to hook back up. Do you realize that the Bible says that when Christ died, He died for all of your sins and broke the power of sin in your life?

Remember when they put that placard above the head of Jesus on the cross? Do you know what that was for? Those were the charges for which he was being executed. Now on that same plaque, I want you to realize that all of your sins that you have ever committed, are committing, or will ever commit, have been nailed to the cross. And the blood of Jesus covers them all. You say, "You mean to tell me that I don't have to sin?" If you know Jesus, that's right — you don't have to sin. You say, "Then why do I feel like I'm still hooked up?" It is because of where you are looking with your spiritual eyes.

I have a distinct memory of the Ozarks. My grandfather had a ranch when I was a little child, and I remember spending Thanksgiving there when I was seven years old. It is a vivid memory of a huge rock house in Arkansas with the state of Texas outlined on the side of the home. He was a native Texan. On Thanksgiving morning, my dad was given the responsibility of killing a goose for our main course. That morning held something I would never forget. "Come with me, son. I want to show you something," he said.

After catching a goose by the neck and grabbing a hatchet, he then stretched the goose's neck across a stump that had been sawed off as a chopping block. Then he said, "Watch this goose. Don't close your eyes. Keep your eyes open. I want to show you something." He took that goose, held its head with its neck across the stump, raised the axe up, and let it fall swiftly, severing the head from the neck! The goose's head stayed on the block and as he let go of the neck of the goose, the goose took off. As I watched it flop out of control and even run, I heard him say, "Son, go get the goose." I said, "I'm not going to get that goose. That goose is not dead!" He said, "It's dead. Look at the head!" I said, "Yes, sir, but his body doesn't know it.." I will never forget that scene. The goose's head was on the block. The head wasn't moving, but the rest of the goose was out of control!

Do you capture the picture now? When you gave your life to Christ, He cut off the head of the sin nature in your life. And the reason you struggle with sin is because you choose to hook up with a sin nature that has been severed by the cross. The Bible tells us what to do: *"Count yourselves dead to sin, but alive to Christ."* Keep your eyes not on the body of the goose that's flopping, but on the head that is on the block. In other words, keep your eyes on the cross where your sin was nailed and where you were totally forgiven and set free. The cross gives you the power to live in the new way of the Spirit, in the flow of His Spirit, and in His power. You either have a choice to hook up and be in bondage once again, or to celebrate that your old life is dead in Christ. God's Spirit wants to begin to flow through you.

Before Augustine, one of the early church fathers, met Christ, he had many sordid affairs. After meeting Christ, one day Augustine was walking and passed a former lover. "Augustine," she called. Augustine just kept walking. She yelled out again, "Augustine, don't you remember me? It is I!" Augustine stopped, turned around, looked her in the face and said, "Yes, I know. But it is no longer I."

When you meet Christ, a new beginning happens, and you can either focus upon the chain that is still rattling in your flesh or the flopping goose of your desires, or you can see the broken link and the head that has been severed and realize how free you are. Look to the cross!

THE POWER TO SEND YOU OUT

Paul said that he did not come to baptize, but instead came to preach the gospel. He would later say that he did not want to take any glory or boast in anything except the cross of Christ. What was motivating him was this relationship he had with God through the power of the cross. His motivation to do what he did was transformed. No longer was he a performer of legalistic rules and regulations, but a passionate soul flaming with the hot fire of intimacy with God through Jesus.

The ought-ness to do ministry that trudges up the mountain from guilt-laden motivation will fall short in the heat of battle with the evil one. God does not seek to motivate us into service by guilt or expectations from fleshly representatives. That comes from the flesh. The flow of the Spirit of God in your life, out of the relationship you have with Him because of what Jesus has done for you on the cross, will motivate you to share Christ with other people. If there is not a desire to share Christ and to take a stand for Jesus, the problem is not in anything other than the issue of the fellowship of the cross.

Years ago I did a survey where I asked several hundred people to ask themselves, "What keeps me from loving the lost – those people who don't know Christ?" Here are their responses. As you read them, remember these are Christians.

"I don't feel like I love the lost because I'm lazy."

"I'm just too busy."

"I don't have a love for the lost because there's a lack of abundant joy and excitement about my salvation."

"I grew up in a legalistic church with so many rules without relationships that I am just now feeling God's unconditional love in my own life."

"Distractions."

"Lost my first love."

"Programs make me feel that I'm satisfying that need."

"A hardened heart to those who need Christ."

"What keeps me from loving the lost is a lack of time to be trained."

"I'm not good at expressing myself."

"I am concerned about the lost, but not sure of myself doing something about it."

"Don't know any lost people."

"There is no boldness in my life. I'm too complacent. I'm too wrapped up in my own life to focus on lost people."

"Since they don't seem to want to know about the Lord, it is hard to do anything about it."

"Doesn't seem as important as it really is."

"Fear of failure."

"Not enough knowledge of the Bible."

"Fear of invading a person's privacy."

"Busy doing all the right things."

"That's just outside my comfort zone."

"I'm blinded by how good I feel."

"I'm spiritually dry."

"Not remembering that God can guide the conversation."

"What keeps me from loving the lost? There's no sense of urgency in my life."

Bold ministry and service flows from intimate fellowship with Christ! Guilt may empower you for three days to six weeks, but not for a lifetime of effective ministry and joyous service. If there's no going, there is probably no flowing. So instead of beating somebody up about not going, we need to focus in on the problem with the flow. That's why we come back to the cross – to realize what God has done for us at the cross, what Jesus has done for us right there, and understand how accepted we are. It is from this position we will develop the desire to share Christ. That is how God wants it to happen. He wants it to flow from your life.

One of my fondest memories was when Jonathan, our oldest child, was born. We have a little home movie that some friends took of me. I am standing right outside the nursery in that hospital garb, and I'm pointing to him and talking about how wonderful he is, how intelligent he is, and how handsome he is, and how much he looks just like me. I remember that there were people coming through that waiting room in front of the nursery, and I would stop every one of them and say, "Hey, come here. Do you want to see a good looking kid? Right there! He's mine!" Then I would ask the nurse, "Hold him up again," for the umpteenth time. "These people (whom I had never met) need to see him." I couldn't help but share my joy about my son. That was exciting! I didn't have to be motivated. My wife didn't have to say, "Now, Curt, when you leave the delivery room, I want you to go out there, step in front of the nursery window, and make sure you tell every person that comes by how long he is, how much he weighed, what color his eyes are, and don't forget to tell them his full name." She didn't have to tell me anything. It just flew out of me, and you couldn't stop me, because I was excited. I was a father for the first time in my life!

Many of us are living our Christian life based upon feelings, rather than "flowings." We find ourselves living the Christian life based upon a sense of what we know we need to be doing rather than upon the passion that flows because of our relationship with Christ. To live any other way is an invitation to set up your home in the desert.

That's why Paul wrote, "I'm here to live for the cross. It's all about the cross! I'm not going to boast in anything except the cross!" Then he would write again there in 2 Corinthians, chapter five, verse 14: *"For the love of Christ compels me..."* What gives me the desire to tell people about Christ is that I've met Him, I know Him personally, and His love flows through me.

Feel the heartbeat of heaven in the words of Charles Wesley:

And can it be that I should gain
An interest in the Savior's blood?
Died He for me, who caused His pain —
For me, who Him to death pursued?
Amazing love! How can it be,
That Thou, my God shouldst die for me?

Do you sense the passion in these words of Isaac Watts?

When I survey the wondrous cross
On which the Prince of glory died,
My richest gain I count but loss,
And pour contempt on all my pride.
See from His head, His hands, His feet,
Sorrow and love flow mingled down!

Did e'er such love and sorrow meet,

Or thorns compose so rich a crown?

Were the whole realm of nature mine,

That were a present far too small;

Love so amazing, so divine,

Demands my soul, my life, my all.

Come to the cross! It is where we are embraced by His love, fitted with His power, and empowered to serve.

20

WHY DO WE LIFT HIM UP?

Dr. Richard A. Powell

Senior Pastor

McGregor Baptist Church

Fort Myers, Florida

IT'S AMAZING HOW MANY PEOPLE had the audacity to confront Jesus Christ, the very Son of God, on matters of faith. We come to such a passage today.

Why do we lift Jesus up? The passage we will study is set in a moment of time when there was a confrontation between Jesus and the religious leaders of His day. It was early in the Holy Week, the week when Jesus, having been welcomed by cheering crowds into the city streets of Jerusalem, would soon hear those cheers turn into jeers and angry shouts of "Crucify Him! Crucify Him!" A week that would lead to the death of Jesus on the cross, but then on to the wonderful and glorious celebration that is above every celebration for the Christian – Easter Sunday morning, celebrating the fact that our Savior is not dead and in a tomb, but He's alive and in this room.

The Bible says, Now there were some Greeks among those who went up to worship at the Feast. They came to Philip, who was from Bethsaida in Galilee, with a request, "Sir," they said, "we would like to see Jesus." Philip went to tell Andrew; Andrew and Philip in turn told Jesus. Jesus replied, "The hour has come for the Son of Man to be glorified" (John 12:20-23, NIV).

Now this passage means that Jesus is proclaiming that it is time for Him to be crucified. It is time for the Son of Man to be glorified and to be crucified.

◆ 251 ◆

Look at verse 24, where Jesus said,

"I tell you the truth, unless a kernel of wheat falls to the ground and dies, it remains only a single seed. But if it dies, it produces many seeds. The man who loves his life will lose it, while the man who hates his life in this world will keep it for eternal life. Whoever serves me must follow me; and where I am, my servant also will be. My Father will honor the one who serves me" (vv. 24-26). Now, watch these words, beginning in verse 27, where Jesus said, "Now my heart is troubled, and what shall I say? 'Father, save me from this hour'? No, it was for this very reason I came to this hour. Father, glorify your name!" Then a voice came from heaven, "I have glorified it, and will glorify it again." The crowd that was there and heard it said it had thundered; others said an angel had spoken to him. Jesus said, "This voice was for your benefit, not mine. Now is the time for judgment on this world; now the prince of this world will be driven out. But I, when I am lifted up from the earth, will draw all men to myself." He said this to show the kind of death He was going to die. (vv. 27-33) In verse 34, The crowd spoke up (and there is hardly a time in all the Bible when the crowd got it right), "We have heard from the Law that the Christ will remain forever, so how can you say, 'The Son of Man must be lifted up'? Who is this Son of Man (v. 34)?" Well, Jesus had just told them. He had said, "If I be lifted up, I will draw all men unto myself."

So, why do we lift Him up? Earlier in the book of John, there is a wonderful verse where Jesus says these words, "When you have lifted up the Son of Man, then you will know that I am the one I claim to be and that I do nothing on my own but speak just what the Father has taught me" (John 8:28 NIV). In effect, Jesus is saying, "I didn't come to this earth to do what I wanted to do, I came to this earth because I had business to attend to. I came to this earth because God the Father sent me to this earth, and I'm doing what I've been told to do, and I'm doing nothing on my own. I'm going to the cross." And if that's not explicit enough, then notice what He says in chapter 12, verse 32, from *The Living Bible* paraphrase. Jesus says, "And when I am lifted up [on the cross], I will draw everyone to me" [Brackets in original].

Now, I know that many of us who are longtime Christians, who have been coming to church for many, many years, are accustomed to the words of Jesus. And those of you who are new believers or guests, and even those of you who are here because you are searching for something more in life, need to know that those words are very familiar to those of us who have known Christ for a long time. Jesus actually said, "When I am lifted up, I will draw all men unto myself." We glory in those words from our Savior! But, when you take them by themselves, they are extraordinary words. When you think about it, a mere mortal man (in the eyes of many people back in those days), our Savior, stood up and said, "Hey! Look at me! I'm gonna tell you a truth – when I am lifted up, I will draw all men unto myself." Those are extremely bold, incredibly audacious words for a man to say. But we believers don't have any problem with it, because we permit Jesus to say what we wouldn't let others say. As a matter of fact, we expect Jesus to say what we wouldn't expect others to say, because we know who Jesus is. But, taken on their own, those words are extraordinary words. We expect them to come from Jesus, but we would never allow them to come from any other person in all of the history of mankind.

Notice these three things: first of all, we wouldn't let religious leaders say those words. Can you imagine if some other religious leader besides Jesus Christ stood up and said, "When I am lifted up, I will draw all men unto myself?" Imagine if Buddha, the enlightened one who died in 480 BC, had stood before his followers and said, "When I am lifted up, I will draw all men unto myself." It wouldn't make any sense. Instead of his followers following him, they would ridicule him. Or imagine if another religious leader, say Mohammed, who died in 632 AD, having lived a life so violent that it still causes violence today, stood in his day and said, "When I am lifted up, I will draw all men unto myself." We wouldn't allow him to say that. Or suppose Confucius, the wise man of China, who gave us all of those wonderful little quotes and little sayings, had among his sayings, "When I am lifted up, I will draw all men unto myself."

Do you see that it just doesn't make sense coming from the lips of any other religious leader? Because we wouldn't let anybody else say the things that we expect Jesus to say.

Well, it wouldn't make sense if it came from any other religious leader, but it's also the case that we wouldn't let any political leader say those words. Think about Alexander the Great, perhaps the greatest political/military leader who ever lived, whose life is such a fascinating historical study. Here's a man who died in 323 BC at the age of 32, who, a few years earlier, when he came to his time of greatest triumph, when he came to the pinnacle of his life, Alexander the Great, who had conquered all of the known world of his time, stood weeping on a mountain above a battlefield and said, "There are no more worlds to conquer!" But imagine if he'd stood on that same mountain and said, "When I am lifted up, I will draw all men unto myself." We wouldn't allow him to say it, even though he's Alexander the Great.

Or what about some much more recent political leader? What about someone who is a part of our history in America? Suppose General George Washington, the highly articulate father of our country who said such things as "Every post is honorable in which a man can serve his country," had said,

"When I am lifted up, I will draw all men unto myself." We would discount him as a political leader. We would discount him as a military leader. We would discount him as an American leader. Or what if Lincoln had said it? Or one of our more modern leaders, like Roosevelt or Reagan? If any one of them stood up and said, with boldness. "When I am lifted up, I will draw all men unto myself," we surely would not consider him much of a leader. In fact, we would not allow any of them to say that. We would not allow others to say what we allow Jesus to say.

Look with me at a third group. We wouldn't even let the followers of Christ say those words. What if Paul had said it? The great apostle Paul, who wrote 13 books of our New Testament, was perhaps the greatest follower of Christ from the first century until today. Under the inspiration of the Holy Spirit, he wrote half of the New Testament. He was a great missionary; he was a great soul-winner; he was a great preacher; he was a great church leader. What if Paul had stood up and said, "When I am lifted up, I will draw all men unto myself." We probably would rip the pages that he wrote right out of the Bible! Instead of a great believer, we would call him a great blasphemer. What if somebody not from Jesus' day, but from our day, made that statement? You would probably have no problem getting a consensus that the most well-known, and best-respected, Christian leader of our generation is Dr. Billy Graham. But, what if Billy Graham, having preached all of his evangelistic sermons to millions all over the world, stood up in a crusade and just one time said, "Oh, by the way, if I be lifted up, I will draw all men unto myself." He'd be ruined. All of his massive credibility would go right in the tank.

What if it were John Wesley? What if it were Dwight L. Moody? What if it were Calvin or Zwingli or any one of the great, beloved followers of Jesus Christ? We wouldn't allow any of them to say what we allow Jesus to say, because He alone is worthy to be lifted up. We allow Him to say those kinds of statements because the only person who can say such statements is the One about whom they are true. It's the Lord of all the universe, the Lord Jesus Christ. And the reason we lift Him up is because He's worthy. The reason we worship Him is because He's worthy. The reason we focus our lives upon Him is because He's worthy. So, we know why we lift him up, but how do we lift up the Lord Jesus? Oh, He's lifted up on the cross, yes, but how do we lift Him up in our lives and in our hearts?

Let me tell you how we're supposed to do it. Let me give you four ways. First, we are to lift Him up exclusively. When I say that we are to lift him up exclusively, I mean we are supposed to help answer the same question that was being asked about Him in His day, "Who is this Jesus? What do we do with this Jesus?" Well, we lift Him up exclusively. We lift Him up in our lives like nothing else in our lives. He's got sole possession of first place in our life. Here's the verse, John 12:32, from *The Living Bible*, "*When I am lifted up on the cross...*(John 12:32 LB) In the original language, the word "I" means "I alone." It's an emphatic first person pronoun. He's saying that you can't lift Him up along with something else. It can't be Jesus plus the denomination, or Jesus plus the church, or Jesus plus any institution. Further, it can't be Jesus plus my own or and Jesus plus my own opinions. It's not to be, "Well, I'm going to have goals, and I'm going to have accolades, and I'm going to accomplish a few things in life, and, oh, yes, by the way, I'm also going be a Christian, and I'm going to live like I'm supposed to live." No, no, a thousand times no, my dear friend! One of the things that we must learn is that Jesus Christ is to be absolutely preeminent in our lives. And God demands of those of us who are believers in Him that we lift Jesus Christ up to a status and to a place of exclusivity so high that there is nothing that ever competes with Jesus Christ. He is to have the solo spotlight in our lives, a place not shared with anybody or anything else. There are other people in our lives to whom we give respect, but to Jesus we give reverence. There are others in our lives with whom we fellowship, but Jesus we worship. There are others in our lives for whom we reserve dignity, but Jesus alone is deity in our lives. We worship only Him. And so, the great application for your life and for mine is simply this question, "Is there anything that we love, worship, adore, appreciate, and value, in any part of life, that is set equal to the Lord Jesus Christ?" Some of you will say, "I'm not certain that I have Jesus Christ in the top place." If that's true, then that's a point of concern in your life, because the Bible says that we're to worship and lift Him up exclusively. He's to be in the stratosphere all by Himself. Oh, yes, I have family, I have friends, I have loved ones, I have hobbies, I have habits, I have a career, I have goals. But the most important thing in my life, without question, is my relationship to Jesus Christ. That's what the Christian life is all about.

So, we lift Him up exclusively, but also we're to lift Him up redemptively. Now what in the world does the word "redemptively" mean? That's one of those big, 50-cent church words. So what does it mean to lift Jesus Christ up redemptively? If you don't mind admitting that you are old enough perhaps, like me, you remember parents or maybe grandparents a long time ago going to the grocery store and giving you not only your change back, but also those little sticky stamps that you'd put in books that you could turn in for prizes – S&H Green Stamps, remember those? Well, for those who can't remember, it went like this: they would give you these stamps, and then it was always the kids that got the job of licking them and putting them into these little booklets. And when you'd finally get a bunch of books of stamps together, you'd take them to the S&H Green Stamp Store and redeem them for the gift or the prize of your choice. You could get an iron for the house or you could get a pair of roller skates or a set of golf clubs, or whatever else you wanted. You'd redeem them. Well, the Bible says that we need to lift Jesus up redemptively. That is, we need to allow His death on the cross to redeem us, to be exchanged for the sins of mankind. And not just for the sins of mankind, but for my sins. See, I take my sins and I take them to the foot of the cross and I say, "Jesus, would You do me a big favor? Would You please forgive me of all of my sins?" And Jesus says, "I offer you this: I will redeem my blood and forgive you of all of your sins."

It's a great, great gift from God the Father through Jesus Christ.

So we are to lift Him up redemptively. Look at John chapter 12, verse 33, He said this to show the kind of death He was going to die. Have you ever considered that the most important thing about Jesus is His death? I know that's unusual, but it really is the truth. As a matter of fact, there are two major things I want to share with you. First, it's true that the value of most people is in their lives, but the value of Jesus Christ is in His death. There have always been those who want to look at the life of the Lord Jesus Christ and say, "Well, look at all that He did, look at all the years when He was living. He fed the 5000. He fed the hungry. He clothed the naked. He gave sight to blinded eyes. He healed the leper. Look at all that Jesus did! Therefore, the most important thing in the Christian life is to emulate the life of Jesus Christ!" No, it's not! Certainly, it is important for us to study and honor the life of Jesus and obey His words and teachings, but His life story is not the most important thing. The most important thing about Jesus Christ is His death and His resurrection. And so the most important thing about our Christian life is to identify redemptively with His death and resurrection. That means we need to place our faith in Jesus Christ so that His death and the shedding of His blood become the payment for our sins. Only then can we know that our sins have been forgiven and cleansed by the blood of Jesus Christ, and we have a personal relationship with Him wherein we can be saved. His life is important, but His death and resurrection secure our eternity.

A second thing you need to see is this: unless you focus on His death, you will miss the purpose of His life. See, for most of humanity, most of the influence we'll ever have is while we're living. Most people, when they die, their influence wanes. Their influence diminishes. By the way, we're seeing in the newspapers almost on a daily basis where there are people who are intentionally killed over in the Middle East. The founding leader of the terrorist group Hamas, Shaikh Ahmed Yassin, was assassinated by the Israelis because the Israelis knew that this particular man was influencing the people of Hamas to commit terrorist acts. And so on March 20, 2004, the Israelis removed him. Why? Because when you're dead, your influence diminishes. Unless you're Jesus. Because, you see, when Jesus died and then rose from the dead, those acts magnified, they verified, they validated the impact and influence of His being exactly who He said He was. Most people's influence diminishes when their life is over. For example, Charles Haddon Spurgeon. Now, in 1854, at the age of 20, he became pastor of the church that would grow to be named The Metropolitan Tabernacle in London, England. In his twenties, he was preaching to 10,000 people in several morning worship services. And Sunday after Sunday, with crowds overflowing into the street outside, with no sound system and no glorious music, he had London standing at attention to listen to the Word of God. But there was one great problem with Spurgeon – he died. And his influence diminished. And now London is not being influenced by Spurgeon, and even though you may be a very committed Christian, you've probably barely heard of the name of Charles Spurgeon. Or there are many other examples, there's a man by the name of John Keats. He was a British poet who lived in Rome until he died at the age of twenty-five. He was a brilliant man. But he's only known in literary circles because he died.

Then there's a man by the name of Hans Schubert, who was an Austrian composer. He was acknowledged as a great prodigy until he died at the young age of 31. But his name and his influence have diminished because he died, and now his name and even his music are known only to those who are classical music enthusiasts, because most people's influence diminishes when they die. But the Lord Jesus Christ's influence has increased because of His death and His resurrection. As a matter of fact, if all you emphasize when you know about the Lord Jesus Christ is His life, "Oh, look at what He did, look at the miracles He performed, look at what He said," you'll miss it. If all you do is study His life, the irony is that you may well miss His great purpose in life. Because, you see, as unique as His life was, Jesus Christ's greatest impact happened not because of His life, it happened because of His death. And we must emphasize His death and His resurrection because that's the only way that we can be saved. Friend, if you've never given your heart to Jesus Christ, you've never trusted Him, you've never been saved, you can't get saved just by coming and sitting in a worship service, you can't get saved by saying, "Well, let me open the Bible, and maybe God will bless me; maybe God will do something miraculous in my life." I'll tell you what God will do: God will point you to the death, burial, and resurrection of the One who can forgive you of all of your sins. God in His Word will point you to Jesus Christ, because the Bible says that without the shedding of blood there can be no forgiveness of sins. So, friend, that means that you need to give your heart to Jesus Christ. Why? Simply this – because of His death and His burial and His resurrection, He has the right and the power to be your Savior, and He wants to be your Savior. You can invite Him in, and when you do, you'll be saved, and you'll be a believer, and you'll go to heaven when you die. And it won't be because you examined the teachings of His life, but because you've trusted Him by faith as your Lord and Savior. See, we've got to lift Him up redemptively in our own personal lives.

And the third thing is this: we also have to lift Him up compassionately. That means we've got to love Him. We must love Him with all of our heart, with all of our soul, and with all of our mind. That's what God wants us to do.

And it's not just Christ, but it's Christ and the cross. We don't just look at the life of the Lord Jesus Christ, we look at the life of the Lord Jesus Christ and we look at the death of the Lord Jesus Christ. They come together as a duet. They come together as a package. And now why is that so important? Because Jesus Christ came not only to live, but He came especially to die. He came to give Himself on the cross for the sins of all the world. Now, if there had been some other way, if there had been something else that He could have done, then He would have done it. Had there been some other way that He could have given His love to us, in deed or demonstration, He would have chosen it. Had there been any way to say, "I love you," except for the cross, He would have said it that way.

I heard a story one time, many years ago, about an incredibly talented Soviet ballerina. Her name was Pavlova, and she could dance ballet in a way that caused people to say that she literally told a story with her dance. One day she danced a beautifully exquisite dance that left all the audience breathless, and afterward, she was outside the theatre, where her fans had gathered, signing autographs and being congratulated, when a reporter walked up to her. He was cynical in his heart, a critic of the worst kind, and he said, "So you wowed the audience and you supposedly told a story with your dance, but I didn't get it. Tell me – what was the story in your dance?" And here's what she said. She said, "Sir, had I been able to say it, I would not have danced it."

When Jesus stretched out His arms on the cross, do you know what He was doing? He was telling us stories from God. He was demonstrating to us and accomplishing for us the only way whereby we can be saved. And when you look up at Jesus and say, "Jesus, tell me what I must do," Jesus says, "I can not merely tell you, I have to show you." Please realize this: God's love for us is more than just words. Had just saying it been enough, He would not have sent His Son to do it. But it's not a matter of just going through the story one more time, reminding ourselves about what Jesus did. In fact, the great danger is that we become almost numb because the story is so familiar to us. We know what happened on Palm Sunday. We know what happened on Friday at His crucifixion. We know what happened on Easter Sunday morning. We know the old, old story. But our Bible knowledge is not the main point. The point is to trust the Savior of the story to be your Lord and Master. Have you lifted Him up? Not just from the pages of the Bible, but have you personally, have you compassionately, lifted Him up in your own life, so that He's changed you forever and ever?

That leads me to the fourth and final thing. We need to lift Him up personally. Oh, if you could hear anything that I'm going to say, I want you to hear this: the story of the crucifixion of Jesus Christ, the story of the resurrection of Jesus Christ, is not just a story for the history of all the ages, it is a story that will change your life personally. There are committed Christians who would stand up and say, "You know what? From the time when I invited Jesus Christ to come into my heart, my life has never been the same. And I've been exploring His love for me and praising the Lord Jesus ever since, because of what He's done in my life. My life is filled with joy and meaning and peace and purpose and happiness because I've met Jesus Christ." But, friend, you've got to do that personally. Let me show you how personal it is. Notice this verse in the Bible, John 12:36, and look at all these personal pronouns: *"Put your trust in the light while you have it so that you may become sons of light." When He had finished speaking, Jesus left and hid himself from them.* When Jesus left and hid Himself from them, it is as though He were saying, "Now that I've shared with them that it's a personal decision, they must trust me as their own personal Savior, they must live a life of commitment to the things of God, so I'm just going to withdraw, because they need time to make a decision. They need time to decide for themselves – are they going to put their trust in the light of the world? Are they going to do the only thing that will absolutely, radically, change their lives for eternity?" And by the way, isn't it absolutely a miracle to know that God has been changing lives through Jesus Christ for centuries? And He always will be changing lives, as long as people will trust Him as their Savior.

Let me tell you a great story. In 1983, there was an article in the magazine *Christianity Today* about how the central Communist Party of the Soviet Union had issued an order to the KGB. Understand that in the Soviet Union, the KGB was like our FBI and CIA all wrapped up into one. And the Communist Party had issued an order to the KGB, and here's the order: "You must redouble your efforts to snuff out the Christian faith in the Soviet Union." The Communist Party leadership wanted a godless society. But there were little pockets of Christianity that were popping up everywhere, and so the KGB had orders from the highest command of the Communist Party, "You must redouble your efforts to snuff out the Christian faith." A little while later, in the Communist newspaper called *Pravda*, there was an article about that mandate that revealed that the order to snuff out the Christian faith had been a complete and total failure. The reason? Many of the KGB's own agents, when they began to check out the Christian faith, became Christians themselves. And you know why? Because when you lift Jesus Christ up personally, He changes your life forever. And that's why we must lift Him up.

21

DIVINE HEALING: FACT OR FICTION

DR. PAIGE PATTERSON

President

Southwestern Baptist Theological Seminary

Fort Worth, Texas

ILLNESS IS A COMMON HUMAN EXPERIENCE, which, its ubiquity notwithstanding, is almost universally resisted. When afflicted, Christians visit physicians and not infrequently seek the intervention of God through prayer. For not a few, a visit to a faith-healer is on the menu. They wish to be healed of a malady and are wonderfully resourceful in their search.

But there is a kind of "Divine Healing" available to all. The disease that it conquers is far more devastating if untreated than the most debilitating virus or crippling form of cancer. I call this disorder "contracted spiritual heart failure."

In chapter 3 of the gospel of John, an event with eternal significance unfolds. And because it has become so critical and because even people who claim to be born-again believers no longer want to embrace this truth, we must study it.

There was a man of the Pharisees named Nicodemus, a ruler of the Jews. This man came to Jesus by night and said to Him, 'Rabbi,' which means *teacher*, 'We know that you are a teacher come from God; for no one can do these signs that You do unless God is with him.'

♦ 265 ♦

You know that this conclusion is inaccurate. You can never say something is true just because it is accompanied by a "miracle." Remember when Moses threw down his rod and it became a serpent, an Egyptian cobra? Pretty impressive? Then Jannes and Jambres, the Egyptian magicians, threw down their rods. Guess what? They also became serpents, but this miracle was not of God. The only difference was that Moses' rod was hungrier and ate the other two! The Egyptians did make something out of the ordinary happen. In fact, the Bible warns that in the last days there will be signs and wonders so that, if it were possible, even the elect would be deceived. Yet God never deceives anybody; so those signs and wonders must be coming from a source other than God. That can only be the devil. So Nicodemus' consideration here is in error. But it sounded impressive to him, and he's trying to be impressive and right.

Jesus answered and said to Nicodemus, "Amen, amen," translated sometimes, "verily, verily..." In the text, the Hebrew word *Amen* is used, which is one way to give emphasis in Hebrew. It underscores some statement or ensures your understanding of the importance of what has been said. So Jesus was saying,

'Most assuredly, I say to you, unless one is born again, he cannot see the kingdom of God.' Nicodemus said to Him, 'How can a man be born when he is old? Can he enter a second time into his mother's womb and be born?' Jesus answered, 'Most assuredly, I say to you, unless one is born of the water and the Spirit, he cannot enter into the kingdom of God.'

This strong statement does not say that Nicodemus "*may*" not enter the kingdom but rather that there is "*no*" way he may enter the kingdom of God. Some condition in the heart of Nicodemus makes it impossible for him to find acceptance with God. Jesus continued.

That which is born of the flesh is flesh, and that which is born of the Spirit is spirit. Do not marvel that I said to you, 'You must be born again.' The wind blows where it wishes, and you hear the sound of it, but cannot tell where it comes from and where it goes. So is everyone who is born of the Spirit.

Nicodemus answered Jesus and said to Him, "How can these things be?" And Jesus answered and said to him,

Are you the teacher of Israel, and do not know these things? Most assuredly, I say to you, we speak what we know and testify what we have seen, and you do not receive our witness. If I have told you earthly things and you do not believe, how will you believe if I tell you heavenly things? No one has ascended to heaven but He who came down from heaven, that is, the Son of Man who is in heaven. And as Moses lifted up the serpent in the wilderness, even so the Son of Man must be lifted up.

Why is that?

That whosoever believes in Him should not perish but have eternal life. For God so loved the world that He gave His only begotten Son, that whosoever believes in Him should not perish but have everlasting life.

A few years ago I received a telephone call from the Fox television

THE LAST SERMON I WOULD PREACH

network. They asked me, in light of a much-publicized confrontation between the Baptists and their Jewish friends, if I would be willing to come on nationwide television and have a discussion with a rabbi from Los Angeles. Of course I am always interested in seeing what these folks have to say, so I agreed to appear on *The O'Reilly Factor*. It began something like this. Mr. O'Reilly said to the Jewish rabbi, "Rabbi, tell us, what is all this flap about anyway?" And the rabbi said, "Well, it's about these Baptists. Why are they praying for us? It's like the Holocaust all over again." Well, Mr. O'Reilly knew that was absurd, so he said, "Rabbi, give me a break, what on earth are you talking about? These are Baptists, not Nazis, and they're praying for you, not gassing you. What on earth are you talking about?" And the rabbi realized that his first trial balloon had hit the ground pretty quick after launch, so he thought he had better try another route. He said, "You don't understand, Mr. O'Reilly, that other guy on the television over there believes that we're going to hell." And Mr. O'Reilly said, "Rabbi, that's the craziest, most absurd thing that I've heard in all of my life. Why on earth would you say anything like that? Reverend, tell him!" This statement was the prelude to great difficulty and trouble!

When I explained not only to the Jewish rabbi, but also to Mr. O'Reilly and to everyone else watching, that anyone who did not come through Jesus Christ of Nazareth would not make heaven, but would go to hell, Mr. O'Reilly was greatly offended. And he spent the rest of the program assailing me in every way he could. And in one sense he is absolutely right, i.e., the position I was advocating is the most arrogant, unreasonable, and unacceptable position in the whole world today, UNLESS it is true.

If this position is true, then it is not unreasonable. There is a government facility in Nevada that often gets attention. Especially those who believe in UFOs and are certain that beings from other galaxies have visited the earth suspect that the evidence is hidden in Area 51. People slip up and try to look

♦ 268 ♦

over the mountains and see what's going on at this United States Air Force base. And because of the government's secretiveness, people are further stimulated. There are those who say UFOs have visited here, and there are others who will say there are no UFOs at all. Both positions cannot possibly be right. Nor is there an "in-between" position that is right. There are not "almost" UFOs. There either are or there aren't. Visitors from other galaxies have either visited the earth or not. It is not partly one or partly the other. As someone pointed out many years ago, a woman cannot be partly pregnant. That is not possible: she either is or she isn't. In John 3, Jesus is either correct in what He said, or else He is the biggest fabricator who ever lived. The time has come for evangelical Christians to decide which of these things is true.

A man named Nicodemus was a Pharisee. There was never a more religious and "church-focused" group in all the world than the Pharisees. When you hear about them, you dismiss them because you remember all the times that Jesus talked about their hypocrisy. And indeed, they were often guilty of hypocrisy. Whereas they may not have been able to walk their talk, they were undoubtedly intensely religious. They were "churchmen" to the core, and they were morally head and shoulders above those around them. Not only that, but they were also people of prayer and of profound spiritual commitment. The man who came to Jesus by night was a Pharisee, a religious and moral man. He complimented Jesus by saying, "You must be a great teacher because nobody can do these miracles except that God were with him." Most of you would have said, "Thank you for the obviously shrewd observation." But Jesus knew that this encounter was not the time for responding to flattery, so He changed the subject and astonished Nicodemus in the process. He said, "Amen, amen, I say to you that unless one is born again, he will never be able to see the kingdom of God." That statement is either true or false. If it is false, you are wasting your time worshipping each Sunday. If it is false, following Jesus Christ of Nazareth or anything in this Bible one step further is incredibly senseless. Go do anything you want to do, be anything you want to be, act any way you want to act, and it will all be okay in the end.

That position is the popular opinion in the world today. The world, as Mr. O'Reilly, believes that as long as you are sincere and essentially good and some sort of practitioner of religion, you are okay. Every Muslim believes that. Every Hindu believes that. Every Buddhist believes that. Well, you say, "We may be thankful that Christians don't believe that;" but actually the vast, overwhelming majority of people who claim the name of Christ believe that very same thing. They have different religious books, and they have different religious duties, but the fact is that 90 percent of the people in the world, who now number 6.5 billion, believe that very thing. However, Jesus of Nazareth, who claims to be the God-man, God in human flesh, who died on a Roman cross, and who said, "If *I* be lifted up, *I* will draw all men to Me," clearly had a claim unique to Him. Jesus testified that all other religious effort would take you straight to hell. The Lord is not trying to be unkind. The oncologist who informs you that you have cancer is not doing something unkind to you. He is telling you that you have a problem; and if you will take his words seriously and accept the prescribed treatment that he has to offer you, he may be able to save your life. Better than the oncologist, Jesus says that you are afflicted with a serious cancer of sin, and our healing from sin is totally and completely impossible for humans. You can never do enough things to make yourself acceptable to a holy God.

Let me illustrate this for you. Suppose you go to medical school. You become a physician; you stay a little longer and become a surgeon; then you stay a little longer and become a cardiac surgeon. You are going to do some of the most delicate surgery in the world. You graduate and begin your surgical career. Before long, you are doing quite well. One morning you are going to go do surgery. You get in your Rolls Royce and drive to the hospital. There is a special place for you in the doctors' parking lot.

You walk into the hospital to begin your surgery. You go straight to the medical file room and pick up the records, and you look over everything that you need to know about your patient and his medical history. Having satisfied yourself once again that you are fully aware of the situation, you go to the scrub room. You scrub yourself thoroughly because you don't want any germs to contaminate your patient. Then they bring a green beret and put it over your head; they put a mask over your nose and mouth; and they put a green gown around you. And they even have green moccasins to put over your shoes. Then they bring your surgical gloves. You are careful not to touch anything or anyone. The operating room has doors with automatic eyes that can see you coming, and the doors open automatically. Your patient is on the operating table, and the surgical team is gathered around. You are ready to begin the surgery, and you say to the nurse, "Take away the sheet." She takes hold of both corners of the sheet and pulls it back to expose the chest of your patient. As she does, three cockroaches scurry across the chest of the patient. Awful? That's why my wife doesn't like this illustration.

What would you do as a surgeon? You would be furious. "Who is responsible for this? I cannot operate in a room like this. Even if I do my work perfectly, this patient is going to die if I have to operate under these conditions. I must have an antiseptically clean operating room."

The revulsion that you would feel as a cardiac surgeon toward that invasion of unsanitary conditions in an operating room is miniscule compared to what a holy God thinks about one sinful thought! Even one unholy thought is enough to separate you from a holy God forever. A holy God cannot bear the presence of evil. There is nothing you can do to make yourself acceptable to a holy God. You have forever obliterated that possibility. You cannot do anything to make yourself acceptable to God.

Becoming a Buddhist or a Hindu or a Muslim will not impress God. Merely placing your name on a Baptist church roll will never satisfy the righteous demands of Almighty God! There is nothing you can do. No church you can join, no good deeds you can perform – there is no way that you can ever DO anything to make yourself acceptable to a holy God. Believe me, if you could, Nicodemus would have done so. The text notes that he was, in fact, a good man. He was a noble leader of the people. And he was a man who was a churchman and a man of prayer and of high moral standards. And to that man, Jesus said that except a man be born again, he can never see the kingdom of God.

Nicodemus asked the logical question, "How can a man enter into his mother's womb when he is old and be born a second time?" Jesus replied that "unless a man is born of the water and of the Spirit, he can never enter the kingdom of God." What did Jesus mean by that? Although the field of obstetrics was not so far advanced then, the ancients in some ways understood physical birth better than those in the modern era. Most ancients had often witnessed physical births. One reason so many people today are willing to have abortions is that they have never seen a physical or live birth of any kind. Just to see a dog give birth will forever change your perspective. Have you ever seen the birth of a giraffe? That is the most amazing thing you have ever seen. I love going to Africa. You see so many unbelievable things. Mama giraffe gives birth to her baby giraffe standing up. The first experience for that newborn is an eight-foot drop to the ground. Talk about a rough beginning! And as soon the little giraffe hits the ground, the mother is kicking him, nudging and pushing him around, because she has to get him up and get him running in twenty minutes, or he will soon be lion breakfast. It is a rough beginning but an incredible event to watch.

Everyone in antiquity knew that birth was preceded or accompanied by a flow of water from the womb of the mother. Thus, it was common to speak of the physical birth as the water birth. What Jesus says to Nicodemus is that physical birth is not enough; you must have a spiritual birth as well. He was saying, "Do you not know that you have to be born of the water physically and of the Spirit?" You may ask, "How did you come to that interpretation?" The next verse says, "Because that which is born of the flesh is flesh" – that is the water birth – "and that which is born of the Spirit is spirit" – that is the spiritual birth.

The analogy is perfect. In a physical birth, at least in the human species, after conception there are nine months leading up to the moment of physical birth. But that physical birth occurs at a given moment. For example, your birth certificate, if you can find it, says something like mine: "Leighton Paige Patterson, born October 19, 1942, at 11:55 p.m." That is very specific! So I ask people, "Have you been born again?" Some reply, "Oh, yes, many times." And I say, "Oh, really. Well, how many times were you born physically?" And they say, "What? What are you talking about? Everyone knows you are only born once physically." And you are only born once spiritually. And just as your physical birth takes place at a moment in time, so your spiritual birth takes place at a moment in time. Just as there are nine months leading to a physical birth, there may be many factors that lead to a spiritual birth. Perhaps over a long period of time you hear the gospel, and gradually the Spirit of God begins to work His convicting power in your heart; or that timing may be very compressed and you hear the gospel the first time, and your heart is quickened, and you immediately respond to the Lord. But there will be a time leading up to it. And then just as a physical birth results in maturation, the same thing should happen after the spiritual birth. There should be spiritual growth. Unfortunately, some Christians remain spiritual infants all their lives. They are not hard to identify. They are murmuring and complaining and crying about anything and everything. Nothing is ever right; they are determined to have their way.

Nevertheless, hopefully you grow out of spiritual infancy and into the spiritual teenage years. Those are dangerous years, as you know. But then, you are growing into spiritual maturity. However, the spiritual birth like the physical birth occurred at one moment. If you are going to heaven, there was a moment when you were born again. If you are saved today and right with God, there was a moment when you were born again.

You may say, "I can't remember the moment; I don't know the date." I am not concerned whether or not you know the date. Most people do not think to write down the day they were saved. But, if you have been born again, you know when it happened. You may not know the date, but the experience was unforgettable. My salvation is more vivid to me than what happened to me yesterday, and I was only nine years old when I invited Christ into my heart. I was sitting on the third pew in the auditorium of the First Baptist Church in Beaumont, Texas. I was under so much conviction that I did not know what the preacher said; I did not hear a thing he said. God was speaking to my heart that night. I had been under conviction for three years, and I was totally miserable. I had a three-year gestation period. These years between ages six and nine were the most miserable years of my life as I struggled every day with the Spirit of God speaking to my heart. Finally, as a nine-year-old boy, I slipped out that night and went forward. I was not saved when I got to the front; I was saved the second I said, "Oh, Lord, I trust you." Monumental things happened in my nine-year-old heart. I have not gotten over it yet, and my conversion is as vivid to me as if it happened yesterday. Unless a man is born again, he can never see the kingdom of God.

Nicodemus asked, "Lord, how can these things be?"

Jesus said, "Okay, Nicodemus, see that tree swaying back and forth?"

"Yes, I see it!"

"What causes that, Nicodemus?"

"Elementary question. The wind causes it, of course."

"Good for you, Nicodemus, you finally got one right, didn't you? Well, now, Nicodemus, let's push this a little further. Can you see the wind?"

"Well, no, I can't see the wind."

"Not to worry, Nicodemus, tell me where it's coming from."

"Well, I don't know where it's coming from."

"Don't worry about it, Nicodemus, just tell Me where the wind is going."

"Well, I don't have a clue where the wind is going."

"Nicodemus, is there something wrong with you? You told me the wind causes that tree to do that, and now you tell me that the wind is something you can't see. You don't know where it comes from or where it goes, and yet you still believe in the wind?"

Nicodemus responds, "Lord, I don't see the wind, and I don't know where it's coming from, and I don't know where it's going, but I do know it's there because I see the evidences of the wind as the tree moves."

The Lord says, "Ah ha! There you go, Nicodemus! Now you are beginning to understand that the new birth takes place when somebody who has been hooked on drugs is suddenly set free in the power of the Lord Jesus Christ. You know that the Spirit of God has moved when someone who is a slave of alcohol suddenly has the chains broken and has been set free from that alcoholism. You know that the Lord's Spirit is there when someone burdened with the lust that comes with the flesh suddenly breaks free from that in the freedom that is in Christ Jesus."

You may be unaffected by some of those outward forms of sin, but your heart produces wicked acts because "the heart is deceitful and desperately wicked. Who can know it?" When that heart undergoes a change, you see the evidences of it. You know the Spirit of God is there.

"Maybe, but Lord, how does it happen?"

"I will tell you how it happens. As Moses lifted up the serpent in the wilderness, even so must the Son of Man be lifted up. Whoever will believe on Him will not perish, but have everlasting life."

Do you remember the incident? The children of Israel were in the process of demonstrating that they were all Baptists. They were griping and complaining because some of them did not like the Wednesday night meal, others did not like the color of the choir robes, and many of them thought that they should have built the tent of meeting larger since the people had to stand on the outside for the services. They were complaining and murmuring about everything, and the Lord God said, "I've listened to about as much of this as I want to hear." The Bible says that God sent among them fiery serpents — Egyptian cobras.

Why does He call them fiery serpents? An Egyptian cobra's poison is not hemotoxic. It is not carried in the bloodstream; it is neurotoxic and cytotoxic, which in essence means that it affects your nervous system, and even the cells of your flesh begin to break down. When you are bitten by one of those snakes, at first you feel nothing; but within about three seconds, it feels as though someone has taken your arm and thrust it in a flame of fire and held it there. The fire begins to spread up your arm until it eventually embraces your entire body. Or it moves up your leg until finally your body feels as if it has been attacked by a blowtorch. The agony of the flame of that fiery serpent is the closest thing to hell on this earth. And unless you get antivenom within one and a half to two hours after that bite, you may die. When the snakes attacked in the wilderness, there was no antidote. A bitten man was a dead man. A bitten child was a dead child. All over the camp of Israel, people were dying. They were crying out to God, but dying as they did. God heard from heaven, and He said, "Moses, I will not destroy all the people; I will give them a remedy. I want you to take some bronze and fashion it like one of those Egyptian cobras. Put it atop your staff, Moses, and go to the highest spot in the camp. Stick the staff in the ground and tell the people to look and live. Anyone bitten by one of the cobras can look at the bronze cobra on Moses' stake. When he looks at it, God will heal."

A 16-year-old girl is racing through the camp as fast as she can run. She does not stop for any well-wisher, she bypasses anybody who has anything to say to her because she is running as hard as she can. Suddenly, she gets to the outer boundary of the tents of the children of Israel, and there lies a man in front of the tent. Perspiration is broken out on his brow; there is blood from the side of his mouth; he has been bitten by one of those cobras; and he is not far from death. He feels his whole body is on fire, and that little sixteen-year-old girl suddenly falls to her knees beside her own father. She reaches him and cradles his head with her hands and says, "Dad, I have good news, wonderful news. You will not die. You don't have to die. God told Moses to put a serpent on the stake over there, and I can see it from here, Dad; and if you'll just look right over there, when your eyes fall on the serpent, you will be made whole." Do you know what that man probably said? He said, "I know you mean well, Honey, but I'm 55 years old, I have been able to handle everything that has ever come along in my life so far, and I can handle this, too. I'm not about to believe that something as silly as looking at some snake on a stick is ever going to make me whole." A few moments later, as his daughter weeps, he breathes his last breath and dies.

A mother is running through the camp. Nothing can deter her. Her little nine-year-old boy has been bitten and does not really understand. All he knows is that he is in terrible agony. She reaches the tent where her little nine-year-old boy is dying, and she sweeps him off his mat from the floor. Just for a brief moment she hugs him as he weeps and she weeps. She says, "Honey, it's going to be okay. God told Moses to make a snake, and he put it on a stake. All you have to do is look at the snake, and the pain will be gone and you will live. I'm going to turn you around so you can see the bronze serpent, and I will lift you up." The little boy's eyes have already begun to glaze over. And he looks, but he can't see it. She says, "Hang on, honey!" And she begins to run through the camp, making every step count, being careful not to stumble herself, running as fast as she can until she gets as close as she possibly can. Then she turns that little boy's head again and says, "Now, son, try one more time. I want you to look right over there. I want you to look and see." In just a split second, the little boy's eyes focus on that serpent, and instantly that little boy lives and the pain is gone.

An unbelievable plan worked because God said that He is the way. And Jesus said, "Just as Moses lifted that serpent up in the wilderness, so must the Son of Man be lifted up." Anyone who would look to Him and Him alone – not to the Koran, not to some religious group, not to the Baptist denomination, not to anything else in this world. But those who look to Jesus on the cross, the moment they look, they are healed; they are born again; they are made right with God, and their destiny is eternity in heaven. And Jesus said, "I am the way, the truth and the life, and no man comes to the Father, but through Me."

22

THE RESURRECTION HOPE

DR. DWAYNE MERCER

Senior Pastor

First Baptist Church

Oviedo, Florida

PEOPLE ALL ACROSS THE WORLD ARE WONDERING…is Christianity true? Is there hope for me after death? All of Christianity really centers on three things. Number one, it centers on a person – Jesus Christ. Secondly, it centers on a book – the Bible. And thirdly, it centers on an event – the resurrection. Everything about the book, and about the person of Christ, really hinges upon this one miracle. And I am going to share with you the reason why.

Scholar Ravi Zacharias said, "There are only two questions that have relevance to this matter of the resurrection. The first is…'did Jesus indeed rise from the dead?' The second is, 'so what?'"

What does it mean for your life and for mine? Rollo May, who was a world-famous psychologist, was in Greece one Easter. While there, he attended a Greek church. And, during the service, the pastor stood up and shouted out, "Christ is risen!" And the congregation responded, "He is risen, indeed!" He said it again, and the congregation responded with "He is risen, indeed!" Suddenly, Rollo May was struck with the thought…what if Jesus Christ really did rise from the dead? What would that mean for our world today?

As we look in Mark, chapter 15, I want to begin reading in verse 37. because I want to lay the stage for what happened right before the resurrection.

My message is very simple – it's going to have three points – basically, what happened? how do we know it happened? and so what? In Mark 15:37-41 we read,

> And Jesus uttered a loud cry, and breathed His last. And the veil of the temple was torn in two from top to bottom. When the centurion, who was standing right in front of Him, saw the way He breathed His last, he said, "Truly this man was the Son of God!"
>
> There were also some women looking on from a distance, among whom were Mary Magdalene, and Mary the mother of James the Less and Joses, and Salome. When He was in Galilee, they used to follow Him and minister to Him; and there were many other women who came up with Him to Jerusalem.

Then He was buried, as we could have read in the next few verses. But, let's continue in chapter 16, verse one:

> When the Sabbath was over, Mary Magdalene, and Mary the mother of James, and Salome, bought spices, so that they might come and anoint Him. Very early on the first day of the week, they came to the tomb when the sun had risen. They were saying to one another, "Who will roll away the stone for us from the entrance of the tomb?" Looking up, they saw that the stone had been rolled away, although it was extremely large. Entering the tomb, they saw a young man sitting at the right, wearing a white robe; and they were amazed. And he said to them, "Do not be amazed; you are looking for Jesus the Nazarene, who has been crucified. He has risen; He is not here; behold, here is the place where they laid Him."

Let's look first of all at this event. What happened that weekend, when Jesus Christ was crucified and He rose again? Jesus Christ was tried by Pilate. Pilate asked the question, "What shall I do with Jesus? He's done nothing wrong." The only thing that Jesus was crucified for was the fact that He claimed to be God – that He claimed to be the Son of God in the flesh. Therefore, the Jewish leaders wanted Him crucified.

As He was crucified, He was first scourged. Scourging consisted of taking a piece of wood with nine leather straps coming out from it, with little pieces of bone and metal on the ends. They would stick that to a person's back and drag it down, or simply flog Him with the whip. It was against the law to give more than 40 stripes, because more would certainly kill a man, and so the Romans would usually go to 39.

Then the Bible says that they put a crown of thorns on the brow of Jesus Christ. They laid Him on a Roman cross. They placed spikes in His hands, and in His feet, and they hung Him between heaven and earth (on the cross) from nine in the morning until three in the afternoon. Two Roman executioners pronounced Him dead. They took Him off of the cross, and they wrapped Him from head to toe with wrappings, so that you could not see any part of His body. Then they placed Him into a borrowed tomb.

Now, three days later, the anointing came. Why the anointing? It was a tradition among Jews to anoint the dead. It was believed that the spirit left the body four days after it died (this is not Scriptural, it was just their belief). Therefore, they wanted to anoint His body before that four-day period was up. The women were concerned…"Who is going to remove the stone for us?" Not only was it heavy, but there was a Roman seal on it as well. It was against the law to break that Roman seal. As the ladies approached the tomb, an angel was waiting for them, saying, "Christ is not here. He has risen."

I want to bring out something else very important as well. Let's look in

John 20:6-9.

And so Simon Peter also came, following him, and entered the tomb; and he saw the linen wrappings lying there, and the face-cloth which had been on His head, not lying with the linen wrappings, but rolled up in a place by itself. So the other disciple who had first come to the tomb then also entered, and he saw and believed. For as yet they did not understand the Scripture, that He must rise again from the dead.

Now, what does all of this mean? What does it prove that Jesus rose from the dead, appeared before the disciples, and 500 other people saw Him after that? It proves God's love for us. The Bible says in Romans 5:8, "But God demonstrates His own love toward us, in that while we were yet sinners, Christ died for us."

The resurrection proves Christ's love for us, because He died for us. But the question is, was He a mere man dying for us, or was He really God in the flesh? Certainly, if Jesus Christ is risen from the dead, it would prove everything about Christ – who He claimed to be, what He claimed to say to us, and the promises of God that He has for us.

And so, I not only want us to see the event of the resurrection, but also I want us to see the evidence for it.

Frank Harber, in his book *Beyond All Reasonable Doubt*, lists nine things that we know about Jesus Christ. Now, I know some of you might be skeptical. You really don't believe that this miracle occurred. How could anyone believe that somebody could be dead and could come back to life?

Let me share with you nine things that we not only know from the Bible, but things that we also know from history. Josephus, and other Roman writers, wrote about this during the first and second century.

What do we know about it?

1. Jesus of Nazareth (a man by that name) died by means of crucifixion.

2. Jesus' body was placed in a borrowed tomb.

3. The disciples were shattered that their Messiah had died. They lost all hope, and did not expect a resurrection.

4. The tomb of Jesus was found empty on the third day.

5. Eyewitnesses reported the bodily appearance of Jesus on several occasions. In fact, there were 500 people who saw Jesus. The emphasis of the biblical writers was never to prove Christ's resurrection as there were many still alive that had seen the resurrected Christ.

6. The shattered faith of the disciples was radically transformed to a bold belief in the resurrection. The disciples, from this point, willingly sacrificed their lives for the cause of Christianity.

7. The proclamation of the early church was unapologetically the resurrection of Jesus Christ. The preaching began in Jerusalem, where Jesus was crucified.

8. The church sprang from news of the resurrection, and Sunday became the featured day of worship.

9. Jesus appeared to James, and to Paul, both of whom experienced conversion as a result of their encounters with the risen Christ.

Then I add number 10:

10. They never found the body of Jesus Christ.

Now, all of these are historical facts – whether you believe in the miracle of the resurrection or not. Maybe you are thinking…"Well, I have a faith, but it's not based on the resurrection, and I really don't believe that miracle occurred." Since these ten facts that I mentioned to you could be traced back through history we have a choice.

We can believe in the bodily resurrection of Jesus Christ, or we need to grapple with what happened that day. Either He rose from the dead or something else happened, because on the third day the tomb was empty, and the body was never found. The disciples' lives were totally and radically changed. So, what happened?

There are two attempts at an explanation that make no sense. One is the "Swoon Theory." Proposed in 1828, it says Jesus never really died. Now of course, that is ridiculous, because of everything that I have described to you already and what He went through on the cross. We have historical evidence that Jesus died.

Then there is another theory…the "Wrong Tomb Theory." This theory came about in 1907, and it said that the Roman guard went to the wrong tomb, and then the disciples went to the wrong tomb, and of course, then the Roman guards were guarding the wrong tomb. And then the Romans went back and checked out the wrong tomb. This theory has been rejected by the most skeptical of scholars.

What are the real options? There are only two. Either Jesus Christ rose from the dead, or someone stole the body.

Let's look at the first option…

All of the historical writings – all the way back to the first century – point to the fact that the tomb was empty, the right tomb was empty, and they never discovered the body of Jesus Christ.

What about our second option? Was the body stolen? In order to have a crime, you have to have a motive, and you have to have opportunity. There are only two groups of people who could have stolen the body of Jesus Christ – His enemies or His friends. Now certainly, His enemies, the Jewish leaders back in that day, were insulted because Jesus called them to repentance. They were insulted because they said that He blasphemed God (because He claimed to be the Son of God), and they felt justified in crucifying Him. They certainly had opportunity. In fact, in Matthew 28:11-15, we find that they paid off the guards to say that the body was stolen. They had opportunity, but what was their motive? Why would they steal the body of Jesus Christ, and make things worse on themselves than they had ever been before? You could say, "Well, they stole the body so that the disciples would get out and preach about the resurrection, and then they could later expose the disciples by producing the body." The problem is, they never produced the body.

That narrows our choices to two alternatives. Either Jesus Christ rose from the dead or His friends stole the body. Again, the story in Matthew 28 was that the Jewish leaders paid off the guards to claim they had gone to sleep and the disciples stole the body. That way, the Jewish leaders would watch their back with Rome.

Now, I have some problems with that. First of all, if they went to sleep, how do they know that the disciples stole the body? Secondly, please keep in mind that the penalty for going to sleep while on guard duty was to be drawn and quartered (that's a horse tied to one hand, and one on the other, and then one onto each leg, and the body splits down the middle as the horses pull in four directions. The limbs go flying in all different directions – a very quick death, a very dramatic death, a very painful death. The Roman guards would face the penalty of death if they had gone to sleep while on guard duty.

If the disciples stole the body, they broke Roman law, and they broke the Roman seal. Why were the disciples never arrested or charged with the crime?

Then, I wonder why the disciples died for their faith. Tradition tells us that Peter was crucified upside down, because he didn't feel worthy to be crucified the same way that his Savior was. James was stoned to death. We could go on and on. These people died for their faith! You could say, "Well, that doesn't mean anything. There are lots of people who have died for their faith. What about Jim Jones and the suicides in Guyana?" Well, here is the difference: if you were to study history, you would find out that everybody who died for a cause believed in their cause. They believed their cause was just and true.

If the disciples stole the body, then it would have been the first and only time in history where people died for a faith that they knew was false. After Christ died, the disciples became cowards and ran away to hide. It was not until the day of Pentecost, just 40 days later, when God's Spirit came into their lives that they became giants for God. They are the ones who began to share the gospel of Jesus Christ with everyone around them. There was a new conviction in their lives. There was a new power in their lives. So, you see, for the disciples to have stolen the body, they would have to have known that it was all a lie, and then they would have died for that lie.

Simon Greenleaf, a famous 19th century professor of law at Harvard, wrote, *"All that Christianity asks of men…is, that they would be consistent with themselves; that they would trust its evidences as they trust the evidence of other things; and that they would try and judge its actions and witnesses, as they deal with their fellow men, when testifying to human affairs and actions, in human tribunals…the result…will be an undoubting conviction of their integrity, abilities, and truth."*

You might be thinking, "Well, I'm not going to believe it anyway… I have other objections." I believe there is a reasonable answer to every reasonable objection you have. However, the final decision must be made in your heart. The heart is where our desire dwells. The heart is what makes us soft to Jesus, as we look and see how much He did for us, as He died on the cross. You see, I can give you all of the intellectual arguments in the world, but it's up to you to decide in your heart.

I was sharing Christ with someone about six months ago. I walked into their garage, and as it turned out, it was the wrong house. Someone had filled out the visitor card and put someone else's address on it. As I shared with this man, he began to object to things before I could even say anything, and you could tell that he was very defensive. So, I was backing off, but he just kept coming, defending himself. Finally, I began to share with him the evidences of the resurrection, and he totally rejected them. Because, you see, you must realize that you must open up your heart to the truth, if the truth is going to affect your life. You say, "Let's just say that Jesus Christ, for argument's sake, did rise from the dead. What does that mean to us today?"

We've seen the evidences, and now, let's look at the effects of the resurrection. If Jesus Christ is risen, it proved who He was. The Bible says in John 1:1, "In the beginning was the Word, and the Word was with God, and the Word was God."

And then later, it explains in verse 14 that the Word became flesh. Who is the Word? It is Jesus. He was with God in the beginning, He was God in the beginning. In John 10:30, Jesus says, "I and the Father are one."

Jesus Christ claimed to be God. You might be saying, "Well, I really believe that Jesus was a good teacher. He was a good man, a man worthy of following." I've heard that before. I remember meeting with one of my college friends several years after graduation. I shared Christ with him, and he responded, "I want you to know that I believe in every ethical teaching of Jesus, and I teach that to my children. I believe He was a good teacher." Well, let me ask you something; if I claimed to be God, it wouldn't give you very many alternatives on what to believe, right? If I claimed to be God, you couldn't go out and say that I was a really good teacher. If I said that I am God, then you're going to have to make up your mind. Either I am God, or I am not God. If you say that Jesus is not God, and you've already made up your mind, then He's not a good teacher. You see, He claimed to be God. Therefore, He's either God, or He's lying to you. Or, He's crazy, He's lost His mind. He's anything but a good teacher. So, He is either (as C.S. Lewis would say) a liar, a lunatic, or Lord. It's got to be one of the three. You either have to accept Jesus Christ for who He is, or you have to reject everything about Jesus Christ.

I remember watching part of the rerun of a movie entitled *Oh, God*. It had John Denver and George Burns in it, and George Burns played God. You don't have to raise your hand if you saw that movie...because it was totally worthless. But, I saw a little bit of it on television, before I turned it off. John Denver's character asked George Burns (playing God) if Jesus Christ was really his son. And he said, "Well, of course he is. And so was Buddha, and so was Mohammed. They are all my sons." Well, dear friends, I want you to know something – Buddha never claimed to be the son of God. Mohammed never claimed to be the son of God. Confucius never claimed to be the son of God. Nobody, no religious, mainline faith that anybody follows today – their prophets or their priests – none of them has ever claimed to be the Son of God. They never claimed to rise from the dead. Confucius died and was buried. Buddha rotted with food poisoning. Mohammed died in 632 A.D. and his body was cut up and spread all over the Near East. Jesus is the only one who claimed to be God. So, either He is or He is not. The resurrection of Jesus Christ proved that He is everything He said He was.

Since Jesus is God and He died for you, then rose from the grave, what does that mean for us today?

First of all, it means that you can be forgiven of everything in your past. Can you imagine being forgiven for everything that you have ever done? Guilt is one of the great negative motivators of life. It's so bad that many psychologists do everything that they can in their therapy to try to rid you of your guilt – except deal with it. But underneath, the guilt continues to work on us. And we all want forgiveness. Forgiveness, perhaps, is the greatest gift that God can ever give to mankind. You and I can be forgiven of everything that we have ever done.

Rick Warren told a true story about a young lady named Jenny. I suppose that Jenny and her parents did not have a very good relationship. Finally, Jenny had a big fight with her parents. She decided that she would leave home. She said, "I hate you, and I never want to see you again." This young teenager packed her bags and she left.

She met a man on the street who promised her all kinds of things. He put her up in an apartment, and she lived a good life for about a year. He taught her how to do "favors" for men. She became a prostitute – a high-priced, underage prostitute. But, after a year of this lifestyle and a subsequent drug addiction, Jenny became worthless to him. He tossed her out onto the street. She had no place to live, and no money to get an apartment or even a room, because all of the money she made had been spent on drugs. Finally, one day, Jenny called home. More than anything else, she wanted to see her parents again. She wanted to return to the comforts of her old room. She wanted to see her golden retriever again. But she wondered if they would ever take her back. She called her parents and only got their answering machine – on three different occasions. The third time that she called, she said, "Mom, Dad, I am coming home on such-and-such a train. As I come through town, if I don't see you at the depot, I am going to keep right on going to Canada. If, however, you want me back, and you are willing to forgive me for the terrible things that I have done, please be there to meet me." All kinds of anticipation went through her heart – all kinds of fear. When she arrived at the train depot, she wondered if they would ever forgive her, would they ever take her back? And there they were, not just her parents, but every uncle and aunt and cousin – 40 different people – waiting on her at the train depot, holding up signs saying, "Welcome Home, Jenny!" As she got off the train she hugged her dad and said, "Dad, please forgive me, forgive me. You won't even believe what I have done – to you and to Mom." He said, "Don't talk anymore. We've got a party waiting for you at home. Everyone is waiting on you."

That's an illustration of the love of God, and how Jesus Christ died on the cross for your sins, so He can have that kind of relationship – a forgiving relationship – with you.

Secondly, we have strength for today. You might be saying that you understand that you can be forgiven, but at the same time, what about tomorrow, when you sin again? Well, you probably will. What about that? What about a change of heart on the inside? Well, Jesus said, "I go away, but I am going to send another comforter to you – another one just like Me." That is the Holy Spirit. And the very moment that you and I trust Jesus as our personal Savior, the Holy Spirit of God comes to live inside of our heart. As He comes to live in our heart, He gives us the power to live the Christian life. He makes the difference. You cannot live the Christian life without the Holy Spirit within you. The very moment that we receive Christ, we receive this marvelous gift.

Thirdly, we not only have a remedy for our yesterdays, we not only have strength for today, but we also have assurance for tomorrow. One of the greatest things that we deal with is fear. Maybe you have the fear of being alone. Maybe you have a fear of the afterlife and what it holds for you.

The biggest fear of all is the fear of death. When they bring the casket into a funeral service, and you stare at the coffin, and you try to deal with all of the emotions going through you, you realize that one day you are going to pass through this life. You might wonder, "Is this life all there is?" Jesus came that you and I might have life. Listen to these wonderful words from the book of John 14:

> "Do not let your heart be troubled; believe in God, believe also in Me. "In My Father's house are many dwelling places; if it were not so, I would have told you; for I go to prepare a place for you. "If I go and prepare a place for you, I will come again and receive you to Myself, that where I am, there you may be also."

Jesus Christ died on the cross, ascended up into heaven, and He is preparing a place for you and me today — a place where we can go to be with Him forever. In that same chapter, though, He said this: "I am the way, and the truth, and the life; no one comes to the Father but through Me."

Well, that makes sense, doesn't it? If there were many ways to heaven, why would the Father in heaven be so barbaric as to send Jesus Christ, His only Son, to die on the cross for us? If there had been any other way, why would He have given up His Son for 33 and a half years? Why would Jesus have to cry on the cross, "My God, My God! Why hast Thou forsaken Me?" if there had been any other way for us to be saved. You can't have it both ways. Either He doesn't promise heaven, or Jesus is not the only way. He said, "I am the way, and the truth, and the life; no one comes to the Father but through Me."

How do you and I receive Christ? We do so, first, by admitting that we are sinners. That's why Christ died for us — so that we can have forgiveness of our sins. It's me. It's not everybody else. It's not my friends or my family that I am blaming. It's me, God. I have fallen short.

Second, we must believe that Jesus Christ, and Jesus alone, will save us.

And thirdly, we must commit to Him by asking Him to come into our heart. The Bible said, "But as many as received Him, to them He gave the right to become children of God..." (John 1:12).

Paul Harvey, the famous TV and radio personality, tells the story of a little boy named Phillip. He was in a classic Sunday School – an eight-year-old in a third grade class. He wasn't accepted by the rest of the students because he had Downs Syndrome, and he had many of the mannerisms that come with that deformity. Well, Easter time came, and the teacher had an idea that everyone should bring in something that reminded him or her of Easter. One little girl brought a flower, and she said that her flower reminded her of Easter, because of the Easter lilies, and everyone thought it was a good idea. One little boy brought a rock. He had no idea what the rock had to do with Easter, but he had it at home, and just wanted to show it to everybody. Finally, the last little gift came around, and it was an egg – one of those little plastic eggs – and when the teacher opened it up, it was empty. Someone yelled out, "That is stupid!" The teacher felt a tug at her shirt...and it was Phillip. Looking up, he said, "It's mine. It's empty. I have new life, because the tomb is empty." The class fell silent. From that day on, Phillip became part of the group. They welcomed him. Whatever had made him different was never mentioned again. Phillip's family knew he would not live long, because there were just too many things wrong with his tiny body. That summer, overcome with infection, Phillip died. On the day of his funeral, nine eight-year-old boys and girls confronted the reality of death, and marched up to the altar, not with flowers. Instead, these nine children, along with their Sunday School teacher, placed on the casket of their young friend their gift of love – an empty egg.

That's why we celebrate Easter. When you open up the grave, it's empty. I've been to the tomb of Christ in Jerusalem, and there are no bones there. It's empty. Jesus left an empty tomb so that He could fill an empty heart.

If you have never trusted Him as your personal Savior and Lord, I want to give you the opportunity to pray and receive Christ.

You and I can know Christ. You and I can be assured of heaven. If that is your desire, pray along with me.

"Lord, Jesus, thank You for loving me. Thank You for going to the cross and dying there for my sins. I open up the door of my heart, and I ask You to come in. Thank You for dying for me. Make me the person that You want me to be. In Jesus' name, Amen."

23

WHO WE ARE!

PASTOR TONY LAMBERT

Senior Pastor

First Southern Baptist Church

Del City, Oklahoma

PETER WROTE ONE OF HIS LETTERS TO SPEAK GRACE and truth to a group that was under great persecution. He wanted them to know that our God is supreme and sovereign. Peter was writing to a group of believers who were struggling with what I would call an identity crisis. They were under pressure to conform, to be like the world. These were not just people involved in activities drawing them away from God, but people who had intense pressure on their lives to conform to the world. You say, "Well, *I'm* under intense pressure." Maybe you are under pressure, but for most of us, in comparison to what these people were facing, we do not understand pressure. These people were dying because of their stand for Jesus Christ, and Peter said, "Listen, the way of the world is this way...but God's grace has changed you." Peter told them very boldly that God had done a mighty work in their lives and they must stand firm.

Peter was writing under the inspiration of the Holy Spirit with words of encouragement – words which are needed just as much today as they were then. It's time that we recognize *who we are.*

I believe we're in an identity crisis in the church in America. Upon his return from a mission trip to London, my former chairman of deacons told me about how most of the erstwhile great churches are almost empty. This is the land God had graced with some of His finest servants in the past. Even the church seems defeated. He told me of having a little bit of an identity crisis being in a seemingly godless society and of God's reminding him in the midst of his trip of who he was. We need to remember who we are. We need to remember the price that's been paid for us. We're being pulled away from the Lord. All around us we're being pushed toward the world. All around us our spiritual models seem less and less like the Lord Jesus Christ and more and more like the world. We must be reminded of who we are.

The context of verse nine is found in verses seven and eight, then rolls into our powerful selected verse, "This precious value, then, is for you who believe; but for those who disbelieve, the stone which the builders rejected, this became the very corner stone, and, a stone of stumbling and a rock of offense..." And then look at this: "...for they stumble because they are disobedient to the word, and to this doom they were also appointed." Then he says in verse nine, "But you are a chosen race, [you are] a royal priesthood, [you are] a holy nation, [you are] a people for God's own possession..." In the midst of a compromising culture and immoral assaults, God says this is who you are!

We are in an identity crisis in America. One research institute that does an intensive study about every five years issued a report of findings in 1995. The report determined through surveying our country how much money it would take for Americans to have all their dreams fulfilled. The average number was $100,000. In the year 2000, another study from the same institute with the same question was given. The response had climbed from $100,000 a year to $1,000,000 a year. I suppose that says a lot of things to us, but I'm going to tell you what I believe it says that we really need to hear. It says, first of all, we have bought the line that if we simply have "more" and if we can fill our lives with enough "stuff" we will be satisfied, we will be fulfilled, and we will have all our dreams met. It also says that we are hungering for more even as we have more and are not being satisfied.

One Christian psychologist has noted that the income in America has doubled since the 1950s. He factored in inflation and all other relevant considerations, and still we earn twice as much as people did in 1950. Yet it is noted that if you ask even Christians in the church today if they are happy, only one third of them say yes. That means that two thirds of all believers would say they are unhappy in life. While we are getting more of what we have been told will make us happy, we are a people who are less happy. Why? Could it be that we do not know who we are? We are out there in the sea of worldliness and materialism. We are out there in a society that is geared more and more simply to fulfilling the desires of the flesh, and yet we are less satisfied than ever. What's the problem?

Randy Stella played football for the University of Nebraska at Lincoln during the 2000 and 2001 seasons. He is one of the best football players that I have personally ever seen play. Due to some personal problems, Stella transferred to the University of Nebraska at Omaha, a Division II school whose team is known as the Mavericks. He sat out for one season and then became part of the Mavericks football team in 2003. In the opening game, Stella was credited with 22 solo tackles. When they interviewed Stella, they asked, "How does it feel to go from one of the premier programs in the nation to a Division II school that really nobody in the country will know much about?" And he said, "Well, quite honestly, I enjoyed the game, but when I was out there it was somewhat confusing as I couldn't remember if I was playing at Lincoln or Omaha. I didn't know if I was a Husker or whether I was a Maverick." I believe that's where a lot of Christians are today – in an identity crisis. Maybe on Sunday we do all right, but when we're out there Monday through Saturday, we don't really know whose team we're on. We're out there doing the best we can, but we have no purpose, we have no vision. We're not even sure who our coach is. There are so many expectations. The pressure, the struggles, the tension we have, and the war we're in, are all intensified by this identity crisis. Few of us have been threatened physically, but if you don't live for the world, your image is threatened. Your popularity is threatened if you don't play by their rules. Your good ol' boy likeability is threatened if you don't live like everybody else. And the tension and the agony that you feel, especially when you're confronted with the Word of God, is because you have an identity crisis.

Peter was saying in those last couple of words, "The world that does not know God, they are like this," and then he said, "But you..." Listen, church, here's the struggle and tension in your home. Here's the tension in your marriage. Here's the tension in your family. Here's the tension in your Bible study. Here's the tension in all our churches. "But you are a chosen generation." God loves us. He's on our side. He cares for us. He wants to pour His glory on us, but He will not do it on our terms. He will only do it on His. God is saying to us that He wants to get us to that place under the spout where the glory comes out, but He cannot pour out His glory until we will line up and say, "God, we're going to do it Your way."

If you are in Christ, you are a chosen generation. Perhaps you don't feel "chosen" sometimes. In fact, you may feel like the devil is kicking your brains out and you don't know what to do. Sometimes you may feel like you're a worthless worm. Sometimes you may feel life is caving in all around you. Sometimes you just feel like you're dying on the inside and you wonder if God is even there, but it does not change what the Word of God says. "If you're in Christ Jesus, you're a new creation," and if you're in Christ Jesus, as the Word of God says, "You are a chosen generation." We need to quit relying on how we feel or what we see. We need to get back to the Word of God and either say "He is God and He is Lord" or "He is a liar."

I love the contrast that He makes. He begins with that little word "b-u-t."

God says, "But..." What does He mean by that? The world is telling you one thing, but the Word of God says another. He is saying, "But in contrast" – in contrast to the world, in contrast to everything else including the fact that you get told sometimes you're worthless, you're not what you ought to be, you're not spirit-filled, you don't love God, and you're messing the world up, Jesus says, "You are a chosen generation." The word "chosen" is a powerful word. It has the same root as the word "holiness." It means "holy" or "set apart" for a special purpose, for God's specific plan. God is saying, "I have chosen you. I have set you apart."

I have an 18-year-old son, the youngest of my children, who is very strong and very helpful to have around when I do projects around our home. Last year, we purchased a pallet of sandstones. As we were pulling them off the truck, we would take certain pieces that were really beautiful and separate them from the others. We placed those special pieces in very strategic, visible places. That is what God has done with you. He has a design for your life. He has a special plan, and He wants to work it in your life. Can you imagine if during the night, those special sandstones, those dumb, inanimate rocks that we had set apart, decided they didn't want to be there, and they moved to some other location? God has formed you. And if you try to do anything other than His will, you're going to face a crisis, an identity crisis.

The word "chosen" can also be translated as "separation, consecration, devoted to His service, sharing in His purity, abstaining from the earth's defilement." We are to be daily sanctified, daily moved, and daily directed by the influences of His Holy Spirit. He knows where you are and He cares for you. He's got it all worked out. It doesn't mean you're always going to feel good. That's not what the Word of God teaches. If we only consider what Jesus told Peter, which was that he was going to die for the glory of Christ, we know His plan may not always be easy. That does not take away the truth that I am chosen by Him. I am called. I am equipped. And He cares for me and He cares for you as well.

Our God is committed to us. Let me illustrate. On one of the most difficult days of my life, I was driving into the office as I had done a thousand times, but this day was different. I did not know if I could face the world. I thought about just giving up, turning around and going home. About that very moment, I looked up at an electronic sign that I routinely pass every day. Out of the blue, I noticed the sign on this secular institution read, "With God all things are possible." Now, let me tell you something, God did that just for me. You see, I'm a chosen generation.

The word "generation" has the root word "*genos.*" It is where we get our word "genetics." It points to our "family of origin." I know we are told we have the bloodlines of our mom and dad. I am personally blessed to have parents who love God. But that is not enough. My blood and yours is tainted with a horrible disease called sin. Unless we both have a spiritual blood transfusion, we will die both physically and spiritually. I've got great news: God can change all that! He can break the chain. Through Jesus we can be made new creatures! The more we mature spiritually, the more we ought to look like and act like our spiritual heavenly Father. I mean, we ought to be a chip off the old block, so that as people look at us day after day, the more and more they see Jesus Christ. I have the genetic makeup of my Lord Jesus Christ. Why? It is because I have had a supernatural blood transfusion. I have been filled with the spirit of God. My blood that was sinful and tainted has been changed and replaced with the life-giving blood of the Lord Jesus. I am a chosen generation.

You know how it is. The devil creeps into your life, whispers in your ear, and says, "You know what? You're really worthless. You see all this stuff going on in your life? You really don't know what's going on. You don't have the answer. You're worthless. In fact, you can't even keep your family together.

How are you going to keep the world together? How are you going to do anything? How are you going to be faithful to God? You haven't got it." I'm going to tell you something, according to the Word of God, that very word "genetics" teaches me that I am like my Father. I choose to believe Him.

Peter says secondly, "but you are...a royal priesthood." I am not only a chosen generation, but I am a royal priesthood. I love that word "royal." It speaks of the kingdom of God. I have been made royalty through the blood of Jesus Christ. It means that I belong to Him. I have been appointed. I have been engrafted and adopted into the family of the King of Kings and Lord of Lords! The base meaning of that word means we are "suitable" for the King. If something has been made royal, it is suitable for the King. Now, listen to this, when that liar, Satan, whispers in your ear telling you those things, when he begins to beat you down, you must remember you are a chosen generation and a royal priesthood. And when he starts to rip you apart and tell you how worthless you are, you know what you can do? You can erect that spine, brush off your coat; stick your finger in the face of the evil one and say, "You are WRONG! I have been made suitable by the King!" No matter what he says, he's a liar. He's a liar. *He is a liar!*

This is also important to remember when temptation comes. The evil one says, "You know, you can go ahead and do this, and nobody will know. After all, you deserve it. It feels good. It will be okay. Anyway, everybody is doing it. You don't want to be ostracized. You don't want to look different. Go ahead. Play the game. Go to church on Sunday and live like you're going to hell the rest of the days of the week." One more time, listen to the voice of truth, and by the power of the Spirit, stand up erect, put your finger in the devil's face and say; "I am suitable for the King. I will not do it. I am too good. I am royalty because of Jesus."

It's time you stop living with an identity crisis, not knowing who you are

THE LAST SERMON I WOULD PREACH

THE LAST SERMON I WOULD PREACH

playing for and just out there struggling in the game of life. You are royalty! I believe in the face of Satan, you ought to strut. I believe you ought to get all up in his face and say, "You can't touch this. I belong to Jesus." But don't miss the other side. You don't strut in the presence of the King. In a self-serving, self-indulgent world, we have lost the concept that in the presence of the King we should never strut. We have been made suitable by the incredible sacrifice of the blood of the Lamb. Sometimes we miss that. Often there is such arrogance even in the Christian culture. We see this manifested when we can freely cast stones at others because we think we're spiritually at a different level. Remember what 2 Chronicles 7:14 teaches us? "If my people, who are called by my name, will humble themselves, and pray and seek my face..." If we will humble ourselves, hunger for Him, and walk in holiness, God says, "then – then – then..." I believe many Christians have been deceived and are living in artificial, emotionally-driven glory, immensely consumed with a self-absorbed materialistic lifestyle. We don't understand that we are royalty but that we are royalty because of Jesus.

The Bible reveals over and over that God has a plan for our lives. That plan is further revealed in the next word of our verse, "a royal priesthood..." We are a part of God's priesthood. Priesthood is a band of brothers and sisters who have been given a purpose, not for fulfillment of the flesh, but to glorify God. The emphasis is upon a select person or group. In the Old Testament, the Levites were the group God set apart to serve as priests. Today those who are born again function as a type of priest under our great High Priest, Jesus. As believers, we represent God before people. We are an example to those not yet in God's kingdom, but also to our fellow believers.

Once again my mind goes back to the sandstones in my yard. Those stones can do nothing but hold the ground upon which they are placed. They have no power or freedom. According to Scripture, we are *living* stones. Life is full of adventure and fulfillment. Christ came to bring us life and to have it more abundantly. He desires to unleash our individualism and creativity for His glory. Jesus is our High Priest. He is the one we live for and die for. Our lives belong to Him.

A story is told by Mark Twain concerning a wealthy businessman from Boston. It seems that the businessman's dream was to go to the Holy Land, climb Mount Sinai and shout the Ten Commandments from the mountain top. Twain told the businessman to save himself a lot of time and money and just begin to live out the Ten Commandments. If we could simply understand who we are and the great calling which is upon our lives as Christians, certainly we would live differently today.

Allow me to touch briefly on a few more words in our verse. "Holy" has the same root as "chosen," yet the word "nation" is an interesting word, the same as the word "ethnos." It identifies a specific ethnicity. One way of understanding the word is to understand its usage in other contexts. One usage is in reference to a flock of birds. To some they may all look the same, but with a closer look they are all different in ethnos. We are a people transformed by Christ and, therefore, we can be identified with His ethnicity. Can the world tell that we are of a different spiritual ethnicity? Is it obvious or has the identity crisis caused us to blend in? This is not putting on your best three-button suit, grabbing a 50-pound study Bible and running around saying, "Praise God!" Rather it is reflecting the very character of Christ in all we do. Those sandstones in my yard are only effective as they are connected! They look different from all the other objects in our landscape, and they are strategically connected to make a path which leads somewhere. We are connected in a new ethnicity which should always point others to Christ.

This last phrase is extremely hard to translate into English. But one truth is obvious – we are purchased by God. We are His possession. Humanistic theology says God is there to serve your purpose. Health and happiness seem to be His responsibility to us according to this philosophy, yet the Bible says God's desire is to reconcile us to the Father, and holiness, provided by Christ, is the only pathway. Christ makes us holy, and the Holy Spirit gives us power to continue on that pathway.

Life is more than how we do in this one game we call today. God sees it as a season, and it is not just you with whom He is concerned. It is ultimately about showing forth His praises to a world that is dying. Scripture tells us that we do not belong to ourselves, but we have been purchased with the price of the blood of Jesus.

Once when we were on a cruise ship, the boat inexplicably stopped. An announcement was made, and we were quickly informed that it was the captain who stopped the ship, and because of his position, he had that right. Our captain Jesus has a great plan for us and we must recognize His authority and release our lives to Him.

Who are we? I want to ask you today, do you know who you are? Some might say, "Oh, I'm a Baptist, or a Methodist, or a Catholic," or something else. But that's not who you are. That just happens to be which fellowship you are aligned with or where you gather to worship, study, or serve.

Is there tension in your life because you have an identity crisis? And could it be that you don't recognize that you're part of a chosen generation and that you, by the blood of Christ, have been made royalty today? I believe He is saying, "Lift up your head, child of God, and live like you belong to the King." Go to a mirror and tell yourself, I have been chosen!

24

THE WORTHINESS OF KING JESUS

DR. JIM HENRY

Pastor Emeritus

First Baptist Church

Orlando, Florida

THE QUESTION WAS ASKED LONG AGO, "What think ye of Christ?" The right answer to that question is the determining factor in your personal relationship with Him. Different people have many different opinions about who Jesus is.

Some say Jesus is a revolutionary, not in the violent sense, not in the political sense, not but in the sense that He moves inwardly to revolutionize a life through the new birth and the indwelling of the Holy Spirit.

Some see Jesus as gentle and meek. The association at this point is that Jesus is weak – and that is not true. Pontius Pilate, who had seen many strong men and knew what a man was, said, "Behold the man!" That is hardly the description of a pitiful specimen.

Some see Jesus as simply a good man. He was a good man, but He is much more than just a good man. He never prayed for the forgiveness of His own sin. The best men I know who walk closest to the Lord are the men who realize the sinfulness of their natures and often find themselves confessing sin in the prayer chamber. There is one thing for sure, when you bring up the name of Jesus Christ, you hear varied opinions. Thinking of Jesus and His many great miracles, many wonderful attributes, many marvelous characteristics, and many great words, thrills my soul, but the picture that captures my heart is

King Jesus.

He is king because of His superiority. There has never been another like Him. He was a unique man of history. John 1:14 says, "And the Word was made flesh, and dwelt among us." When He became man, that helped us to understand God a little better. What a man He was!

When Lawrence of Arabia was seeking to get a following, he was told, "If you would lead us, you must eat the same food we eat, find shelter in the same tents in which we dwell, accept the same risks we accept, meet the same difficulties we meet, live the same life we live, and live it better than we do!" I don't know if Lawrence lived up to that or not, but I do know that Jesus did from every standpoint.

He was a man, yes, but He was also God. John 1:1 says, "In the beginning was the Word, and the Word was with God, and the Word was God." Emmanuel Scott put it pungently when he said, "The celestial dwelt among the terrestrial; the supernatural was naturalized; the ultimate was entangled with the immediate; the supersensory was sensed in the sensory; the 'God up there' became the 'God down here.'"

Jesus is superior in His uncommon offices. He was a prophet. Deuteronomy 18:15 says, "The LORD thy God will raise up unto thee a Prophet..." Peter said in Acts 3:22-23 that Jesus was a confirmation of Moses' prediction. Not only was He a prophet, but He also fulfilled the office of priest. In Hebrews 3:1 we find, "Wherefore, holy brethren, partakers of the heavenly calling, consider the Apostle and High Priest of our profession, Christ Jesus." He is also king, as indicated in John 18:37: "...Art thou a king then? Jesus answered, Thou sayest that I am a king. To this end was I born, and for this cause came I into the world..."

His superiority is also seen in His undeniable character. His detractors tried to accuse Jesus of sin. They did everything to frame Him, but He always came out on top. Even His enemies ended up having to admit that He was a good man.

His superiority is also seen in His unprecedented mission. In Revelation 13:8, Jesus is spoken of as "the Lamb slain from the foundation of the world." Jesus' sacrificial death was voluntary. John 17:18 states it plainly: "As thou hast sent me into the world…" His death was substitutionary, as Peter tells us in 1 Peter 2:24: "Who his own self bare our sins in his own body on the tree…" His death was a final sacrifice; there will never have to be another, according to Hebrews 9:28: "So Christ was once offered to bear the sins of many…" Most men feel they are born to live. Jesus had the mission of being born to live and die – for us.

His superiority is seen in His unceasing ministry. What is Jesus doing now? He is on the right hand of God interceding for us in prayer, according to Romans 8:34: "…It is Christ that died, yea rather, that is risen again, who is even at the right hand of God, who also maketh intercession for us." King Jesus – worthy because of His superiority in every realm of life.

King Jesus brings salvation that is unique. Only He can perform that work in a person's heart. In Acts 4:12 Peter said, "Neither is there salvation in any other: for there is none other name under heaven given among men, whereby we must be saved." Man's basic problem is a sin problem. The only lasting remedy is the forgiving, life-changing, cleansing blood of Jesus. God effected the miracle of the ages when His own Son took our place, our death, our guilt, and our sin, that we might live and become heirs of God and joint heirs with Christ. When I think of the cross of Christ, these two thoughts grip my heart: how much God loved us and what a tremendous price was paid for my sin.

Bobby Mitchell was an outstanding pro football player with the Washington Redskins. In his Christian testimony, he reports that a friend of his was standing on a street corner watching the panic that had occurred in Washington, DC after the assassination of Martin Luther King, Jr. A boy about nine years old came racing down the sidewalk with six cans of tomato juice in his arms. A policeman stopped him and asked him, "Son, what are you doing?"

"Let me go!" the boy replied. "They killed my man, they killed my man."

"What do you mean, they killed your man?"

"Turn me loose, they killed my man."

"Son, who is your man?"

The boy thought for a moment and replied, "I don't know, but they killed my man." The youngster was talking about Dr. Martin Luther King, Jr.

Mitchell testifies that when he heard the story it set him to thinking. He said, "When I was young we were probably the only family in town who went to church seven days a week. My daddy was a minister. But as you get into pro sports and bask in the bright lights and hear the applause, it is not difficult to draw away or to forget your early teachings. This happened to me."

Mitchell continued, "Then I heard about a little boy, who in the midst of a riot, knew only that 'they killed my man.' Then I was home with Daddy again and all the teaching that had just rolled off was suddenly real to me. For I knew that years ago they had killed my man, too. And I knew that this man had willingly given His life for me. My man, Jesus Christ."

The worthiness of Jesus is seen also in His subjection of sin. Throughout the New Testament we read of the Lord Jesus dealing with difficult sins of long standing. Many held in sin's dread sway for years felt hopeless and helpless. The Simon Peters, the Sauls, the Zacchaeuses, the Marys, all found in Jesus a new power. They found that "He breaks the pow'r of cancelled sin, He sets the pris'ner free." Paul in his Roman epistle used chapters 6 through 8 to show that Christ brings sin under subjection in the life of the believer. Jesus not only saves us from the ultimate penalty of sin, but He also delivers us from and gives us victory over our sinful nature in this world.

I remember counseling and praying with a man who had been an alcoholic for several years. He had tried everything he knew to overcome the sin that had so desperately gripped his life and affected everyone in his family. He told me that he had never tried the Lord Jesus. I shared with him how he could let Christ have the victory in his life and give him the power to overcome his slavery to alcohol. We knelt to pray, and he began to cry. In a few moments he sobbed out the words, "I've tried everything else, Lord, now you do it."

Maybe you have tried everything else. Maybe you have a besetting sin in your life, a habit, an attitude, an action. The Holy Spirit has pointed this out to you time and time again. The victory can be yours. He promised in His Word, "Likewise reckon ye also yourselves to be dead indeed unto sin, but alive unto God through Jesus Christ our Lord. Let not sin therefore reign in your mortal body, that ye should obey it in the lusts thereof" (Romans 6:11-12). When a person is in Christ Jesus, he takes on the attitudes and actions of his Lord and Master.

In the musical *My Fair Lady,* Professor Higgins says to the little waif he is trying to transform into a lady, "Act like a duchess, think like a duchess, talk like a duchess." In Christ, we should act like a son or daughter, think like a son or daughter, and talk like a son or daughter of God. How much do you think you're worth? What does your personal portfolio say? Jesus says you are worth everything. Jesus says you are somebody.

We live in a time when men are so alienated from the Lord that there is a desperate search for identity. The crisis of loneliness probably is the prevailing mental illness of America. The feeling of nothingness points to one of the greatest needs of our time.

It is all too evident that Satan would prostitute a person's worth. He begins by making him think he is everything – then at the end of the road, making him think that he is nothing. Jesus begins by taking a person at the point of his nothingness and making him into something. Jesus heard a man's cry and said, "I became the Son of man, that you might become the sons of God." Sons of God! Think of it! No one can look down his nose at me. I belong to the King. My father is God! Cardinal Newman once stated, "There are two and two only, absolutely and luminously self-evident beings – myself and my Creator." Martin Luther said, "It's the personal pronouns that matter."

When I was in high school, I attended the Hopewell Baptist Church with my grandparents and my mother. I was converted in that wonderful church. There was to be an anniversary celebration there. I had persuaded my parents to let my cousin and me thumb our way out to the church, which is about 30 miles from Nashville. We wanted to be there for the dinner on the grounds and to hear the special speaker.

On the outskirts of Nashville we stood beside the road with our thumbs out. In a few minutes we were approached by a big black Oldsmobile. As the car drew nearer I noticed the hat of a state trooper. My heart froze. The brakes screeched as the car stopped; and I thought perhaps he was going to arrest us. As we ran up to the car, I noticed that the license plate displayed the number 1. The thought quickly ran through my mind that this must be a very important person to have a number 1 on his license plate.

The patrolman rolled down the window and said, "Where are you boys going?" I introduced myself and replied, "We're going up to my grandparents' church for a special service." Surely, I thought, he won't throw us in jail if we're going to church. He said, "Jump in, we're headed that way, and you can ride with us." We climbed into the back seat amid briefcases, papers, radios, and other important-looking items. The gentleman seated in the back said, "Hello, Jimmy, I'm Frank G. Clement, governor of Tennessee. I am going up to the Hopewell Church to speak, and I will be glad to give you and your friend a lift. Buckle your seat belts, we're running a little late, and we need to get there in a hurry."

Well, that patrolman let the hammer down on that big black Oldsmobile, we reared back in the seat with the governor, and the closer we got to Hopewell, the bigger and more important we felt. In my mind's eye I envisioned the scene soon to be a reality at the church. My mother and daddy would be there and my younger brother, Joe, plus the friends and neighbors that I had known through the years. Imagine what they would think when they saw Jimmy Henry riding with the governor of Tennessee! Sure enough, the vision soon became a reality.

As we rounded the comer and came near the church at the top of the hill, a great crowd of people awaited the arrival of the governor. The patrolman stopped amid the popping of gravel, the swirling of dust, and the swishing back and forth of the aerials on top of that shiny black Oldsmobile. The crowd enveloped the car. The first one out was me. I jumped out, tipped my hand in the governor's direction, and said, "Thank you, Governor, I sure did appreciate and enjoy the ride. God bless you." I can assure you that I was the envy of my brother and all my buddies from that moment on. I was somebody!

As I have grown older and think back on that exciting moment, I realize that as wonderful as it was, there is something even more precious to recognize: I am a child of the King and can have an audience with my Father at any time! King Jesus gives a sense of personhood and dignity to a person as no one else can.

King Jesus imparts lasting victory to His children who make up His church. Christmas was the day He was born. On Good Friday we remember His crucifixion. Easter is the day that He arose. Whitsunday is the day the Holy Spirit came on the church. There is yet another day coming, the day when He comes for His church. 1 Thessalonians 4:16-17 exults, "For the Lord himself shall descend from heaven with a shout, with the voice of the archangel, and with the trump of God: and the dead in Christ shall rise first: Then we which are alive and remain shall be caught up together with them in the clouds, to meet the Lord in the air: and so shall we ever be with the Lord." The final victory is His.

In the last days of what President Ronald Reagan called "the evil empire" in Communist Prague, Czechoslovakia, word had gone out that at 12 o'clock noon the Czech Republic would no longer be under Communist domain and the people would be free to exercise their liberties. The night before, people began to gather in the Main Square. They came slowly at first, and then by the dozens, twenties, and fifties, and soon the city square was packed. Many held candles, and prayed, and talked with one another. It was the first time in many years they had been able to express their freedom and their religious liberty. As the night wore on and the morning dawned, excitement continued to build. People began to sing the old hymns – hymns they had not been allowed to sing in public. The voices rose to a mighty crescendo as the magic hour of noon approached. And then at 12 o'clock noon, as promised, they were free at last. The church bells all over Prague began to ring out and, for the first time in over 50 years, people heard the bells. The bells had been silenced by the Communist regime, as they sought to cut out all witness of the Christian faith, but now they rang – deep, long, loud – peal after peal rang out. The people wept, shouted sang, hugged and breathed deeply of the refreshing air of freedom. Then they noticed something. In one of the apartments surrounding the square, a lady held out a sheet. She draped it under her window so every eye could see, and what did they see? She had scrawled out in the Czech language, in bold letters, the words THE LAMB WINS! And indeed He has. He has won the war, and one day we shall share the victory in its fullness and completeness with our King of Kings and Lord of Lords.

25

THE ONE QUESTION EXAM

DR. KENNETH HEMPHILL

National Strategist

LifeWay Christian Resources

Nashville, Tennessee

SINCE I AM A "SOMETIMES" PROFESSOR, I can say without malice that professors can be strange folks and thus do the unexpected with regularity. Usually the first question that students ask on the first day of the course relates to the grading scale and the content of the final exam. They want to know what it takes to pass. I once heard of a professor who gave a one-question exam.

Let me help you prepare for your final "final." The one question – "Who do you say that Jesus is?"

You may recall that Jesus once asked Peter this question. The dialogue is recorded in Matthew 16:13-19. Curiosity about Jesus' true identity had led to wild speculation. Some thought He was John the Baptist raised from the dead. Others believed Him to be Elijah, Jeremiah, or one of the other prophets. Look at these pronouncements. They all were willing to believe He was a supernatural figure. They knew that His teaching had the authority of prophecy, thus acknowledging that He was a spokesman from God. Peter, however, was willing to risk a more daring answer – "You are the Messiah, the Son of the living God!" To suggest that Jesus was Messiah was to declare that He was the King, the Redeemer, man's only solution for his sin problem.

The question still stands. And many answers often have the appearance of being correct. But there is only one answer. In our text, Paul was addressing the church at Colossae. This church was located in Asia Minor. When we read both the Colossian and Ephesian letters, we can sense that Paul was protecting the churches from doctrinal heresy. The theological winds were swirling that would soon produce a heresy known as gnosticism. When you study it carefully, you will find that it had many of the components of the New Age thinking of our day. Satan really isn't very creative. He continues to recycle the same old half truths. Paul doesn't attempt to deal with the various aspects of the half truths of the heresy, he goes immediately to the central question – who is Jesus?

I. CHRIST AS REDEEMER (V. 9-14)

This first profound acclamation about the identity and work of Jesus is found in a section where Paul tells them of his prayer for them. He prays that they will have knowledge of God's will and spiritual understanding (v. 9). This will enable them to walk worthy of the Lord, please Him, bear fruit in every good work, and grow in the knowledge of God (v. 10). Notice that knowledge produces fruitful service, and that in turn produces greater knowledge of God. Isn't it wonderful that the Christian life is an adventure of learning that allows us to grow daily into His likeness?

Further, he prays that they will have supernatural strength which will enable them to endure with joy (v. 11). He depicts a life of thanksgiving. Now remember, these early Christians were living in turbulent times where persecution was looming large on the horizon. Why could they be joyful and give thanks to the Father? It is at this point that we hear some of the most beautiful words ever uttered...

HE RESCUED US FROM THE DOMAIN OF DARKNESS

Can you still remember some of those childhood experiences where darkness seemed to be the foreboding enemy? I can still vividly remember one stormy night lying in my bed watching the shadows cast by a weeping willow tree run their "monster-like" fingers across my bedroom wall. In my brain I knew they were just shadows. But my brain couldn't convince my heart. Finally in desperation I called out to my dad. In just seconds I saw his huge figure at the door, and with one flip of the switch, light flooded my room and the monsters dissipated.

But our problem is no illusion of a childish mind. You see, we all belong to "the domain of darkness" (v. 13). This imprisonment was the result of sin. You may recall that Paul put this in clear focus in his Roman letter. "For all have sinned and fall short of the glory of God" (Romans 3:23). This is a terminal problem. "For the wages of sin is death..." (Romans 6:23). But aren't you happy that there is a second half to verse 23? "But the free gift of God is eternal life in Christ Jesus our Lord."

HE TRANSFERRED US INTO THE KINGDOM OF THE SON HE LOVES

Here in our Colossians text, Paul puts it another way. "He has rescued us from the domain of darkness and transferred us into the kingdom of the Son He loves" (Colossians 1:13). We understand what it means to be transferred. Sometimes we are transferred by our employer, and we move from one location to another. "Transferred" renders a word that was used in secular literature of removing persons from one country and settling them as colonists in another country. When you are transferred by God, you no longer dwell in the domain of darkness, you now dwell in the kingdom of the Son He loves. This kingdom is a present reality of the peace discovered when Christ is Lord of our hearts and lives.

We must ask – how could this be possible? If we are sinners and deserve death, how can God transfer us to the kingdom of His beloved Son?

IN WHOM WE HAVE REDEMPTION

Our redemption is not in a church, a religion, or a practice, it is in a person. In other words, our redemption is in Christ. You may not have noticed it in your first reading, but the two words "redemption" and "forgiveness" create something of a holy tension. The terminology of redemption belongs to the slave market. Sin has created an objective problem which must be resolved, and to resolve it requires a price.

This redemptive process is well illustrated by the Old Testament story of the prophet Hosea. Hosea is married to Gomer, who becomes a harlot. As the story progresses we find Gomer in the slave market. It doesn't take much to imagine the scene. The once attractive woman now bears in her body the marks of her sin. She is being auctioned off to the highest bidder to be used and abused as that person desires. She is nothing more than property. In an unexpected turn of events the prophet buys back his own wife. He pays the price to buy her freedom – he redeems her.

In a slightly more modern application we see this principle in action every time we pass a pawn store. Generally an article is pawned because we need the money to pay bills or meet daily living expenses. Our plan is to buy the article back before it goes on sale at a greatly reduced price. We plan to redeem it.

The good news is that God has offered to pay the price to buy you back. You are His by virtue of creation, but because of your sin, your Creator has now become your redeemer. But the cost to redeem fallen mankind was a large one. Peter speaks to this in 1 Peter 1:18-19: "For you know that you were redeemed from your empty way of life inherited from the fathers, not with perishable things, like silver or gold, but with the precious blood of Christ, like that of a lamb without defect or blemish." The redemption price was God's Son. Thus our redemption is found only "in Him."

THE FORGIVENESS OF SINS

Forgiveness by its very nature implies a free act of grace. The literal meaning of the word "forgiveness" is "sending away." Thus, when we are forgiven, the barriers which separate us from a holy God are sent away. When you forgive someone, it is not based on what they deserve, but on grace freely extended.

It is here that we encounter the divine tension caused by our sin and resolved by our redemption. Forgiveness is a free act of grace, but redemption requires that a price be paid. How can both be true? First God's justice requires that a price be paid for redemption. He cannot simply "wink" at sin as if it doesn't matter. But God's mercy causes Him to pay the price for our forgiveness.

To illustrate this truth, the story has been told of the two college buddies who, after graduation, went separate ways and led quite different lives. One applied himself, becoming a lawyer and finally a judge. The other became a petty thief wandering from town to town and from scheme to scheme. One day the crook's behavior lands him in a small town courtroom. To his amazement he looks up to see his college friend behind the desk. Internally he smiles, thinking that his good friend couldn't condemn him. The case is presented, the facts are clear, the man is guilty. The judge pronounces the sentence mandated by the law and then, to the chagrin of the thief, exacts the largest fine possible. But then to everyone's surprise, the judge steps down from the bench, removes his robes, and pays the fine in full. Justice demands that he find his friend guilty, love and mercy demands that he pay his penalty in full.

This is precisely what God has done. Only One who was innocent of all sin could satisfy the demands of God's justice. "He made the One who did not know sin to be sin for us, so that we might become the righteousness of God in Him" (2 Corinthians 5:21). Jesus died in our place so that we could be transferred to His kingdom.

II. CHRIST AS REVEALER (V. 15-17)

In exalting the supremacy of Christ, Paul now declares that Jesus alone can fully reveal God. From creation to consummation, Jesus reveals God. If Jesus had not revealed God, no one would have ever been able to find Him. This is what is meant when Jesus declares, "I am the way, the truth, and the life. No one comes to the Father except through Me" (John 14:6). Paul uses two different images to help us to understand how Jesus reveals God.

HE IS THE IMAGE OF THE INVISIBLE GOD

Christ is the image of God in that He is the exact likeness of God. Like a mirror reflects the image before it, Jesus reflects God's very nature and character. In the same manner that the die stamps its image upon a coin, so God's image is stamped upon His Son. Listen to the writer of Hebrews as he writes about God's Son – "He is the radiance of His glory, the exact expression of His nature…" (Hebrews 1:3a).

The gospel writer John expressed it this way: "No one has ever seen God. The One and Only Son – the One who is at the Father's side – He has revealed Him" (John 1:18). In Christ the invisible God became visible. Christ is fully God. He shares the same substance, nature and character, and therefore He alone is qualified to fully reveal God. All of the so-called saviors and gurus who have ever been cannot reveal God because they do not bear His exact image. Only Christ can reveal God and, therefore, only Christ can redeem man.

HE IS THE FIRSTBORN OVER ALL CREATION

"Firstborn" denotes both *priority* in time and *supremacy* in rank. Christ stands before all creation in terms of time. He is fully God and therefore He has always been.

But the major emphasis is on supremacy. The firstborn child in a family was accorded certain rights and responsibilities not shared by the other children. He was the father's representative, and thus the management of the household was committed to him. Therefore Christ, as firstborn, has the management of all of creation. He is the Lord of creation. "...[A]ll things have been created through Him and for Him. He is before all things, and by Him all things hold together" (v. 16b-17).

Some who have read this passage superficially want to conclude that Jesus was part of God's creation and thus stands on a par with other prophets and teachers like Muhammad or Sai Baba. Such a reading distorts the context which clearly indicates that "all things have been created through Him and for Him." Far from being a part of the creation, He is the very One by whom the creation came into being.

III. CHRIST AS HEAD OF THE CHURCH (V. 18)

Paul's next affirmation may take us by surprise because many today have such a low opinion of the church. But this statement follows logically upon the affirmation that He is supreme over all creation. The church, as the assembly of the redeemed, is His new creation. The head of the church gives it both life and direction.

This affirmation concerning the church indicates first the intimacy of the union which exists between Christ and His people. He is the head, we are His body. Together we constitute one living unit, through which God desires to display His fullness. Further, it suggests that the church is a living organism made up of many diverse members connected to one another but infused with life by Christ Himself. That, in turn, leads to the dramatic conclusion that it is the earthly community through which Christ carries out His kingdom purpose and declares His redemptive plan. Thus to be "in Christ," one will of necessity be in His church, engaged and involved, for the advancement of His kingdom.

Paul further notes that "He is the beginning, the firstborn from the dead." Christ is the very origin and source of the life of the church. He is the wellspring from which it bubbles forth. Earlier Paul declared that He was firstborn over all creation. Now he declares that He is firstborn from the dead. The meaning is clear yet profound. Christ was the first to be raised from the dead, never to die again, and therefore He alone can offer eternal life to those who are "in Him."

Christ's resurrection from the dead declared with no uncertainty that His preeminence is universal. He is Lord of death and life. He is Lord of the old creation and the new. He had always been first – even before creation began – but His resurrection declared in the broadest possible arena that which has always been true. Here is how Paul words it in Romans 1:4 – "...and was established as the powerful Son of God by the resurrection from the dead according to the Spirit of holiness."

What does this mean? It means that neither redemption nor life exists apart from Him. It means that we are without excuse before Him. His resurrection made clear what has always been true concerning Him, and it opened to man the possibility of eternal life.

IV. CHRIST AS LORD OF RECONCILIATION (V. 19-22)

Paul concludes this wonderful hymn on the supremacy of Christ with a magnificent truth. "For God was pleased to have all His fullness dwell in Him, and through Him to reconcile everything to Himself by making peace through the blood of His cross – whether things on earth or things in heaven" (v. 19-20).

This is not only a profound truth but it is also an exclusive truth. Only Christ, who is the fullness of God, can reconcile fallen man to holy God. The heretics of Paul's day parceled out deity among various spirit beings filling the space between God and the world. All communication from man to God had to pass through these spirit beings. Man's quest was to discover the divine spark within. If any of this sounds vaguely familiar, then you must hear the truth.

Christ is not one of many divine beings, He is the one mediator, the only one capable of reconciling God to man because it was God's pleasure for His fullness to dwell in Him. The idea behind the word "reconcile" is to change from enmity to friendship. Man in his sin is at enmity with God. The Greek word here is a double compound which has intensive force. Christ can change your enmity with God so completely that He can remove the enmity forever.

How is this possible? Paul explains that He made peace for us "through the blood of His cross." This points us to the redemptive work of the cross. It underlines the sacrificial and substitutionary nature of Christ's death. The perfect Son of God died a sinner's death so that you could be reconciled to God. He paid the price you owed but could not pay so that you might have the life you desire but could never deserve.

Paul refuses to let the Colossians leave this in the theoretical realm. Look at verses 21 and 22. "And you were once alienated and hostile in mind because of your evil actions. But now He has reconciled you by His physical body through His death, to present you holy, faultless, and blameless before Him."

We were surprised when we walked by the open window of our new neighbor's house. Strange sounds and smells wafted from the window. Our neighbor was burning incense to a small statue. My wife became burdened for her and prayed for an opportunity to share. She openly talked to our neighbor about Jesus. To my wife's great surprise, she smiled and declared that she too loved Jesus. She even declared that she considered Him to be a "savior." My wife was confused. How could she then be burning incense to a false god? As their dialogues continued, she discovered that this woman worshipped Sai Baba; nonetheless, she was willing to accept that Jesus was *a savior*. Perhaps you notice the difference. For her Jesus was one among many, and not even the highest in rank.

Listen, dear friend, Jesus is not one among many saviors, nor one among many holy men. Jesus alone is redeemer. He alone can both satisfy God's justice and express His mercy. He alone can reveal God, for He alone is God. He alone is the head of the church, for He alone is the firstborn of the church. He alone can reconcile you to God, for in Him alone does all the fullness of God dwell bodily. He alone shed His blood on the cross to pay the penalty of your sin.

Will you today acknowledge your need and accept His forgiveness and be reconciled to God?

26

NICODEMUS

KELLY GREEN

Evangelist
Kelly Green Evangelistic Association
Brandon, Florida

IN JOHN 3:1-9 WE READ,

"There was a man of the Pharisees named Nicodemus, a ruler of Jews. This man came to Jesus by night and said to Him, 'Rabbi, we know that You are a teacher come from God; for no one can do these signs that You do unless God is with him.' Jesus answered and said to him, 'Most assuredly, I say to you, unless one is born again, he cannot see the kingdom of God.' Nicodemus said to Him, 'How can a man be born when he is old? Can he enter a second time into his mother's womb and be born?' Jesus answered, 'Most assuredly, I say to you, unless one is born of water and the Spirit, he cannot enter the kingdom of God. That which is born of the flesh is flesh, and that which is born of the Spirit is spirit. Do not marvel that I said to you, 'You must be born again.' The wind blows where it wishes, and you hear the sound of it, but cannot tell where it comes from and where it goes. So is everyone who is born of the Spirit." Nicodemus answered and said to him, 'How can these things be?'"

As an itinerant preacher, you can imagine that I fly a lot. I've already earned about 120,000 miles, and I'm working on 3,000,000 miles, which is probably, as far as I am concerned, 2,000,000 too many. But you're going to have to go through Atlanta if you live where I live in Tampa. To get anywhere you must go through Atlanta, there are just no ifs, ands or buts about it. Here's what is always perplexing to me – why is it when you have a 45-minute connection time, not an hour and a half, you land in Terminal A and you have to go to Terminal E? You never have an hour and a half to go to Terminal E. And it always bothers me that the end of the place you go on an airplane is called a terminal. Nevertheless, I was rushing through the airport one day and, sure enough, I had a close connection of only 35 minutes. I had to traverse at least two terminals, so I was really hustling. As I made my way down the escalator to a tram, above was an advertising billboard. And with not much time to catch your attention, the advertisers only show a picture and maybe a phrase, and that's it. Now remember, I am going down into the belly of the airport to catch the tram, and sure enough, I see this picture of a little precious infant swimming through the water. And the caption read, "Need to be born again?" And I thought, "How did Charles Stanley pull that off? I mean, he's got more influence than I realized!" Well, that sign had nothing to do with Charles Stanley. It was a marketing firm that was hired by a consulting company to send a message to those business people, "Hey, if your company needs a new start, we're here to help." And that company took a wonderful Bible passage about eternal life and they turned it into a marketing scheme to simply say, "We're here to help." Well, if you really want to know what that phrase "born again" means, then why don't we go to the dictionary where it first appears – God's Word. And let's look into the Bible and this interview that Jesus had with a man named Nicodemus. And let's find out what in the world does it mean to be born again.

Now I have quit asking people if they are Christians, at least in America. You want to know why? Because I found out that everyone is one. I mean, if you're not a Communist or a Muslim, I guess you qualify in some people's minds. This goes way past the cultural understanding of religion, because Nicodemus had it. And yet, if you have never been born again, God's Spirit is going to speak to you through the life of this religious man.

Look at what the Scripture says in verse 1, "There was a man of the Pharisees..." A Pharisee was a religious person; he was a leader. In today's terminology, he would be a Catholic priest or a Baptist preacher or maybe a Jewish rabbi. He was a spiritual advisor. So this man was a leader, and it says here, he "was a man of the Pharisees named Nicodemus." The Bible says three things about him here; what he did – a Pharisee – his name, and that he was a ruler of the Jews. We know he was well educated. The name "Nicodemus," interestingly enough, is not a Jewish name, although he was a Jewish leader. So here was a man who had a very diverse background. Here was a man of culture. He was a Jewish leader. Perhaps he had family that was socially connected.

Now look at verse 2. The Bible says, "This man came to Jesus by night..." Now you need to underscore those words, because we are going to come back to them in a just a little while. So the interview that Nicodemus had with Jesus took place at night. Nicodemus was probably a bit nervous. There is not a whole lot that intimidates me, but I remember the first time I had the privilege, many, many years ago, to be invited to go to Billy Graham's crusade in Philadelphia. Several of us got to sit behind him. Right before he got up to preach, about ten of us got to pray with him in a little private room that he uses before he comes out in the golf cart and gets on the platform. Jim Wilson, who is close to the family, asked me to pray for him, and that really spooked me. I mean, that intimidated me. Indeed, here was this incredible man of God, and there's not a lot I even remember about what I prayed, I just know I thanked

God that I got through it. And I hope I said, "In Jesus' name." It was a little bit intimidating standing there with this great man of God, because what is amazing is his humility. He just reeks with humility. And it intimidated me.

Well, you can imagine, Nicodemus had great fear and intimidation, because Jesus was not winning any popularity contests with the Pharisees. If you saw *The Passion Of The Christ*, enough said. And yet something brought his heart there to be with Jesus. There was something that brought his heart into the presence of Jesus. And so he did what you and I might have done when meeting someone that impressive and intimidating. He passed on a genuine compliment. Listen to what Nicodemus said to Jesus here, "Rabbi, we know that You are a teacher come from God, for no one can do these signs that You do unless God is with him." Do you know what that tells me? That statement tells me that, not only was Nicodemus complimenting Jesus (maybe just to calm his own nerves), but he used the word "we." He didn't say "I." So, Nicodemus probably had some buddies in the religious establishment. Maybe there were some closet Pharisees who were asking some hard questions about Jesus. Not all the Pharisees rejected Jesus, but they sure weren't going to come out and let themselves be known. So, Nicodemus was saying, "Some of us know that what You are doing is of God because nobody can do the signs and miracles that You do unless God is with him." So this religious leader recognized something unique and different about Jesus.

Now watch verse 3, because this is an interesting transition. Something intriguing takes place here. Here's Nicodemus complimenting Jesus, maybe soothing His nerves, and watch Jesus' reply in verse 3. Jesus answered and said to him, "Most assuredly, I say to you, unless one is born again, he cannot see the kingdom of God." Now here is what intrigues me about this verse – Jesus answered a question that Nicodemus wasn't even asking. Nicodemus didn't say one thing about spiritual stuff. But Jesus had His own agenda here. And

Nicodemus didn't know exactly what he wanted to talk about, but Jesus was now steering the conversation toward eternal things, because He was saying, "Nicodemus, you can't get into My kingdom unless you are born again."

Here was a well-educated Pharisee. Here was a man who knew the Torah. Here was a man who took pride in living by the law. Remember, between the book of Malachi and the book of Matthew, there are about 400 years. And during that interval, the religious system of the day had added about 1,500 man-made rules and commandments. And here was this man who was living under this unbelievable bondage. He was living by the law. He knew the Old Testament. And Jesus dropped a bomb in his lap. You know what that bomb was? That little phrase, "born again." He had not heard that before.

Now let me tell you what is about to happen next in verses 4 through 8. Jesus is going to dismantle much of what Nicodemus had learned. Jesus is going to put into perspective, in an eternal sense, what this man was searching for. Nicodemus did not even understand yet what Jesus was talking about, because he had never before heard the phrase "born again." Jesus rocked his world. And I watch this happen every time I preach the gospel.

There are times when the Spirit of God must tear down something before it can be rebuilt. I lived under the bondage of Mormonism for 19 years. You know why? Because I grew up in California; I didn't grow up in the Bible Belt. All I heard all my life was join the church, get baptized. Join the church, get baptized. Join the church, get baptized. So I did what my grandmother said. I joined a Mormon church. Then I joined a Lutheran Sunday School when I was 15 because there was a dad there who cared about teenagers. I didn't have a dad. My dad was a drug addict, and he left home when I was young. A friend of mine said, "Look, you need to come to our church, because at our church, this guy really likes teenagers."

So I showed up after partying all night, smoking dope. I showed up in this church with bell bottoms and no shoes on. My hair was in a ponytail. (That was back in the days when I had enough hair to have a ponytail!) I showed up in this guy's church with an attitude. I walked in, and he was gracious and kind to me. He didn't say to me, "Get your act together, clean up, you need to have shoes on, don't come into God's house without shoes." And so six weeks later, I joined a Sunday School class just because he was kind. At the same time, I went to Catholic mass to keep my step dad happy. So, was I religious? I had enough religion to sink the *Titanic*.

Well, Nicodemus was just the same. This guy could read the Bible backward and forward. He knew the Bible better than most of us in the Bible Belt, the Old Testament at least. Yet Jesus, in a gracious way, told Nicodemus, "What you have done is not enough." And that would rock this man's world.

Now, look at verse 4. Nicodemus said, "How...?" Now that's the important word. "How can a man be born again when he is old?" That's so amazing to me. This is a grown adult man. This isn't some child who hasn't attained the age of accountability yet. This is not only a grown adult man, this is a man of culture, a man of intelligence, a ruler of the Jews, a Pharisee. He hadn't understood what Jesus had just said. I mean, it went *whoosh*, right over his head. In essence, he said "You mean, Jesus, I've got to go back and go through that whole physical birthing process again?" Now he was really confused.

Now watch what Jesus did in verse 5. Jesus answered, "...unless one is born of water...." Now that statement is not referring to baptism; it is talking about the physical birthing process. Jesus had just said something that had rocked Nicodemus, so now Jesus was going to relate to him a little bit. He is saying – now look – "You've gotta be born of water" – the physical birthing process – "and of the Spirit." Here is what Jesus is saying, "Look, Nicodemus, there are two births. There is a physical birth that you have obviously experienced, and there is something else that you haven't experienced yet, a spiritual birth." And Jesus amplified that in verse 6, when He was saying, "Now look, Nic, that which is born of the flesh is flesh" – again talking about the physical birth – "and that which is born of the Spirit is spirit." God loved Nicodemus. Jesus just messed him up.

Someone said to me, "Well, you got saved at age 19 from a Mormon background." And I said, "Yeah." And they said, "What happened then?" And I replied, "Well, I got excommunicated. Now I am an apostate." Let me tell you something, when the Spirit of God starts moving, it's going to mess up all kinds of stuff in your life, especially religion. Nicodemus was confused. He might as well have just said, "Whewwww...You lost me there." Well, at least he was honest.

Look at verse 7, "Do not marvel that I said to you..." Now if you allow me to paraphrase; the conversation might have gone like this: "Nic, look, buddy, if you want to come into My kingdom, you've gotta be born again." And then Jesus injected something else that probably seemed a little mystical to Nicodemus' mind. Look at what He said in verse 8. It just gets worse. Jesus was saying, "The wind blows where it wishes. You can hear the sound of it, you've got no control over it, dude, but you can't tell where it comes or goes. You cannot tell the sound of it, you cannot tell where it comes or where it goes." And then Jesus said this, "So is everyone who is born of the Spirit." And instead of walking away and being frustrated and angry in verse 9 (it appears there again as in verse 4), Nicodemus asked, "How can these things be?"

We have a tendency as humans to be event-oriented. But God is not just event-oriented; God is more process-oriented. And God's process had begun in the life of Nicodemus. And the process began when he came to Jesus, because this man was risking something by coming and talking to Jesus. And now God was going to find out what he was willing to risk, what he was willing to take a chance on. Would this man be willing to take a chance on his reputation getting messed up? We don't know based on John, chapter 3, at least in these first eight verses, if Nicodemus was born again. We don't know. All we know in these first eight verses is that the Lord was speaking to him. He got the correct information. He got the truth, and he got his world rocked. He got some of those foundations stripped away. He got some of that garbage, and that junk, and that muck that had been placed in his head stripped away. He didn't get mad and walk away, but it does not say, in this chapter, that the man became a Christian. And yet I believe that I am going to see Nicodemus in heaven.

Nicodemus asked, "How can these things be? I don't understand it, Lord, but I'm still asking questions." You want to talk about the seeker movement? Here was a real seeker. I mean, if religion could do it, what was he doing there? If being good and keeping rules could do it, what was this guy doing talking to Jesus? There was a void in his life, and he knew it. And sometimes the only person who knows it is you and God. Something drove him to come into the presence of the Lord.

Now watch the process of God. It's the same process that you may be in. You've been in a process, and God's going to speak to you just like He did to Nicodemus.

The next place that we find Nicodemus in the Word is in John, chapter 7. Let me tell you what happened there. The chief priests and the Pharisees had their bellies full of Jesus. Now you have to understand that the chief priests and the Pharisees were very powerful people in the Jewish culture. The Romans, even though they were a secular society, had instilled religious leaders into the Jewish society. The temple police were not rent-a-cops. The temple police had authority given to them by the chief priests, and when the temple police came to arrest you, that was a serious matter. With that in mind, watch what happened. The chief priests sent the temple police out to get Jesus and bring him back. Look at verse 45 in chapter 7. The Bible says, "Then the officers came to the chief priests and Pharisees, who said to them, 'Why have you not brought Him?'" The Pharisees said, "Where is he? We sent you on a mission to get Jesus and bring him back. Why have you not brought him?" They were upset because those temple police were supposed to go get Jesus and bring him back, but they didn't do it. Now look at verse 46. The Bible says, "The officers answered, 'No man ever spoke like this man!'" WOW! Then the Pharisees answered and said, "Are you also deceived?" Now look at this religious pride. The Pharisees were saying, "Oh, you guys are deceived also. What is wrong with you?" In verse 48, you can just see them puff up like the NBC peacock. They just puffed up with all those feathers of pride. They asked, "What's wrong with you? *We're* the standard!" I mean, these guys were hacked off. However, look at verse 50. "Nicodemus (he who came to Jesus by night, being one of them)..." He was a Pharisee! He was a religious leader! He was with his peer group and most of them hated Jesus. There was no Bible Belt in those days. There was no comfort zone where everybody spoke the language of Zion. There was no oasis there for Christians. I mean, Jesus was despised among most of the Pharisees, and suddenly, one of the Pharisees, one of the religious rulers, Nicodemus, was standing up for Him. Look at verse 51, here is what Nicodemus said: "Does our law judge a man before it hears him and knows what he is doing?" Well, now, Jesus had nabbed the crowd, nabbed the cops, and now he'd nabbed one of their very own. Nicodemus was speaking up for him. And they answered and said to him, "Are you also from Galilee? Search and look, for no prophet has risen out of Galilee."

I once asked one of my seminary professors, Dr. Roy Fish, this question: "Doc, why did Nicodemus come at night?" He replied, "Yeah, there is a lot of theological jargon that explains why he came at night." But he said, "Let me just give you a down-to-earth practical reason." I said, "That's what I need." He said, "He came at night because he didn't want to be seen by his friends during the day talking to Jesus."

Maybe you've come to church before and sat in the back row. Maybe you've come and hidden in the balcony; but suddenly the wind has begun to blow. What happened? The process of God. This man came from looking over his shoulder, worrying about his friends seeing him. Now he's in front of his own peer group, who despised Jesus; they didn't want to have anything to do with Him. Suddenly, Nicodemus is standing up for Jesus and saying they weren't being fair. WOW! What happened? The wind started blowing.

The next place in Scripture we find Nicodemus is in John, chapter 19. After our Lord was crucified, the Bible says in the later part of that chapter, two men went to the Roman authorities, and here's what these two men said, "Give us the body of Jesus." The first man who said that was Joseph of Arimathea. Joseph of Arimathea was a very wealthy business merchant. He had earned a lot of money. I believe living in the community that he did, he knew Jesus was controversial. He knew that if he sided with Jesus, it might cost him some business. He knew it might cost him some family relationships. He knew it might cost him some fans. Now watch this, in a parallel passage, Joseph of Arimathea is called – this is interesting – a secret disciple, a closet Christian. Now I am not being a smart aleck, and I'm not making fun of him. You say, "What is a closet Christian?" You know, one day I was praying, and I said, "Lord, help me here. What is a secret disciple?" And the best way I could figure it out is this: a secret disciple is someone who has made a commitment of his life for Christ privately, but has not come out openly yet. So these guys have a lot to lose – their reputation, maybe their family's reputation, their health, their livelihood. Now the Bible doesn't give us a clear definition of what happened, but I believe that somewhere in the life of Joseph of Arimathea, he finally died to what the crowd thought; he finally died to his reputation. He was willing to take a risk because he must have committed his life to Jesus. You don't lay all that out on the altar unless something has been transformed. And when you get changed, it will not matter what everybody else says. You won't care what anybody else thinks, because as for me and my house, we're going to serve the Lord! And that's what this man did. He came out and he said in front of the whole world, "Give me the body of Jesus."

Well, I said there were how many men? Two. Guess who was the second dude? You got it, Nic. I usually don't title my sermons; but I've got a title for this one, "Nic at Night." Do you see the process of God here? Do you see the men seeking and reaching out? Taking a risk? What risk are you going to take today? What risk will you take today? Is this the day? I'm not sure. Nicodemus wasn't sure either, even though he was much better educated than we are. Not many are as well educated as this guy. He took a risk. What brought him to that point? He went from a private conversation in John 3:2, at night, to a small group meeting in front of his peers, and that must have been very, very difficult in John 7 to say to his friends, "You aren't being fair to him, as a matter of fact; we've got a double standard. We have certain ways, and the law says that we are not to judge a man, and we are not even giving Jesus half a chance." So now, watch this, in front of the whole world, he goes with Joseph and he says to the Roman authorities, "Give me His body."

But let me show you what happened after that. Look back at chapter 3, verse 9. Twice, in verse 4 and here in verse 9, Nicodemus says, "How...?" Let me ask you something: Are you at the "how" stage right now? or are you at the "what" stage? I mean, I don't know where you are. Are you still gathering information, or are you are you ready to ask the question, "God, what do I need to do? Show me how to do it." Now there are some folks at the "what" stage; they're gathering information. That's fine, that's great! God bless you. We are going to pray that you get past that. Because the next stage is tough; the next stage steps on pride. The next stage steps on the fear of man. The next stage does not care what anybody else thinks. The next stage is a desperate stage. The desperate stage of "God, I've gotta have You, and You alone, and I don't care what anyone else thinks."

Now watch what God showed me. Jesus is now going to answer the how-to. In verse 10, Jesus answered, and He said to Nicodemus, "Are you the teacher of Israel, and do not know these things?" He is sort of reprimanding him, and then Jesus said in verse 11, "Most assuredly, I say to you, we speak what we know and testify what we have seen, and you do not receive our witness." I mean, this is pretty strong. As one ol' boy once said, "This is as strong as dog's wood." But it is the truth; watch this. He said, "If I have told you earthly things and you do not believe, how will you believe if I tell you heavenly things? No one has ascended to heaven but He who came down from heaven, that is, the Son of Man who is in heaven." Finally, Jesus is going to say something and Nicodemus is going to respond, "Oh, finally, He said something I understand." The wind, the Spirit descended from heaven, the Son of Man, he got it...but the process of God is going to come to an abrupt conclusion. God is setting him up. You know what? Because God loves you, God is setting you up today. Verse 14 says, "And as Moses lifted up the serpent in the wilderness, even so must the Son of Man be lifted up, that whoever believes in Him should not perish but have everlasting life."

In verse 14, Nicodemus is going, "Oh, yeah, man." Remember this guy was a Jewish scholar, well educated. Nicodemus knew the book of Numbers. In the book of Numbers, chapter 21, the people had been disobeying God. They had been murmuring, rebelling, and God said to Moses, "Moses, here is what I want you to do..." It says right here in verse 6, "I'm so sick and tired of this complaining and disobeying, I'm going to send fiery serpents." So the Lord sent "fiery serpents" – Numbers 21:6 – "among the people" – now watch this – "and they bit the people, and many of the people of Israel died." Therefore, the people came to Moses, and they said, now watch this, "We have sinned, for we have spoken against the Lord and against you; pray to the Lord that He take away the serpents from us." So, thank God for the mercy of God. Moses prayed for the people. They recognized their sin. And those fiery snakes had come and gotten their attention. There was judgment. Then the Lord said to Moses (remember, Nicodemus knew this whole story, this is the story Jesus is referring to in John 3:14), "Make a fiery serpent, and set it on a pole; and it shall be that everyone who is bitten, when he looks at it, shall live." Now here we go, verse 9, Moses did what God said: "So Moses made a bronze serpent, and put it on a pole; and so it was, if a serpent had bitten anyone, when he looked at the bronze serpent, he lived."

Here's what happened. God said, "Okay, Moses, I'm gonna give My people" –here is grace in the Old Testament – "I'm gonna give My people another chance. They have admitted their sin, they have agreed. Now here is what I want you to do, Moses, I want you to take a long pole; and on that pole I want you to put a serpent which represents their sin, and that serpent is not just to be a snake or a serpent, but that serpent is to be a bronze serpent." Now why does the Bible call it a bronze serpent? Let me tell you why. Bronze, in the Old Testament, represents judgment. And here is what God is telling Moses to do, "You look out there at that pole, and that bronze serpent is my judgment upon their sin, and here's the deal, you tell them don't go giving their sacrifices, don't go killing more lambs, don't go sacrificing more birds, don't give me any turtle doves, you tell them by faith that those who hold that pole up, and those who by faith get past their good works, and get past all the other religious activity, by faith when they look at that pole, they shall be healed." Amen?

Now watch this, let's bring this puppy home. Let's land this 737 on this runway. You're about to get blessed. Watch this! Now you ask, "What's that got to do with Moses? And what's it got to do with me?" God has set you up, because there is a process of God's movement. Now why? Why?

I'm so glad that one time I obeyed God. I'm so glad God showed me this. It is so stinkin' simple. Watch. Why did Jesus drop John 3:14? Because he wanted Nicodemus to know, "I've given you a lot of information here that you haven't even gotten yet. But I'm going to plant another seed in your soul." Now watch. Do you remember *The Passion of the Christ?* Do you remember when they had our Lord nailed to that cross? Do you remember seeing Mary, his mama? Broken-hearted, shocked, amazed – there was her baby. And then there was the other Mary, and there was John out there. And the second time I saw it, I looked, and I said, "Who's that other guy at the cross?" There were a bunch of them. I believe it was Nicodemus. I'm going to tell you what happened. God planted a seed in Nicodemus' mind. From John 3 to John 7:50 to John 19, the wind started blowing.

Now watch when the wind blows. One more time the wind's gonna blow; and now it's going to change his life. Because I believe with all my heart, as Nicodemus came and as he looked at the cross, I believe the process and grace of God came and crashed in, because when he looked up and he saw Jesus; he finally understood what verse 15 meant: You can't believe until you see the Son of Man high and lifted up. And there is judgment on sin, and Numbers 21 has now come to fruition on the cross of Christ. And when He took our sin, and when He died for our sin, finally the Son of Man purchased our salvation, and I believe that at the cross, that's when Nicodemus finally said, "That's the Son of Man. That's what it means to live by faith. He took my punishment. He is my Redeemer. He is my Lord. He is my Savior. No wonder He is dead. Give me the body of Jesus. Give me His body!"

So what are you worried about? What are you risking? What are you willing to lay out for Him? What reputation do you want to die to? You've gotta come to Jesus by faith.

27

WHAT TO DO WHEN THE STORM COMES

DR. FRED LUTER, JR.

Senior Pastor

Franklin Avenue Baptist Church

New Orleans, Louisiana

I INVITE YOUR ATTENTION TO MARK CHAPTER 4:35-41. Something happened in my life and the life of our city that changed me forever. I have cried more these last eight weeks than I have in the 48 years of my life. I have questioned God. I have asked God why. If the truth be shared, I knew there were some things that God was not pleased with, not really excited about in New Orleans. But I said, "God, why not just take out some of those things? Why not take out Bourbon Street? Why not take out the strip clubs? Why the whole city? We had a great city. We had an awesome city. We had great schools like Xavier, Denner, Tulane, Mayolia, but now they're all gone. We had great restaurants, great businesses. We had great churches. But now the whole city is just gone — devastated.

And as I looked at the news reports each and every night, I just couldn't believe this was happening to the city I grew up in. To see that all gone in a matter of days literally brought tears to my eyes. But it got to the point where I began asking God why. God, I don't understand this. I don't understand You destroying the entire city. All the churches. All the schools. I was having a very difficult time with it.

As often happens when I ask God questions, He oftentimes will share with me a passage of scripture that will someway, somehow make sense and answer my "why" questions – to make sense of the things that I may not understand about what's happening on this side. But God in His mercy and His grace and in His sovereignty always gives me the answer to the things that I really don't have the answer to.

Now I want to share that with you from Mark chapter 4. It is a passage of scripture that God used to answer my "why" questions during this time of storms. During this time of Katrina and Rita. During this time of displacement of hundreds and thousands of citizens from the city of New Orleans. One of the reasons He gave it to me was because I believe He wanted me to share it with other members of the body of Christ.

Mark chapter 4, verses 35-41, is a very familiar passage of scripture. It talks about a storm and how that these individuals had a very difficult time dealing with storms in their lives, despite the fact that they had a relationship with God and knew God. I want to talk to you about how that if it happened to them, it can happen to us. It can happen to anybody. The Bible says...

And the same day, when the even was come, he saith unto them, Let us pass over unto the other side. And when they had sent away the multitude, they took him even as he was in the ship. And there were also with him other little ships. And there arose a great storm of wind, and the waves beat into the ship, so that it was now full. And he was in the hinder part of the ship, asleep on a pillow: and they awake him, and say unto him, Master, carest thou not that we perish? And he arose, and rebuked the wind, and said unto the sea, Peace, be still. And the wind ceased, and there was a great calm. And he said unto them, Why are ye so fearful? how is it that ye have no faith? And they feared exceedingly, and said one to another, What manner of man is this, that even the wind and the sea obey him?

Jesus said to them, "Why are you so fearful? How is it that you have no faith?" I want to preach on this subject: "What To Do When The Storm Comes."

Storms are bound to happen to every believer at one time or another. Every child of God sooner or later in his life will face storms. It doesn't matter how long you have been saved. It doesn't matter how long you have been born again. It doesn't matter what age you are. You can be an adoring child or tender teenager. In your tempting twenties, your tantalizing thirties, you firm forties, your fading fifties, your sorry sixties, your free seventies, your achin' eighties, or your restless nineties. It doesn't matter your age. Sooner or later, storms will happen to you. It really doesn't matter your vocation or your profession. You can be a schoolteacher like my daughter and an attorney like my wife, a business owner, a homemaker, a preacher, a carpenter, an electrician or a judge. It doesn't really matter. Sooner or later, storms are going to happen to you. It doesn't matter your denomination. You can be Southern Baptist, National Baptist, American Baptist, Four Gospel Church of Christ, Church of God in Christ, Church of God, or maybe you are like a number of folks that I pastored for years in New Orleans, Bedside Baptists. But sooner or later, storms will happen to you. It doesn't matter what race you are. You can be Anglo, Hispanic, Asian, Indian, African-American, but sooner or later, my brothers and my sisters, I promise you, storms will happen to you. Somewhere along your Christian journey, somewhere between the time that you were born and the time that you die, sometime during the time that God breathes life into you and 'til the time that you go home to be with glory, somewhere along your life a storm will come your way. Somewhere from the time that you are born on this earth until the time that you die, heartaches, trouble, and pain will knock at your door. And to be honest with you, my concern is not that we have storms. My concern is not that we have trouble. My concern is not that we have discrimination. My concern is what will you do when the storm comes?

The issue is not whether we will have storms, not whether we will have tough times, not whether we will have troubles and trials in our lives, but what will we do when the storm comes.

I have discovered that in spite of all the scriptures we know by memory, in spite of all the past miracles of God in our lives, in spite in all the testimony we have heard through the years, I have discovered that many of us still don't know what to do when the storms of life are raging. Many of us don't know what to do when the troubles of life are knocking at the door.

So the question of the hour is…how do you handle storms? How do you handle troubles in your life? No, all of you didn't go through Hurricane Katrina. You didn't go through Hurricane Rita. But you have had some storms in your life. How do you handle the storm of a divorce? How do you handle the storm of an unfaithful spouse? How do you handle the storm of an unexpected death? How do you handle the storm of sickness? How do you handle the storm of jealousy and envy and financial hardships? How do you handle tough times in your life? Not somebody else's life, but your life. Not somebody else's marriage, but your marriage. Not somebody else's son, not somebody else's daughter, your son or your daughter. Your home, your life. How do you handle the tough times in your life?

Single person, how do you handle those times in your life when the enemy is coming to get you? How do you handle tough times on your job? How do you handle tough times in the church? How do you handle those times when things are not the way they should be? When it is difficult to worship? How do you handle tough times in your life when the deacons are devilish? And when the trustees get tricky. When the choir gets cranky. When the members get messy.

When the ushers act ugly. When the preacher gets pushy. How do you handle those tough times in your life?

Do you know what I have discovered? I have discovered that when trouble comes our way...when the storms of life are in a rage...I have discovered that faith is the first area that the enemy works on. I need to be candid; when I was sitting there on a couch in Birmingham, Alabama, watching my city on television...watching the house that my wife and I had built ten years ago...watching the church that we were able to build and use to touch so many lives across our city...as I watched the horrendous things done there at the Superdome and at the Convention Center, I must admit that my faith was shaken. The enemy came to me and sat next to me on that sofa and said, "Preacher, where is your God now? Preacher, how could a loving God allow something like this to happen? Preacher, where is your faith now?" I must admit, he had me going there, because I began to question God and ask, "Why?" I began to say to God, "God, this is not right." I began to ask, "God, why didn't You do anything?" "God, why didn't You hold back the rain?" "Why didn't You hold back the levees?" "God, why a Hurricane?" "God, why is this happening?" My faith was shaken, even though I have been preaching the faith for 19 years. This preacher had faith for 19 years. I have been telling people to have faith in God, and there I was on a couch in Birmingham, and my faith was shaken. Tears were running down my eyes and I was wondering, "God, why didn't you do something?"

I have discovered that when tough times and storms come in your life, faith is the first area that the enemy works on. It reminds me of a story I heard years ago of this man who fell into this bottomless pit. And all he was able to do was to hold on to a branch. He looked down and realized he couldn't get out of this hole. He looked up and saw that he couldn't climb out. So he cried, "Hey, is anybody up there?" Nothing. He cried even louder, "Hey, is anybody up there?"

Still nothing. "Hey, is anybody up there?" After a while, a voice responded and said, "I'm here." And the guy says, "Who is it?" The voice says, "This is God." The desperate man yells back, "I knew you were coming to my rescue. God, I knew you would save me."

God said, "Do you believe I can save you?"

"Yes, God I believe you can save me."

God said, "Do you believe I can deliver you?"

"Yes, Lord!"

God said, "Do you trust me?"

"Yes, Lord!"

God said, "Do you have faith?"

"Yes, Lord! I have faith."

God said, "Then let go of the little branch."

There was a long silence. Then after a while, a voice came back, "Hey, is there *anybody else* up there?"

Oh, I don't understand it all, but I have discovered that every now and then God will allow you and me to get into a situation, and He'll say, "Let go of the branch." Every now and then God wants to see if you really trust Him by faith. I hear you preach about faith, but do you believe it? I hear you singing about faith, but do you believe it? I hear you teaching about faith, but do you believe it? Every now and then, God will allow us to get in situations and then He calls us to let go of the branch! Let go of the branch! Let go of the branch!

I have discovered that fear is the opposite of faith. If the enemy can get you to fear, he can get you to doubt. And I must admit that fear came across my mind. What am I going to do now? I don't have a church to pastor anymore. I am unemployed. I still have a son in college. We still have bills to pay. God, what am I going to do? What is my wife going to do? What's our church family going to do? What about the individuals who have no one else to look after them? God, what are we going to do? At that moment, my faith was replaced by fear. And when fear comes into your life, the devil can get you to doubt. If he can get you to doubt, he can get you to doubt the Word of God.

That's what is happening here in this text. These disciples didn't know what to do when the storms of life were raging. They didn't know what to do when tough times came their way. These disciples didn't know what to do when troubles knocked on their door.

Now keep in mind, these brothers had been with Jesus for several years now. They had seen his miracles. They had heard his great sermons. They knew there was nothing too hard for God to do. Yet, in spite all that their eyes had seen, yet in spite of all the things that their ears had heard, these disciples of Jesus Christ didn't know what to do when the storms of life where raging.

My brothers and my sisters, if it can happen to them, if it can happen to me, it can happen to you. So I want to show you three things you must never forget when the storm comes into your life. These are the things that God had to remind me of there in my daughter's apartment in Birmingham. Everything that I have been trying to share with our members as I am traveling every Sunday now across the country, meeting and greeting, crying and hugging with all the displaced members of our church. Three things we must never ever forget in the midst of our storms. Three things you must never forget when tough times come to your life.

First of all, when the storms of life are raging…

REMEMBER THE PROMISES OF JESUS.

Look at verses 35 of Mark chapter 4. The Bible says on the same day, when the evening had come, Jesus said unto them, "Let us go over unto the other side." Jesus said before He went to sleep, let us cross over to the other side. Beloved, when the storms of life are raging, remember the promises of Jesus. Let me tell you a secret: Jesus didn't come to drown. As a matter of fact, He couldn't drown. He had to be betrayed by Judas. He couldn't drown. He hadn't been denied by Peter yet. Jesus couldn't drown, because He had not gone through the unjust court system. And then He couldn't drown because He had to walk up that hill called Calvary and put nails in His hands and nails in His feet. He couldn't drown because He hadn't cried those seven cries from the cross – the first being, "Father forgive them for they know not what they do." He couldn't drown, because He had not cried that second cry from the cross, "Today thou shall be with me in paradise." He couldn't drown, because He hadn't cried the third cry from the cross, "Woman, behold thy son. Son, behold thy mother." He couldn't drown, because he hadn't cried that fourth cry from the cross, "*Eloi, Eloi, lama sabachthani?* My God, my God, why have thou forsaken me?" He couldn't drown. He had not cried that fifth cry from the cross, "I thirst." He couldn't drown, because he had not cried that sixth cry from the cross, "It is finished!" He couldn't drown, because he had not cried that seventh cry from the cross, "Father, into your hands I commit my spirit." He couldn't drown. He couldn't drown!

They had not yet put him in shawls and laid him in a tomb. He couldn't drown. He had not stayed dead all night Friday night, all night Saturday night. He couldn't drown. He had not arisen on Sunday morning yet with power in his hands. That's why He asked, "Why are you fearful?" He couldn't drown, so that is why He said, "Boys let are go to the other side!"

When tough times come in your life, when storms come in your life, remember the promises of Jesus. God's Word is full of promises for his children when the storms come. Psalm 37:25 says, "I have been young, and *now* am old; yet have I not seen the righteous forsaken, nor his seed begging bread." That's a promise!

Psalm 34:19 says, "Many *are* the afflictions of the righteous: but the LORD delivereth him out of them all." That's a promise!

Isaiah 26:3 says, "Thou wilt keep *him* in perfect peace, *whose* mind *is* stayed *on thee*: because he trusteth in thee." That's a promise!

Isaiah 40:31 says, "But they that wait upon the LORD shall renew *their* strength; they shall mount up with wings as eagles; they shall run, and not be weary; *and* they shall walk, and not faint." That's a promise!

Isaiah 43:2 says, and this one is special, "When thou passest through the waters, I *will be* with thee; and through the rivers, they shall not overflow thee: when thou walkest through the fire, thou shalt not be burned; neither shall the flame kindle upon thee." That's a promise!

Isaiah 54:17 says, "No weapon that is formed against thee shall prosper." That's a promise!

Matthew 11:28 says, "Come unto me, all *ye* that labour and are heavy laden, and I will give you rest." That's a promise!

Romans 8:28 says, "And we know that all things work together for good to them that love God, to them who are the called according to *His* purpose." That's a promise!

Philippians 4:6-7 says, "Be careful for nothing; but in every thing by prayer and supplication with thanksgiving let your requests be made known unto God. And the peace of God, which passeth all understanding, shall keep your hearts and minds through Christ Jesus." That's a promise!

Romans 8:38-39 says, "For I am persuaded, that neither death, nor life, nor angels, nor principalities, nor powers, nor things present, nor things to come, Nor height, nor depth, nor any other creature, [not even Hurricane Katrina!] shall be able to separate us from the love of God, which is in Christ Jesus our Lord. Nothing, nothing. Nothing. Nothing. Nothing!

Ya'll step right up for the love of God which is Christ Jesus, our Lord!

Thinking about God's promise, a songwriter said it best, "I've seen the lightening flashing, I've heard the thunders rolling and I've felt the breakers dashing, trying to conquer my soul. But I've heard the voice of Jesus, telling me to still fight on." Why should I? "For he's promised never to leave me, never to leave me alone." That is why he said, "Boys, let's go to the other side." Oh ladies and gentleman, brothers and sisters, when the storms of life were raging, remember the promises of Jesus.

The good news is the second thing in the text. When trouble comes into your life, when storms come into your life, when difficult times come into your life...not right across the street...not somebody else's family, but your family...not somebody else's home...but your home...not somebody else's marriage...but your marriage...when tough times call, you must not only know the promises of Jesus, but secondly...

REMEMBER THE PRESENCE OF JESUS

Look what the Bible says there in verse 36 of Mark chapter 4, "Now when they had left the multitude. They took Jesus alone in the boat." Notice Jesus was right there in the boat. Ladies and gentlemen, notice what Jesus did *not* say. He did *not* say, "Listen guys, this is a great crusade and you've sung like you've never sung before. You all planned like you have never planned before. Listen guys, you pack up the equipment and get ready for our next crusade. I am tired and I am just whipped. I have got to take a nap. You all pack it up. I'll just walk on the water and meet you on the other side..." He could have said that, but He didn't. The Bible says, that He was right in the boat with the disciples.

Oh, ladies and gentleman, when the storms of life come your way, not only remember the promises of Jesus. But remember the presence of Jesus. If you have accepted Him into your life, if you have asked Him to be the Lord and

Savior of your life, guess what? He's living in you. I don't care what you are going through. No matter what the issue is…no matter what the stronghold is…no matter what the set back is…no matter what the sickness is…if you have accepted Him into your life, He is living in you. He's walking with you. He is talking with you. His grace is with you. His mercy is with you.

But don't just take my word, there are some witnesses here today who can testify about his presence. Ask Noah about His presence, and he will tell you that when God had him build the ark, everybody was laughing at him, but God's presence was with him. Ask Moses about his presence. The Red Sea was in front of him, the Egyptian army behind him, and mountains were on both sides of him. And God's presence was with him. Ask young David about his presence as he went up against that giant, Goliath, with just a sling shot and some rocks, and God's presence was with him. Ask Gideon about His presence and how God reduced his army from 32,000 to 300. Ask Elijah about His presence, as he stood on Mount Carmel against 450 false prophets. Ask Shadrach, Meshach, and Abednego about God's presence as they were thrown into the fiery furnace. And they said, "Wait a minute! didn't we send three? Yes! But wait a minute, I see *four!* The fourth looks like the Son of God!

He will be there with you! Not only David, not only Moses, not only Gideon, not only Elijah, not only Shadrach, Meshach, and Abednego, but I promise you, there is somebody here today who can tell you about His presence.

Oh, my brothers and my sisters, when you thought you were down and out, God came in just in the nick of time and rescued you and gave you something that you didn't deserve. He gave you another chance. I thank God for another chance and that He came just in the nick of time. That's why we sing Amazing Grace. Not just grace. *Amazing* Grace. How sweet the sound that saved a wretch like me. I once was lost but now am found. I was blind but now

I see! His presence is with you.

I should be dead sleeping in my grave, but God gave me something I didn't deserve. He gave me another chance. His presence is with you. Whatever you are going through…whatever the issue…whatever the stronghold…whatever attack of the enemy, remember the presence of Jesus Christ.

There is one last thing. What do you do when the storm comes? What do you do when tough times come in your life, in your marriage, in your home, in your family, in your church? Remember the promises of Jesus. Let's go to the other side. Remember the presence of Jesus. Remember He was right there in the boat. And if you have accepted Him into your life, He is living in you. No matter what the situation or storm you are dealing with. And now there is one more thing…

REMEMBER THE POWER OF JESUS

Look at verses 37-41 of Mark chapter 4. "A furious squall [think Hurricane Katrina] came up, and the waves broke over the boat, so that it was nearly swamped. Jesus was in the stern, sleeping on a cushion. The disciples woke him and said to him, 'Teacher, don't you care if we drown?' He got up, rebuked the wind and said to the waves, 'Quiet! Be still!' Then the wind died down and it was completely calm."

Look at verse 40 – very interesting: He said to his disciples, "What's up with ya'll?" Now that is the first mood of translation. "Why are you so afraid? Do you still have no faith? What's up with ya'll? 'Why are you so fearful? How is it that you have no faith?"

Ladies and gentleman, use your imagination. Picture the scene if you will. Jesus is tired from His last crusade. He is physically drained. He is so tired that the Bible says He brought his own cushion and He is sleeping in the boat while a storm comes raging. The winds begin to blow, and the boat begins to rock from side to side. Waves are coming down and water starts coming into the boat. And listen to these disciples: "Doesn't He care if we parish? How can He sleep? We are about to drown! Why doesn't He do something?" Can you see John on the boat? Peter looked at John and said, "John, why don't you wake Him up – you're His favorite. He likes you."

John said to Peter, "You are always up there talking. You have a big mouth. Why don't you wake Him up? I got rebuked yesterday, and I am not going to get rebuked no more."

Peter looked at Andrew. Andrew looked at Thomas. Thomas looked at Bartholomew. And they all said, "Water! there is water in the boat. Why doesn't He do something? We are about to drown! Doesn't He care if we parish?"

Ladies and gentlemen, don't point a finger at these boys, because if the truth were told, this was me less than seven weeks ago. As I was watching the newscasts about my home, my church, our city, I was just in wonder. I said, "God why don't You do something? People are dying. They are drowning. God, don't You care about our city. Why don't You do something?" This is the same scene in this passage.

Now what amazes me is that these were the same boys who, just a few years earlier, followed Jesus by faith. Jesus said, "Come, follow me. You, follow me. You. You. You follow me." And the Bible says they dropped everything, and they didn't even ask how much there were going to make. Didn't even ask how many hours do I have to work. Didn't even ask if there are benefits in this job. They dropped everything and followed Jesus. That moment He was healing the sick, they were all right there. That moment He made the lame walk, they were all right there. That moment He was feeding them with fish and chips, they were all right.

But now listen to their cry: "Why doesn't He do something? Doesn't He care if we perish? Doesn't He know we are about to drown?" In the midst of their bickering, in the midst of their arguments, in the midst of their faithlessness, Jesus wakes up. He was wiping the stuff from His eyes. He was probably yawning. He asks the question we all ask when we go on a trip, "Hey guys, are we there yet?"

He looked at John. John looked at Andrew. Andrew looked at Bartholomew. Jesus said, "What a minute. I asked a question. Are we there yet?" The disciples reply, "You see, You don't understand. The storm began to rage. And the water..." Jesus replied, "What a minute. Time out! Guys, answer my question. Are we there yet?" Again the disciples reply, "But sir, You don't understand. The boat began to..." And Jesus responded again, "Wait a minute! Did not I promise you before I went to sleep that we were going to the other side? Have I ever promised you something and it didn't come to pass? Am I invisible? I am right here in the boat with you. My presence is here. I didn't leave you guys. I didn't walk on the water and leave you by yourself. I am right here with you." And he looked up at them and said, "Peace, be still." And the winds ceased. The world obeyed God. Then Jesus looked at those disciples and said, " Why are you so fearful? How is it that when your faith is tested you forget everything I have taught you? How is it when the storms were raging, your faith was shaken? How is it when your faith is really put to the test, you flunk the test? Why are you so fearful? How is it that you have no faith? Peace!" And the winds ceased.

Ladies and gentleman, never forget that Jesus can bring peace to the storms in your life. He can bring peace to your situation. He can bring peace to your circumstance. Never ever forget about the power of Jesus. The power of the Holy Ghost has come upon you, and you shall be His witnesses in Jerusalem, and in Judea, and in Samaria, and to the end of the end of the age.

Oh my brothers and my sisters, Jesus can bring power in your life. Power to walk right. Power to talk right. Power to sing right. Power to pray right. Power to preach right. Power to say right. He can give you power that the world can't give you and the world can't take away. Oh yes He can! He has power over your situation.

I know we have had a tough time. We have been called refugees. We have been called evacuees. We have been called all kind of "ees." But remember when the tough times come in your life, when the storms come, remember the promises of Jesus, to get you to the other side. Remember the presence of Jesus. He is living in your life and heart. And remember the power of Jesus. He gives peace in whatever your situation may be.

I remember growing up in the city of New Orleans. I tell you one of my favorite pastimes was Saturday morning television shows. And one of my favorite shows was Superman. How many of you remember Superman? I am talking about Clark Kent. He looked kind of nerdy. Him and Erkle could be brothers. You know they are the nerdy kind of guys. They had the glasses and hat and the coat on. And if trouble ever comes to the *Dailey Planet*, if Perry White gets in trouble or Jimmy Olson gets in trouble or if Lois Lane gets in trouble, Clark would dash to the nearest telephone booth. He would take off his tie. He would take off his glasses. He would take off his hat. And anybody going to the telephone booth would see him coming out as Superman. He came out with that red and blue outfit and that big old "S" on his chest. Superman. Faster than a speeding bullet. More powerful than a locomotive. Able to leap tall buildings in a single bound. SUPERMAN!

What Clark Kent could not do, Superman could...because he was changed and he was transformed. Well, I want to tell everybody that when tough times come, when storms come, when difficult times come...you don't have a phone booth you can go inside, but as a child of God, you have a prayer closet. And I tell you to go into your prayer closet. I tell you to get on your knees and tell

God all about your troubles. And tell God all about your storms. Tell God all about the things that you are going through. Just a little talk with Jesus will make it right. And you will come out of that prayer closet, and you won't have on a red and blue outfit and an "S" on your chest. Yet you can say, "I'm saved! I'm saved! You have an "S" to say I am sanctified. I'm somebody. I am special. I'm a soldier in the army of the Lord. Yes, a soldier. I am a survivor. I am a survivor. I am a survivor!

Hang in there church. Hang in there brothers. Hang in there sisters. You are going to make it. You are going to make it. You are going to make it. YOU ARE GOING TO MAKE IT. YES! You are going to make it. And the reason you are going to make it is that when the storms show up, so does the Savior.

28

FUTURE CHURCH IN THE END TIMES

DR. RONNIE W. FLOYD

Senior Pastor

First Baptist Church

Springdale, Arkansas

ESCHATOLOGY IS THE STUDY OF LAST THINGS. Therefore, when you hear that term "eschatological" or "eschatology," you will understand that it is a term relating to the last events of the world.

However one interprets last things, one cannot ignore the key verse in the Revelation. It's found in chapter 1, verse 19. It says these words, "Write the things which you have seen, and the things which are, and the things which will take place after this."

What I am going to do is give you an image. I'm going to give you a graph that might help discover how you will interpret last things in the eyes of the book of Revelation. For example, we start with the term "what you have seen." This is found in Revelation 1:9-20. Remember what the Revelation said? John saw the exalted, glorified, Jesus Christ while he was exiled on the Isle of Patmos.

Then you will notice "the things which are." You find that in Revelation 2:1-3:22. You see that those are the pictures of the churches which represent the church age.

Then you find the third category – again going back to the interpretive verse of chapter 1, verse 19, "the things which will take place after this." So from Revelation 4:1-22:21, you find the "things which will take place after this."

Now let's attempt to break down some of those major moments in last times concerning the things which will take place after this. Well, we find and discover the heavenly vision. We find that in Revelation 4:1-5:14. And then we move into the tribulation period, which lasts for seven years. We find that in Revelation 6:1-19:21. In those chapters there are two periods of the tribulation. There is the initial tribulation, the first three and one-half years, which you find in Revelation 6:1-14:20. Then you find the second part of the tribulation. It is called the great tribulation, which means it is greater than the first three and one-half years, and we find that in Revelation 15:1-19:21. After the tribulation, we will discover the millennial kingdom. This is what we call the 1,000-year reign of Jesus Christ on this earth. That section is found in Revelation 20:1-10. And then we come to the Great White Throne Judgment. That is not the judgment of the saved, but the judgment of the lost. We discover that in Revelation 20:11-15. Finally, we come to the new heaven presented. This is when eternity begins, Revelation 21:1-22:21.

As you consider this timeline, where is the church in the end times? Where is the church in the seven-year tribulation period? Many scholars believe that the church will go through this seven-year tribulation. I just don't think that dog will hunt. So what does it mean? Does the church go through the seven-year tribulation period? I want to describe for you the future church in the end times, answering that question, "Where is the church in the end times?"

I believe you have in the Revelation 4 what I am calling the Supernatural Transition. You find it in Revelation 4:1-2. These two verses serve as our key text. "After these things..." After what things? The heavenly vision. After what things? After the age of the church, "I looked," John said, "and behold, a door standing open in heaven. And the first voice which I heard was like a trumpet..." Remember that – a trumpet. The text continues, "...speaking with me, saying, 'Come up here, and I will show you things'" – notice this phrase –

"'which must take place after this.'" After an event, after a series of moments, the heavenly vision, the age of the church. Then he tells us in verse 2, "Immediately I was in the Spirit; and behold, a throne set in heaven, and One sat on the throne." After the vision of the exalted and glorified Christ, Jesus walked among the seven churches in the Revelation, representing Jesus' involvement in the church age. And notice what He said in Revelation 4:1: "I looked." This is a new vision coming upon John, something he had not seen before. I believe it is a fulfillment of the final words of Revelation 1:19, when the Scripture says "the things which will take place after this." In other words, those things are now about to take place.

And he saw a door standing open, indicating that John, when he looked up, saw the door wide open. And the trumpet was speaking like an invitation trumpet, "Come up here." Come up where? Where the aliens live? Are there any aliens? Is there such a thing? No. He was saying, "Come up here," meaning "Come up here to heaven and I'm going to show you the things which will take place after this." In other words, He was saying, "John, come up here and I am going to show you the end of the world."

John was in this ecstatic experience. And as he was experiencing this spiritual ecstasy, this spiritual trance, he saw a throne set in heaven. John was having a vision of what heaven would be like. And right here in the midst of this vision occurring, he sees Jesus on the throne. When Jesus is on the throne, He is controlling and He is ruling.

This world will go into complete chaos one day, but you had better remember that Jesus is still ruling, and Jesus is still controlling, even in the midst of that chaos. What you see here in the Scripture is the supernatural transition. The supernatural transition occurs in the church. John is a spokesman of the church, representing that the church age was being closed in the Revelation, and some new era now exists.

There are many learned scholars who debate Revelation. But I want to share with you that regardless of what their view would be about the church's involvement before the tribulation, during the tribulation, or at the end of the tribulation, they must deal with this fact. Here is the hole in much of their theologies. Here is the fact: The church is absent from Revelation 4:1 all the way through Revelation 19:7. You never see the church mentioned. Therefore, you cannot explain that away and just say, "Well, he meant this or he meant that." No, it's a fact. The church is not mentioned. In fact, in Revelation 19:7, John doesn't even use the word "church." He references the Marriage Supper of the Lamb. But then the word "church," the literal word church, does not appear until Revelation 22:16.

So the question is, "What has happened to the church?" I mean, the church was prominent in chapters 1, 2 and 3, until chapter 4, verse 1. Obviously something is going on. What? Where is the church in the end times? Well, let me put it this way. I believe in the rapture of the church. What does that mean, the rapture of the church? We find it talked about in Revelation 4:1-2. Then we find the apostle Paul talking about in 1 Thessalonians 4:16-17.

There is a transition that goes on, something occurs, and I want to say that it is a supernatural transition. The church has been raptured. The church has been caught up. The church has been snatched away. What Jesus was saying in Revelation 4:1-2, because it was written to the churches of the Revelation, Jesus was saying, "Church, come up here, and I'm going to show you the events of the end. Come up here, and I want to show you what it is going to be like when the end actually begins."

What is the church doing in heaven? While the seven-year tribulation is going on, what is the church doing? Well, I want to point out three things to you...

I believe the church during that seven years is going through, first of all, the Judgment Seat of Jesus Christ. Every one of us will stand before Christ. If you do know the Lord, you will answer to God for your life and what you spent your life doing, even though you know the Lord. If you do not know the Lord, you will go through what is called the Great White Throne Judgment following the seven years of living hell on this earth, if you even make it through that, which you probably won't.

Also, what will the church be doing? The church will be preparing for and experiencing the Marriage Supper of the Lamb. The Marriage Supper of the Lamb is that glorious experience when we as a church have now gone through the judgment, experienced a little bit of heaven, and are then being cleaned up and robed in robes of righteousness, our garments are as white as snow, and then one day, thanks be to God, one day Jesus is going to be introduced as the bridegroom to us, the church being the bride. Remember what Paul said, that bride will be given to Him "*not having spot or wrinkle...*" That is some kind of bride!

Then what else will you do in heaven for those seven years? You're going to have the privilege of experiencing the Foretaste of Heaven. The Bible tells us in 1 Thessalonians 4:16-17, the reference I talked about a moment ago. Listen to what God says, "For the Lord Himself will descend from heaven with a shout, with the voice of an archangel, and with the trumpet of God. And the dead in Christ will rise first. Then we who are alive and remain shall be caught up together with them in the clouds to meet the Lord in the air. And thus we shall always be with the Lord." And if we are fortunate enough to be living when the Lord so comes, then we who are alive and remain, shall be caught up together. About the time they are coming out of the grave, God is going to catch you up just in time to go with them.

And we will "meet the Lord" – where? – "in the air." And here is the key phrase – "And thus we shall always be with the Lord." From the moment we go to be with the Lord, then never again, never again, never again will we be separated from the Lord in the history of all of eternity.

The Greek word for "caught up" that you read there in 1 Thessaloanians 4 is the Greek word *harpazo,* which means "snatched up." It is translated "caught up." It could also be translated "snatched away," meaning that one day we are going to be snatched away. We are going to be caught up. The word "rapture" is not found in the New Testament, but it is the concept of being caught up or snatched away. So where does the word rapture come from? That's a very good question. Let me attempt to answer that. Those who translated the Greek New Testament into Latin used the Latin word "rapture" to describe being caught up or snatched away, because this experience is to be a joyous experience. So that's how the word rapture came about, those who wanted to translate the Greek New Testament into Latin used the word "rapture" rather than the term "caught up."

So the question is, who will be raptured? Who will be caught up? Who will be taken up? If you have been born again by the Spirit of God, if your sins have been forgiven, if there has been a time and a place when you have knowingly and willingly acknowledged Jesus Christ as your Savior and Lord, if there has been a moment when your life has been changed by the power and the grace of God, then you will be snatched away. You say, "What if I'm busy enjoying something I'm doing, am I going to want to go?" You're not going to have a choice. I know when I was engaged, my prayer was, "Lord, if the rapture comes, let it happen after my honeymoon!"

Can you think back to that momentous moment in human history, on September 11, when about 3,000 people died in this nation? Devastation occurred to this country. One event devastated the economy. One event plummeted the stock market. I wonder if it will be like that when the rapture occurs? The loss of almost 3,000 had a devastating effect on everything. But let's say 30 percent of the American population is raptured, which is pretty generous. Let's say that everybody who calls themselves a born-again, evangelical Christian, really is a born-again, evangelical Christian, then that means that almost 100 million out of the estimated 300 million Americans will be taken out of this nation. And let's generously say that out of the six billion people alive in the world today, what would happen if one billion of them had truly been saved, had truly met Christ, had truly experienced salvation, what do you think would happen to this nation and happen to this world? I can tell you one thing. It will not be good.

Can you imagine what will occur when major jet airliners who carry hundreds of people have pilots who are saved? Can you imagine sitting in first class or in coach, and all of a sudden people begin to disappear? Can you imagine the media attempting to broadcast what has occurred? I'm afraid they will not be able to spin their way out of that one. And can you imagine the number of meetings that would be taking place in corporate America and all across the world, and suddenly in hundreds of executive conference rooms, and conference centers, hundreds of people are sitting there and suddenly the speaker is gone? Can you imagine what it would be like if it happened on a Sunday morning across America, and there would be so many in the church who were religious, practiced the sacraments, observed the holy ordinances, and yet all of a sudden, certain people would disappear out of the choir, probably not all of them, certain people would be left alive and well in every congregation, because we would probably not all disappear. I pray that none of you is left behind.

What I'm saying is, if you do not know that you are going up in the rapture, you will go through the seven-year tribulation, which will be living hell and devastation. And the moment you think it's about to break, it will intensify. Everyone you know in your family, everyone you know in your business, your acquaintances and your friends will go through that horror if they do not know the Lord. You say, "Do you really believe the New Testament teaches and verifies that?" Oh, absolutely.

In fact, let me take a moment to give to you some...

SCRIPTURAL SUPPORT

The Bible says the church will be supernaturally taken out of here. What does the New Testament say about this? Does it support the event? Well, in 1 Thessalonians 1:10, notice what the Scripture says "and to wait for His Son from heaven, whom He raised from the dead, even Jesus who delivers us from the wrath to come." Will the church go through the seven-year tribulation? Some believe it will go through half of it. Many believe it will go through all of it. Some would even discredit the tribulation saying, "Oh, it's an allegorical type of thing." Why don't you try to allegorize the cross? Why don't you try to allegorize the blood of Christ? And allegorize the authority of Scripture and the creation of mankind? I'm sorry; if you start there; you just end up nowhere.

Then 2 Thessalonians 1:10, one book over, says "...when He comes, in that Day, to be glorified in His saints and to be admired among all those who believe, because our testimony among you was believed." That means that Jesus will be admired among all of those who believe. That's what heaven is. Heaven isn't a football game or a golf game; it isn't the cooking channel, ladies. Heaven is one thing – admiration of the living Lord Jesus Christ.

Also, we understand today that in that pleasure, in that moment, it happens because our testimony is that we were believers. Our life pictured that we belonged to Christ. John 14:1-3 verifies the truthfulness of this text: "Let not your heart be troubled; you believe in God, believe also in Me. In My Father's house are many mansions; if it were not so, I would have told you. I go to prepare a place for you. And if I go and prepare a place for you, I will come again and receive you to Myself; that where I

am, there you may be also."

You remember when Jesus ascended to heaven? He went up into where? The clouds. That's why the Bible goes on to say, "...Men of Galilee, why do you stand gazing up into heaven? This same Jesus, who was taken up from you into heaven, will so come in like manner as you saw Him go into heaven." You know what the rapture is? The rapture is the fulfillment of those words in Acts 1:11. How did He go up? He went up personally. It was no one else other than the Lord Jesus who went up, and He will personally return. He went up physically. It was not some phantom that had been raised from the dead. No, physical death had occurred, physical resurrection had occurred, and now physical glorification was in our eyes as He went upward into heaven. One day He will physically come back in the clouds, and guess what else? He went up visibly. They saw Him. One day everyone will see Him again. "Behold, I tell you a mystery: We shall not all sleep, but we shall all be changed..." (1 Corinthians 15:15).

Then we read this powerful text over in Titus 2:13. This is a key text. You really need to note it in your Bible: "...*looking for the blessed hope and glorious appearing of our great God and Savior Jesus Christ.*" The blessed hope is the rapture of the church. That is in reference to Jesus' coming back in the clouds. Is the glorious appearing the same thing? No, the glorious appearing is another event. It's the second coming of the Lord when He will literally put His feet back on this earth again. In the rapture, He comes in the clouds. At the end of the tribulation, He will come back to this earth to reign for 1,000 years.

Be careful. Do not confuse passages about the rapture with passages about the glorious appearing. They are two different events at two different times, talking about the same Lord Jesus, King of Kings and Lord of Lords. So today, we see the supernatural transition of the church. We see that the New Testament scripturally supports it.

SUCCINCT ACTIONS

Now what are some succinct actions that we need to take as Christian men and women, as Christian students today? What about those of you who do not know the Lord and you are questioning, "Will I go up in the rapture? Will I be left behind?" What are some succinct actions, concise actions you need to take? I just want to tell you that based on our theology of the Revelation and of the rapture of the church, there are some actions that must occur, such as *live right*. If you are a Christian today, I just want to urge you, you better start living right. Some of us, we're banking on having a notification before the Lord comes. I'm sorry; He is going to come at a day and hour that no one knows. You need to start living right. You better get your life right with the Lord, and you had better understand that the Lord's coming is imminent, meaning that He can come at anytime, anyplace, anywhere, any day.

If you do not know Christ as Lord and Savior, if you do not know that you are going to be a part of the rapture, I want to tell you something: If you do not know that you're ready for the rapture, I beg you, I plead with you, give your life to Jesus Christ now. If I were you, I would not even wait. I'd accept Jesus right now. Your first step of living right is letting Jesus Christ come into your life. Would you?

Not only had you better live right, you better *love others*. Are you in love with other people? You see, loving others shows that you love God...loving others enough to help them get ready for the rapture. Do you love people enough to help them get ready for the rapture? A whole bunch of Christian churches have said, "If you come to our church, we're going to have rapture exercises." I remember seeing a notification like that. What are rapture exercises? You only need rapture exercises if you're counting on yourself to take you up. I'm not counting on myself taking me up. I can't go up past this squatty body anyway. I'm telling you, the only way I'm going up is when He takes me up. The exercise every Christian needs to do in relationship to the rapture is to get your relationships with lost people to such a strong point that you can share the Lord with them and inform them, "The Lord is coming. The Lord is coming. The Lord is coming! Are you ready for the coming of the Lord?"

One of the problems with the church today in this nation is that our eschatology has become so nothing, meaning that we don't believe what I just shared...that it is not transforming our personal lives to the point for evangelism to occur. Some of you say, "It's not my gift to evangelize." I'll tell you what your gift is. It's ignoring the truthfulness of the Word of God. That's your gift. When you get your eschatology right, the study of last things, your heart will burn to win people to Jesus Christ. Your heart will burn to take the gospel to the world. Your heart will burn deep within you to make sure everyone knows that everyone has the opportunity to say yes to Christ.

Love others as a Christian. Do you love others as a Christian today so that when Christ comes there is no unforgiveness? When Christ comes, there are no relationship issues? Could you imagine what will happen in some churches that are so full of conflict today? What is going to happen when the Lord comes and the church is filled with nothing more than conflict? What is going to happen in your family? I'm telling you, the reason the church is in conflict all across the country is that families are messed up. We glorify that condition by saying, "We're just dysfunctional." No, you're not. You're sinful. Jesus didn't create you to be dysfunctional. He created you to be functional. When you love Christ, you love others. When you love Christ, your family loves Christ. I want to challenge you. Love your family enough to tell them Jesus is coming.

Do you love them enough?

Live right, love others and *look up*. You better learn to look up. Jesus is coming for us. The rapture of the church could occur at anytime, any day, anywhere, at any moment. And we need to live our lives looking up. You need to look where? To the clouds. When is He coming? Don't know. Where is He coming? Coming in the clouds. Wouldn't that be awesome if you were up there, 40,000 feet up in some jet. You look out, and about the time you're going up, He is coming down and you meet Him right there. Won't that be awesome? You won't have as far to go.

Every Christian man and every Christian woman, every student who loves the Lord today, you need to learn to live your life on your tiptoes. Learn to live your life ready. Are you ready? Are you busy getting others ready?

Jesus is coming.

29

THE GREAT AND GLORIOUS INVITATION

DR. BOBBY WELCH

Pastor Emeritus

First Baptist Church

Daytona Beach, Florida

THEN JESUS TOLD A STORY TO A MAN WHO HAD BEEN INQUIRING about the kingdom of God…

"…A certain man made a great supper, and bade many: And sent his servant at supper time to say to them that were bidden, Come; for all things are now ready. And they all with one consent began to make excuse. The first said unto him, I have bought a piece of ground, and I must needs go and see it: I pray thee have me excused. And another said, I have bought five yoke of oxen, and I go to prove them: I pray thee have me excused. And another said, I have married a wife, and therefore I cannot come. So that servant came, and shewed his lord these things. Then the master of the house being angry said to his servant, Go out quickly into the streets and lanes of the city, and bring in hither the poor, and the maimed, and the halt, and the blind. And the servant said, Lord, it is done as thou hast commanded, and yet there is room. And the lord said unto the servant, Go out into the highways and hedges, and compel them to come in, that my house may be filled. For I say unto you, That none of those men which were bidden shall taste of my supper" (Luke 14:16-24).

In other words, they missed the opportunity at this invitation. If you have a marginal reference right there at the top of verse 15, it probably says something about the great supper. I think it could equally be said that it is the great summons, the great invitation.

Let me ask you two questions: Question number one, did someone share the gospel with you, and after they had done the best they knew how, they asked you if you would like to receive Jesus Christ and be saved, and you did? Or were you at a public assembly or church and somebody gave the invitation, the opportunity to come down the aisle or take a stand publicly before the group, and you accepted that invitation and came forward and stood? If you said *yes* in either case, you and multiplied millions of other people here and around the world are living proof of the value and importance of the invitation.

I want to preach today on the great and glorious invitation. The powerful and wonderful part is that the invitation is something that God has given us. I am talking about the invitation to ask people to come to Christ and not to be ashamed and stand publicly for the Lord. That is what I mean when I say the invitation. The invitation is a call and an encouragement for a person to make his or her sincere commitment to Christ immediately without any further delay. That is what an invitation is. Whether you do it in the front seat of a car with a friend, or whether you are on a creek bank, or whether you are in a living room of a home, or whether you are at a family reunion, or whether you stand before a handful of people at a Sunday School class or multiplied thousands in a large assembly, the invitation is the call and the encouragement.

When you look at the Word of God, you'll see that God opens His Word with an invitation, and God closes the last book of the Bible with an invitation.

And this Word of God overflows, from cover to cover, with appeals, entreaties, exhortations and pleadings, all of which are mountains that turn into an overwhelming avalanche of God's love to lost man and His yearning and calling of them to come from their sin and receive the love and the glory of God. The Bible is a book of invitation. Jesus Christ certainly gave the invitation, and it seems that His very favorite word was come, C-O–M-E, come. That is an invitational word, isn't it? When Jesus extended that invitation, He seemed always to be willing and wanting to say to His mankind in their struggles, "Come. Zacchaeus, come down. Lazarus, come forth. You who are weary and harassed and beaten up, frustrated and confused, come unto Me. Those of you who know Me and say you love Me, watch out for that world out there that's full of sin. Come out from among them and live a life separated. Those of you who know Me and love Me, come, come, come after Me and follow Me and I will make you fishers of men." And in Revelation, Jesus said, "Come up here where I am."

Beloved, I submit to you that the last invitation is the practical reason for the other invitations. Jesus calls us to give the invitation so He can call people to the last invitation. Come. So the point and purpose of this message is to give you an invitation. I want to extend to you an invitation to reaffirm and recommit yourself to go everywhere and on every occasion and at every opportunity share the gospel and give the invitation. I am asking you to do that. That is the invitation today. I am preaching on the invitation about the invitation. Go everywhere and at every opportunity and at every occasion share the gospel and give the invitation to every man, woman, boy or girl to accept the love of God.

Now just so you won't walk away and forget it, let's go over that again. Here is the subject today. Share the gospel and give the invitation. And one of the primary reasons you are going to share the gospel is because it is providential.

THE INVITATION IS PROVIDENTIAL

Some people have said that the invitation is of recent origin. I oppose that completely. The invitation is as ancient and as old as the first man. God gave the first invitation. He gave it upon the first sin and gave it immediately to the first man. "Adam, where art thou?" That was the invitation. God was not saying to Adam, "I can't find you, I don't know where you are." God knew where he was. He had no interest in what he had done. He already knew what he had done. What God was saying to the first man who had committed his first sin was, "Adam, come to Me with that sin. You need to come to Me now because this is where your hope and help lies." No, it is not a recent occurrence that we give an evangelistic invitation. It is of divine origin caught in the foreknowledge of God and let loose when the very first sin was first committed, and God intends for you and me to give that invitation until the last man has committed the last sin and is called home.

Here are some invitations. God gave the invitation. He said to Adam, "Where art thou?" Moses gave the invitation to his people, "Who is on the Lord's side?" That was a pretty straight call, wasn't it? Joshua gave an invitation to the nation of Israel, "Choose you this day whom you are going to serve." Ezra gave his invitation to the people of God when he said, "I want you to swear publicly that you are going to live for God and stand for Him." Nehemiah, to the older people, said, "I want you to take a stand now for your loyalty for the Lord." Jesus gave an invitation to Peter and Andrew and Matthew and all the others when He said, "Follow Me and I will make you fishers of men." Paul gave the invitation when he said to his listeners, "Day and night I stayed with you attempting to persuade you and call you where you need to go." He was extending an invitation. Peter gave an invitation when he said, "Come here and be baptized, this is the time you need to take your stand for the

Lord." The apostle at Pentecost said, "Listen, you need to come and be saved, be saved, be saved." That was an invitation. They are all through the Word of God, and many, many others come to mind now. No, no, the invitation is not of recent origin, the invitation comes right out of the heart and mind of God for us today.

We need to learn to share the gospel, and what? Give the invitation because there is a world out there that is dying without Christ and needs to be saved. We have our mandate. We are the lifeboat needed to bring lost souls to the grace of God and the love of God through salvation in Jesus Christ. But this great huge lifeboat of ours cannot afford to be one without a compass. It cannot afford to be one that is tossed by every wind reduction or moved by every wave of distraction. Beloved, I am here to tell you, we have a helm to hold, we have a course to follow, it is to share the gospel and give the invitation, and we have a port to make, and that is to be faithful unto God as long as we have breath in us and show up one day at a fair haven called heaven with a boatload of lost people who got saved by the grace of God. And when they get saved, you share the gospel and what? Give them the invitation.

Our unity of purpose is evangelism. It is nothing else. As far as I am concerned, that is the need of the evangelical church in North America. The world knows what we are against. And I want them to know what we are against, and that's a good thing. The world knows how we differ inside, all of our diversities. What a lost and dying world needs to know, what it desperately needs to know more than all of that is, we have found purpose, commitment, unity and focus in sharing the gospel in a way that the people of the world can discover the claims of the gospel of Christ and receive the Lord Jesus unto their lives and be saved. That's what this world desperately needs. And you and I need to make up our minds that we do have a purpose, and we do have a commitment, and that is to share the gospel and give the invitation.

Look at Acts 26:28. The man here said to Paul, "Almost you have persuaded me to be a Christian." Well, beloved, I want you to know why he was almost persuaded. Paul was trying to completely persuade him. Paul was sharing the gospel with the man, he was pleading with the man, he was calling on the man, he was giving the man the gospel, and he was giving him an invitation. The invitation, this great and glorious invitation that we are to be giving in God's name, this invitation is not only providential, but also...

THE INVITATION IS PRIVATE

I mean, they are in the confines of a royal household. This is a private place.

One of the huge mistakes that a speaker made once at a pastors' conference was when he came to the conclusion of his message. He took a quantum leap with some good statistics and polling information and said, "I am prepared to say with certain authority that the day of going into private places and into people's homes and visiting and sharing the gospel – that day is all over." The truth of it is, God is still working in people's lives. Do you know what is happening? Lay people are rediscovering the power of the gospel unto salvation, and they have lost friends and relatives whom they cannot get to church. This facility-based evangelism idea is killing us, where you have to get them to the church to get their lives changed. But the church at large can win North America and the whole world. You have to be willing to go to those private places. People say, "Well, it won't work." Well, of course it won't work if you sit in your car and drive by them.

I once went out along with others to the boardwalk on Main Street in Daytona Beach, Florida. I had the joy and privilege of sharing the gospel there on the street corner, and three fine people prayed to receive the Lord. Well, you say, they were bums. Don't worry; they weren't bums. They owned and worked in gift shops there, and they were responsible people. And while I was out there, others were in people's homes, and when I got back, the report was that during that time, 141 people had prayed to receive Christ that night. Nobody knew where they were going; they just went out and went at it. One woman with tears in her eyes grabbed me and said, "I have been saved 42 years and this is the first time I have led anybody to Christ." I said, "Well, what do you say about that?" And she said, "Yahoo! I can't wait to get to my unsaved family because, you see, my family isn't going to come to Daytona Beach, but I'm going to go to my family." In those homes, privately, personally, the gospel can be shared. We need to tell people, go to those homes, wherever you go and whatever opportunity, whatever occasion, share the gospel and give the invitation. People will respond every time.

Not only is it providential, not only is it to be private, but also…

THE INVITATION IS PERSONAL

For example, Phillip and the Ethiopian eunuch. Personal. Now what I mean by personal is that we are to be personal. We are, as I just said, to share the gospel with people personally. We are to do that, one-on-one, face-to-face, personally. But I also want to fortify and emphasize that what I mean by "personal" in the invitation is that it should be their part to be personal as well. The one who is seeking the Lord is to be personal. They must, as you well know, personally accept Christ as Lord and Savior. I cannot do it for them, I have no interest in trying to do it for them, I am just sharing the gospel and giving the invitation. That's it. They must respond to the gospel, not me. Somebody said, "Aren't you worried about faulty evangelism? Aren't you worried about sharing the gospel with the wrong person?" I have never had one thought about that. You know what I am thinking all the time? Dear God, why did I not share with that woman at 7-Eleven? Dear God, why did I not share with the woman who came to our house to work? Dear God, why did I not share with the man in the yard? Dear God, why didn't I ask that policeman? I spend too much time worrying about all those that I don't share with to worry about those who may get the wrong gospel. Besides, you cannot carry the gospel to the wrong person. Share the gospel and give the invitation and make it personal, and that's where the sinner's prayer comes in.

There is no official sinner's prayer; we all have a version of it. But I hope at some time you prayed, "Dear Lord Jesus, I am a sinner, come into my heart, save my soul, forgive me of my sins, I repent of my sins, I can't explain it, but I believe You were resurrected from the dead, and I want You in my life now, and I ask You to change me and save me." Have you prayed that prayer? Did it work? Well, yeah, it worked, because it was personal to you. It was personal.

One of our teachers gave this story to me the other day, I don't know if this is really true or just something that was picked up off of the Internet or something. It doesn't matter, the point is still wonderful. It's talking about how to go to heaven. The story says, "I was testing the children in my Sunday School class to see if they understood the concept of getting to heaven. I asked them, 'If I sold my house and my car and had a big garage sale and gave all my money to the church, would that get me into heaven?' And they all said with this great enthusiasm, 'No, no!' I asked, 'If I cleaned the church every day and mowed the yard, kept everything neat and tidy, would that get me into heaven?' Again, with a huge exclamation – the class was getting the idea – they said, 'No!' Well, by then I was starting to smile, and I said, 'If I were kind to animals, and gave candy to all of the children, and loved my husband, would that get me into heaven?' And again, they said 'No, no!' And by now I was just bursting with pride for them, and I said, 'Well, then, how can I get into heaven?' And at that moment, a five-year-old boy jumped out of his seat almost in disgust and said, 'You've got to *die* to get to heaven!'"

Of course, there is a little more to it than that.

I once heard someone's exaggerated definition of what we need to do to receive Christ. The man clearly implied that to be saved, you should first have at least three to four weeks of daily Bible study of an hour or more with someone. When you get to the end of that time, if you cannot explain and understand the virgin birth and the resurrection, probably it isn't time for anyone to talk to you yet about being saved. If that were true, Jesus would have to apologize and send the thief on the cross back from paradise. He didn't have a week of Bible study time ahead of him. Now I am not saying that's not a good thing, but I am saying you shouldn't wait to give the invitation and share the gospel until you have had Bible study with someone for a month. Most people who are saved didn't spend four weeks in Bible study, and most of them can't explain and understand the virgin birth and the resurrection. I can't explain it, but I'll tell you that as a boy, I fell down on my knees, and I believed the Word of God, and I called on Christ and, bless God, He saved me. I didn't have time for four weeks of Bible study, but I had time to get the gospel, and somebody shared the gospel and gave the invitation, and I got it. And I got a full dose of it. And 95 percent of the people who are saved are in the same shape. If you will confess with your mouth the Lord Jesus, and if you will believe in your heart, not explain it, not understand it, if you will believe in your heart that God raised Him from the dead, you shall be saved. Bless God, that's what we need. That's all we need. Thank God if we get more, but bless God, we better not require more. We need to share the gospel and what? Give the invitation. That's exactly right. Share the gospel and give the invitation.

So I said it is providential, I said it is private; I said it is personal, but I want to say it is public as well.

THE PUBLIC INVITATION

The response to the invitation is to be public. When you read Ezra 10:4-5, you will see a public invitation. When Jesus called Zacchaeus down out of the tree, He didn't say, "Zacchaeus, here is a note; could you meet Me somewhere?" Would Zacchaeus have come down out of that tree? Jesus said, "Today is the day; I want to go to your house." And do you know what? I don't have any record that Zacchaeus got embarrassed or took a poll. He just shimmied down that tree with a smile on his face and took off. He went to Jesus publicly, and there are many, many more examples in the Bible. Matthew entered when Jesus called him. He called him by name, He said "Follow Me," and you know what? Matthew did. That's how I got there. That is how it works.

Now listen to this. I want to say this carefully; it is my conviction that a personal and private acceptance of Jesus Christ and the gospel that is not strong enough to stand up in public will in fact be powerless in public to change the public for the gospel's sake. Let me say that again just for emphasis. I am not saying you are not saved, I am saying a personal and private acceptance of the gospel in Jesus Christ that is not strong enough to stand publicly in the church will never be powerful enough to stand up in public where they need to see and hear the gospel to be saved. People need to learn to stand publicly in the church so they will not fail to stand publicly when they go out of the church. Share the gospel publicly.

Jesus did not die hidden away behind some secret closed-door place. He did not. Jesus died publicly. Just like Jesus walked, talked, and stood, He died out there in public. And we all ought to know this for certain. For certain we should know that the gospel that required the life of Christ has every right to require each of us to be willing to stand publicly with our lives for Christ and the gospel. Are you with me? If the gospel took Jesus' life, He had to give it, it required His life, beloved, don't you think it has a right to ask us to be willing to stand up with our lives for that same gospel? I assure you it does. That's why I say our goal is to share the gospel and give the invitation. When you go to homes and share and talk to people, share the gospel and give the invitation. When you are at the 7-Eleven or wherever you get gasoline, share the gospel and give the invitation. Share the gospel and give the invitation!

The last thing I want to say on this subject is, not only are we to share the gospel everywhere at every opportunity, not only are we to share the gospel and give the invitation because it is providential, we are to do it in private, it should be personal, and it should be public, but I also want to say to you, the invitation is overwhelmingly practical.

THE PRACTICAL INVITATION

Look at Joshua 24:15, as well as Nehemiah, chapters 9, 10 and 11. Those are some of the places where they gave a practical invitation. And by the way, if you want an argument for a decision card, you will find it in those places. They all had to sign their names when they came down. I mean, Joshua was in earnest because God was in earnest. Nehemiah was in earnest because God was in earnest. The invitation is the most practical thing imaginable. Think of the fisherman who goes out in his boat, and you see him going along there, clouds in the sky, and the waves. He's got his net, and he's got his equipment and all of that, and he lets down the sails, and he stops and drops anchor, and then he waits for a moment in true anticipation and expectation to do what? Throw out the net. Throw out the net. That's why he came.

Think of a father and a mother who live their lives so wonderfully for the Lord, and they have prayed with their children, read the Bible to them and loved on them and encouraged them and tutored them along the way in the gospel, and now one night they are called to the bedside and hear, "Mommy and Daddy, can we talk a little bit more about Jesus?" And then they explain everything, and the child is there with eagerness and excitement on the edge of the bed, and his or her eyes are bulging out, and he or she is just waiting, saying, "What's the next step, Daddy? What do I do next, Mommy?" How can we walk away, they are begging for the invitation. It's the most practical thing in the world. And for someone to share the gospel, and people are on the edge of their seats, and the Spirit of God is moving, it's begging for an invitation. They are expecting an invitation. It's practical, practical. If we fall back on giving an invitation, we're going to have to call back from heaven everybody who has ever gone there at the invitation. You cannot give up the invitation. It's providential, it's to be private, it's to be personal, it's to be public, but it is so practical. Right out of the pages of the Word of God. We should believe in evangelism, soul winning, reaching people, keeping them out of hell, getting them on the road to heaven, and we should believe in sharing the gospel everywhere, every time at every opportunity, and we should give an invitation.

Recently I read some documentation on the sinking of a ship called *The Princess Alice*. *The Princess Alice* was a ship in olden days that sailed around England and plied the rivers around London. It was an excursion ship. It wasn't big enough to be called a cruise ship but it was a forerunner of that. On a particular cruise late into the night and the early dark hours of the morning, the lights were on and everybody was having a great time on board, but suddenly something went wrong and the ship immediately began to sink. And it did sink. Just as that ship began to sink, a boatman on the shore saw and understood something bad was about to happen. And instinctively, he jumped into this huge rowboat of his, grabbed each oar and began to bow his back and push toward where this ship was listing. But before he could get there, the ship was out of sight. Some of those on deck had already leaped into the water, and they were fighting to find their loved ones, and screaming in the night. Others were bobbing up, choking and sputtering and spitting, as they had somehow broken loose from the ship that had now hit the bottom. Others drowned outright, trapped inside their cabins. It is told that this man, upon encountering these desperate souls who were fighting for their lives, did what you would do. He began to call to them, "Come, come, come, over here, come, come get in the boat." And then they came. They fought each other to get there. They practically capsized the boat. In fact, there were so many in the boat that the boat began to take on water, and people began to say, "This boat is going to sink, too." Suddenly the man realized that he had to go. He couldn't help the rest of the survivors, even though they were screaming, "Wait!" He took hold of those huge oars, and it said that the man with supernatural strength bowed his back and leaned into those oars, so much so that the boat and the oars creaked and cracked under the weight. And then they say that the people fell deaf and silent as they heard this man attempting to row this load. The noise coming out of him was "Oh, oh, oh," and they thought that this load was too heavy for him to row. But that wasn't the case, because in the next round they caught what he was doing. What he meant, what he was saying was, "Oh, oh, oh, if I just had a bigger boat, if I just had a bigger boat." The man was weeping in agony because of how many were being left behind because his boat was not big enough to carry them all.

If you don't hear anything else today, thank God our boat is big enough. Our boat is big enough. The boat has come. There is still room for one in this gospel ship. The boat is big enough, but hear me now, our problem is not with the size of the boat, our problem is, we don't have enough goers and enough rowers. That's our problem today. Goers and rowers. Row and go and share the gospel, and what? Give the invitation. Share the gospel and give the invitation. Go and share and on every opportunity and in every place share the gospel and give the invitation. God wants us to do it.

30

HELL IS NO JOKE

DR. ERNEST L. EASLEY

Senior Pastor

Roswell Street Baptist Church

Marietta, Georgia

IF I KNEW THAT JESUS WAS COMING TOMORROW, and I had one last message to preach before being raptured with the saints on earth, I would preach with all of the passion of my soul on the subject of hell.

More than likely, it would be the first time many people would ever hear a message on the subject of hell. Hell has all but disappeared from the modern-day evangelical pulpit. Charles Spurgeon, the prince of preachers, said, "Preaching that ignores the doctrine of hell lowers the holiness of God and degrades the work of Jesus Christ."

Too many preachers are dancing around the subject rather than declaring hell's reality in fear of offending and running people off. First, the gospel is offensive. The apostle Paul, quoting Isaiah 8:14 in Romans 9:33, says, "As it is written: 'Behold, I lay in Zion a stumbling stone and rock of offense, and whoever believes on Him will not be put to shame.'" Jesus is not only "a stumbling stone," He is a "rock of offense." Second, by preaching on hell, where are you going to run people off to? Hell number two?

We desperately need a generation of preachers who will passionately and compassionately declare the whole counsel of God, including the truth about the place called hell. It should come as no surprise the condition of our communities and country today. If we had more "hell" in the pulpits, we would have less "hell" in the streets!

The subject of hell may be out of date with today's preachers, but it is not out of business. The truth is that people who die without a personal relationship with Jesus Christ go to the place called hell. There are no exceptions! Hell is no joke!

From Psalm 9, I want to show you what the Bible says about the place called "hell." Why doesn't hell seem to be as hot as it once was? Why has hell all but disappeared from today's pulpit? Well, the devil is no dummy. He knows that if he can water down the subject of hell then hell will be perceived as having gone out of business.

For instance, people use the word "hell" in *referring to violence*. During World War II, General George Patton was nicknamed "Hell on Wheels" because of the havoc his division caused on its way to Berlin.

In 1989 during the revolution against communist Romania, one observer said, "All hell has broken loose." I hear people saying, "War is hell." War is bad...but war is not hell. Hell is the separation of your soul and spirit from God!

So the word "hell" is often used today in reference to violence. But not only in violence, but in *victory*. Somebody wins a great athletic event and they say, "We beat the hell out of them."

So...the word "hell" is used today to refer to victory and to violence, but it is also used *in vain*. When Jack Nicklaus was interviewed on his 50th birthday, he said, "My dad was 56 when he died. I certainly hope to hell that I will be around beyond 56." Now you tell me – What does that mean? That makes about as much sense as saying, "I certainly hope to Alabama that I will be around beyond 56." Or when Graham Gooch, captain of the Australian cricket team, said, "Winning beats the hell out of losing." That makes as much sense as saying, "Winning beats the Denmark out of losing."

The devil has launched a demonic campaign to distort and deny the name for the place where the "worm never dies and the fire is never quenched." You may hear a lot of jokes about hell, but I want you to know today that hell is no joke! Hebrews 10:31 says, "It is a fearful thing to fall into the hands of the living God."

Now there are several things about hell that the Word of God tells us. First, the Bible tells us about...

I. THE CERTAINTY OF HELL

In the early 1970s, Beatle John Lennon, had a smash hit with a song that included these words: "Imagine there's no heaven; it's easy if you try. No hell below us, above us only sky."

So which is it, fact or fiction? Literal or figurative? Dr. W. A. Criswell, longtime pastor of the First Baptist Church of Dallas, Texas, said, "If you say there is no hell, you say the Bible is not the Word of God."

You ask, "Ernest Easley, what do you believe? Is hell fact or fantasy?" I believe in a literal place called hell because Jesus did, because Paul did, and because John did. I believe it because the Bible tells me so!

Now some would say that I am narrow-minded or even cruel. I like what Dr. R. G. Lee said on the subject. He said, "I have no desire to be any broader than Jesus was. As to being cruel, is it cruel to tell a man the truth? Is a man to be called cruel who declares the whole counsel of God and points out to men their danger? Is it cruel to arouse sleeping people to the fact that the house is on fire? Is it cruel to jerk a blind man away from the rattlesnake in the coil?"

And then he said, "I had rather be called cruel for being kind, than to be called kind for being cruel." The cruelest thing I could do is not to warn you about what the Word of God says about hell!

The same Bible that tells us that there is a literal place of beauty and bliss called heaven, tells us that there is a literal place of gloom and doom called hell. In fact, Jesus Christ had more to say about the place called hell than He did about heaven! Evangelist, D. L. Moody, said, "The same Christ that tells of heaven with all of its glories, tells us of hell with all of its horrors." To believe the Word of God is to believe in hell.

Now, if you end up in hell, you will be there as an intruder! You will be an uninvited guest! Jesus said in Matthew 25:41, "Then He will also say to those on the left hand, 'Depart from Me, you cursed, into the everlasting fire prepared for the devil and his angels." Hell was originally prepared for the devil and his angels! Hell was never created by God with you in mind!

Here are the words of Jesus: "And these will go away into everlasting punishment, but the righteous into eternal life" (Matthew 25:46).

"And do not fear those who kill the body but cannot kill the soul. But rather fear Him who is able to destroy both soul and body in hell" (Matthew 10:28).

"The Son of Man will send out His angels, and they will gather out of His kingdom all things that offend, and those who practice lawlessness, and will cast them into the furnace of fire. There will be wailing and gnashing of teeth" (Matthew 13:41-42). Then verses 49-50 go on to say, "So it will be at the end of the age. The angels will come forth, separate the wicked from among the just, and cast them into the furnace of fire. There will be wailing and gnashing of teeth."

Fifty-four times you read throughout the Bible about the certainty of hell! If you believe John 3:16 where the Bible says "For God so loved the world that He gave His only begotten Son, that whoever believes in Him should not perish but have everlasting life," then you have to believe Psalm 9:17, "The wicked shall be turned into hell, and all the nations that forget God."

Hell is no joke!

II. The Conditions in Hell

Don't go to hell! You won't like it. You do not want to go to hell. The Bible describes hell's condition as *a place of suffering.* Jesus said in Mark 9:43-44, "And if your hand causes you to sin, cut if off. It is better for you to enter into life maimed, rather than having two hands, to go to hell, into the fire that shall never be quenched – where their worm does not die and the fire is not quenched."

The Greek word *asbeston*, translated "quenched," is where we get our English word "asbestos." Asbestos is a material that burns and burns and never burns up. Asbestos cannot be destroyed by fire. Hell is a consuming, lasting fire! Here is how the Bible describes the suffering of the place called hell: *Matthew 25:41* describes a place of "everlasting fire." Matthew 25:46 describes a place of "everlasting punishment." Matthew 13:41-42 says that hell is a "furnace of fire." Revelation 20:15 calls hell the "lake of fire." 2 Thessalonians 1:8 says, "...in flaming fire taking vengeance on those who do not know God, and on those who do not obey the gospel of our Lord Jesus Christ."

The Bible also describes hell's condition as *a place of separation.* Do not let the devil deceive you into thinking that hell is a place of comradeship, a place where you can hang out with your buddies for eternity. Hell is a place of isolation and separation!

Jesus said in Luke 13:28, "There will be weeping and gnashing of teeth, when you see Abraham and Isaac and Jacob and all the prophets in the kingdom of God, and yourselves thrust out."

Jesus went on to say in Luke 16:26, "And besides all this, between us and you there is a great gulf fixed, so that those who want to pass from here to you cannot, nor can those from there pass to us."

In hell, you will never again feel the touch of a loving mother or father or ever be held in the arms of a devoted mate. You say, "But I want to go to hell because my spouse is there or my friend is there." Your spouse or friend may be in hell, but in hell there is no fellowship or friendship. Those who die without Jesus Christ are forever separated from their lost loved ones as well as their saved loved ones. Eternal isolation! But even worse is being forever separated from God!

The apostle Paul said in 2 Thessalonians 1:9, "These shall be punished with everlasting destruction from the presence of the Lord and from the glory of His power." Forever separated from His grace and goodness. Forever separated from His presence and peace. Forever separated from His fellowship and forgiveness.

Yet, the cynic says, "I would rather go to hell to be forever separated from the hypocrites in the church." Well, granted, there are hypocrites in the church. In fact, there have always been hypocrites in the church. Judas, one of the original disciples, was a hypocrite. But I would rather spend some time here on earth with some of the hypocrites than to spend eternity in hell with all of them!

The Bible also describes hell's condition as *a place of sorrow.* Jesus said in Matthew 13:42, "...There will be wailing and gnashing of teeth." Hell is a place of great sorrow and devoid of joy. You will never hear anybody laughing in hell. You will never see anybody smiling. There is nothing that delights. There is nothing that pleases.

In the Old Testament, David spoke of the "sorrows of hell." Nobody is happy in hell. Hell is a place of everlasting weeping and wailing, cursing and bitterness. You may hear jokes about hell here on earth, but not in hell, for hell is no joke!

And what makes hell a place of great sorrow is that it is a place of everlasting dying. The Bible tells us that hell is where "the worm does not die and the fire is not quenched." People in the process of dying, yet never able to die. Oh, the agony! The helplessness! The hopelessness! In hell, hope is gone forever. In hell, help is gone forever. When you step into hell, you step into a helpless and hopeless place. You see, hell is no joke!

III. THE CROWD IN HELL

Who will make up the crowd in hell? The crowd in hell may surprise you. John said in Revelation 21:8, "But the cowardly, unbelieving, abominable, murderers, sexually immoral, sorcerers, idolaters, and all liars shall have their part in the lake which burns with fire and brimstone, which is the second death."

So, who will make up the crowd in hell? Well...there will be *rebellious people* there. You would expect to see the rebellious in hell. But it may surprise you to find in hell some *religious people* there. Let me tell you something about the crowd in hell — there is no denomination that can keep you out of hell. Somebody says, "Are you one of those narrow-minded preachers that believes only Baptists are going to heaven?" I am more narrow minded than that! I don't believe a lot of Baptists are going to heaven!

No denomination can keep you out of hell! Once you physically die, your denomination tag will either fall off or burn off. If you go to heaven, it will fall off. If you go to hell, it will burn off!

You can be a Baptist, Church of Christ, Methodist or Pentecostal, and die and bust hell wide open! There is not a creed or a church that can keep you out of hell. There is only one way to avoid hell, and that is through a personal relationship with the Lord Jesus Christ.

You say, "But you don't know what I've done." There is not a sin so bad that the blood of Jesus Christ cannot cleanse and wash. There is only one sin that can keep you out of heaven and that is the deliberate rejection of Jesus Christ after the Holy Spirit has revealed to you who Jesus is.

I decided when I was nine years old that Ernest Easley was not going to hell. That was settled back when I invited Jesus Christ into my life and repented of my sins. Now, I've not always done the right thing. I've not always been faithful, but He has always been faithful to me.

Hell is no joke. One day a man asked a preacher, "Can you tell me where hell is?" The preacher thought about it for a moment and replied, "Sir, hell is at the end of a Christless life." God has done everything necessary for you to miss hell and make heaven! If you end up in hell, it will be because you fought God all the way. For God is not willing "that any should perish, but that all should come to repentance."

One of the saddest verses in the Bible is Jeremiah 8:20, "The harvest is past, the summer is ended, and we are not saved."

Once you are in hell, you are there to stay. There are no exits from hell. There are no windows, no doors. Once you are there, you are there to stay. There is no such thing as a "second chance" once you die.

You don't have to go to hell. God does not want you in hell, He wants you in heaven. He is "not willing that any should perish, but that all should come to repentance" (2 Peter 3:9), including you! God tells us in Ezekiel 33:11 that He takes "no pleasure in the death of the wicked, but that the wicked turn from his way and live." God does not want one person to end up in hell! Not one! He wants everybody with Him in heaven! That is why Jesus came. That is why Jesus died! That is why Jesus arose from the grave, so that you might have life!

Suppose, while out at sea, you fall overboard. Not being a swimmer, you do all that you can to keep your head above the water. Suddenly, a friend on the boat throws you a life preserver. And rather than taking it, you refuse it and die.

Whose fault is it that you died? It is your fault, and here is why: you could have been saved! You could have lived! But instead, you rejected the life preserver.

If you die and go to hell, it will be only because you refused God's life preserver, and His name is Jesus Christ.

We read in Romans 10:9, "that if you confess with your mouth the Lord Jesus and believe in your heart that God has raised Him from the dead, you will be saved." And then in verse 13, "For whoever calls on the name of the LORD shall be saved."

Hell is no joke.

31

Now You See Me,

Now You Don't

DR. FORREST POLLOCK

Senior Pastor

Bell Shoals Baptist Church

Brandon, Florida

FORTY YEARS AGO, AMERICA WATCHED a weekly comedy show called *Laugh-In*, staring comedians Rowen and Martin. Among its many vignettes, the show often featured a "News of the Future" segment in which Rowen and Martin pretended to be newscasters in the distant future, and they would report the most farfetched and impossible stories imaginable.

Ironically, in one of the segments from 1968, their news of the future included predictions that Ronald Reagan would be president of the United States from 1980 to 1988 and that the Berlin Wall would fall in 1989.

We now live at a time when yesterday's impossibility is today's reality.

Likewise, in the world of prophecy, yesterday's impossibility is today's reality. For example, who would have thought a century ago that the Jews would ever have a homeland? But in 1948 the Nation of Israel was born in a single day...just as Revelation 12 prophesied. Yesterday's impossibility is today's reality.

Two centuries ago, crossing America in a covered wagon took 166 days. Today the space shuttle can take you coast to coast in under eight minutes...just as Daniel 12 prophesied. Yesterday's impossibility is today's reality.

Scholars used to scratch their heads and wonder aloud how the two witnesses spoken of in Revelation 11 could be attacked by the Antichrist and be seen by every people, tribe and nation as their bodies lie in the streets of Jerusalem. But today we have satellite news networks and the Internet. Yesterday's impossibility is today's reality.

As we study God's final word on the future, Revelation, we find that it is a book where yesterday's impossibility is today's reality.

To understand Revelation, it's important to grasp that the cross is the "hinge of history" on which the world swings in a completely new direction after Jesus was crucified. You see, when Jesus Christ said "It is finished!" he ushered in what is called the Church Age. That's what you and I are experiencing right now. That's what Jesus was talking about in Revelation chapters 2-3, when He addressed the seven churches.

Now each of these churches really did exist, but they also prophetically represent a period of time during the last 2000 years. Ephesus, for example, represents the apostolic period that followed Jesus. Smyrna represents the persecution of the second and third centuries. Pergamos represents the state church under Constantine. Thyatira represents the papal church period. Sardis represents the reformed church period. Philadelphia represents the missionary church period. And which church represents our era? That would be the seventh church, the Laodicean church. That's the church that disgusted Jesus so much that He said,

...you are neither cold nor hot. I wish you were either one or the other! So, because you are lukewarm—neither hot nor cold—I am about to spit you out of my mouth (Revelation 3:16).

The problem with this lukewarm church is that they had acquired great wealth and felt they didn't need anything. But Jesus said they did not realize that they were "...wretched, pitiful, poor, blind and naked (Revelation 3:17)." Do those words describe the Christian church in America today? I think yes.

When a Christian denomination can promote a practicing homosexual to the office of bishop and then celebrate and sanction homosexual marriage, the church is wretched, poor and blind. When another Christian denomination can encourage its members to consume alcohol and gamble away a life's savings, the church is wretched, poor and blind. When still another denomination can champion a so-called minister of the gospel to run for president of the United States who supports partial birth abortion, the church is wretched, poor and blind.

And so we are living in the last period of the Church Age, the Laodicean period. Therefore, the end must be near. I don't know when, and I can't even speculate – remember that God's in management, I'm only in sales – but who can deny that the end is imminent?

The Bible teaches that the very next event on the end-times timeline is the rapture. We're not waiting for any more *signs*, we're listening for *sounds* – the sounds of a loud command, with the voice of the archangel and the trumpet call of God.

Soon millions of Christian people will suddenly and startlingly vanish. The Bible says the end will come unexpectedly, "like a thief in the night." Just imagine what that moment will be like. Telephone conversations will end in mid-sentence. Cars will collide on the Golden Gate Bridge and semi trucks will plunge into San Francisco Bay. A football team will be driving down the field when suddenly the quarterback vanishes! Meanwhile, the cheerleaders arrayed in a pyramid formation will collapse as half the squad disappears.

The Bible calls this worldwide "catching away" of the church *the rapture*. That's what Jesus was talking about in Matthew 24:41 when He said, "two men will be in the field: one will be taken and the other left. Two women will be grinding at the mill: one will be taken and the other left."

One day Jesus will appear in the clouds and call His church home. It will happen in an instant, in the twinkling of an eye — *that's one-thousandth of a second.* If you are a saved person, the rapture will be a great and glorious moment. You can expect to receive a new spiritual body and be reunited with passed loved ones in the air. But if you're not saved, imagine the horror and regret you will feel after being left behind. Tragically, you'll remember the countless times you heard the gospel and all the times you said no. Imagine the shock and unspeakable grief of losing every family member you love instantly. Imagine the horror of knowing that a seven-year hell on earth, called the tribulation, lies ahead with indescribable suffering. This is the rapture after the rapture — the blow-up after the go-up.

Evangelist Billy Graham speculates that fully 75 percent of church members will be left behind when Jesus returns — good, decent, moral, upstanding, church-going, tax-paying people who are lost. They were only professors, not possessors. They went under the water, but never went under the blood.

If you don't know Christ, I hope the portrait the apostle John paints of the rapture in Revelation will move you to receive Christ as savior and Lord today, while there's time.

As the aged John was exiled on the lonely isle of Patmos, God gave him a vision of the future in Revelation 4:1...

After this I looked, and there before me was a door standing open in heaven. And the voice I had first heard speaking to me like a trumpet said, "Come up here, and I will show you what must take place after this."

You might underline some words in verse 1. First, underline the first two words of the verse and the last two words of the verse. Twice, we see the words "after this." The first verse of chapter 4 is crucial to a correct interpretation of the rest of the book of Revelation. It's like the buttons on a man's dress shirt; it is imperative to get the first button right. If you don't, you'll be wrong all the way down. So, it is important for us to understand just exactly the transition which is taking place in verse 1.

The Holy Spirit gave us an outline of the book of Revelation back in chapter 1, verse 19. John is specifically told there that he is to "Write, therefore, what you have seen, what is now and what will take place later." Following this clue, when we come to chapter 4, verse 1, we discover that we have a transitional verse. The verse begins by saying, "after this." It concludes with "after this." These are the same two words that are used in Revelation 1:19. It is as if the Holy Spirit put the words at the beginning of the verse and at the end of the verse to make very sure that we do not misunderstand the transition which is occurring here.

The natural question arises...after what things? I believe John is speaking about the time after the disappearance of the church. In chapters 2 and 3 of Revelation, Jesus speaks to the seven churches in Asia. Some churches he praises, others he rebukes. But now we have a transitional statement that helps us understand that the church is gone. John says a door was opened in heaven. His vision is now turned upward. He hears a voice. He compares the voice to a trumpet. The trumpet voice says, "Come up here, and I will show you what must take place after this." And so John takes us by the hand and lets us go with him into heaven so that every Christian can see what happens when we are raptured.

In the verses that follow John does his best to describe the indescribable, but there's no way he can adequately do it. So he uses comparisons. Look how John describes what he sees in verses 2-4:

> At once I was in the Spirit, and there before me was a throne in heaven with someone sitting on it. And the one who sat there had the

appearance of jasper and carnelian. A rainbow, resembling an emerald, encircled the throne. Surrounding the throne were twenty-four other thrones, and seated on them were twenty-four elders. They were dressed in white and had crowns of gold on their heads.

Here we see all of the Old Testament and New Testament redeemed. In the book of Revelation, when you get to the new Jerusalem, the Bible talks about the names of the 12 tribes of Israel and the names of the 12 apostles. You add 12 and 12 and you have 24. Therefore, we see here a picture of all of the redeemed. Then verse 5 says,

From the throne came flashes of lightning, rumblings and peals of thunder. Before the throne, seven lamps were blazing. These are the seven spirits of God.

John reports that he saw lightning and heard thunder, which occurs at least three other times in Revelation, signifying that a storm is brewing. That storm is the tribulation, a seven-year death sentence for the earth. It is the floodtide of God's wrath unleashed against sin in a mighty fury of anger.

The tribulation is going to be an object lesson for the whole universe of how much God hates sin. There will be hail, fire, natural disasters, locust attacks, scorpions that sting, and blood running in the streets. And no matter how excruciating the pain, no one will be able to escape it. Revelation 6:16 says that people will be in such agony, they will beg the "...mountains and rocks, "Fall on us and hide us from the face of Him who sits on the throne and from the wrath of the Lamb!"

Scripture sheds light on other Scripture. And when the apostle Paul was writing the young Thessalonian church to encourage them, he gave a fuller understanding of what to expect on the day of the rapture. This letter was written about 51 AD, and these believers had been waiting for Jesus' return, but they were becoming disillusioned because some of their loved ones were dying before the Lord had returned. In these two insightful verses from 1 Thessalonians 4:16-17, Paul gives a preview of coming attractions.

> For the Lord himself will come down from heaven, with a loud command, with the voice of the archangel and with the trumpet call of God, and the dead in Christ will rise first. After that, we who are still alive and are left will be caught up together with them in the clouds to meet the Lord in the air. And so we will be with the Lord forever.

Evidently Paul wants these believers to know that the rapture is right on schedule, and that all believers, both living and dead, will be summoned into the sky to meet Jesus on that glorious day.

Though these events will happen almost instantaneously, Paul here describes the four phases of the rapture.

1. THE REENTRY OF THE SAVIOR

The Bible says in verse 16a,

16aFor the Lord himself will come down from heaven...

For the first time since His ascension 2000 years before, Jesus Himself will reappear in the eastern sky. The one coming is the same one who went away. But notice that Jesus isn't ready to touch ground yet. Yes, this is Christ's return all right, but this is only *phase one*. Phase two will happen at the end of the tribulation when Jesus returns in glory to defeat Satan at the Battle of Armageddon.

It's significant to note that Jesus Himself is coming back personally. That means a lot to me. Let me illustrate why: Anybody who has ever dropped off a child for the first day of school knows it is a heart-wrenching experience. (Take it from me; I've done it six times.) You drop off that little tike at the big schoolhouse with strange rules, a strange schedule, and strange people. And I must tell you that all six times that I have done it, there has been crying, screaming, wailing, begging, and stomping of feet.

And that was just *my behavior*!

Actually, the children did pretty well. But what helped us get through it all was when I would reassure the child by saying, "Daddy's just leaving for a little while. I'm going to return again and receive you unto myself...so that where I am...you can be also." Just knowing that Daddy himself was going to return was all it took to calm the heart of that frightened child.

Likewise, Jesus Himself is going to return for us, His children. And when He does, He'll be fulfilling His promise in John 14 that says He will come again and receive us unto Himself.

Isn't it exciting to know that Jesus Christ is coming again! If you have been saved, the second coming will be a blessed, joyous day! That's why I am looking for the second coming, longing for the second coming, and living for the second coming, because Daddy's coming home!

After the reentry of the Savior, there's...

2. THE RESURRECTION OF THE SAINTS

A frustrated preacher once assured his flock that they would be "the first to be taken up in the rapture because the Bible declares 'The dead in Christ shall rise first.'" He got that from verse 16b of our text which says…

…with a loud command, with the voice of the archangel and with the trumpet call of God, and the dead in Christ will rise first.

Perhaps tomorrow, Jesus is coming again in the air, and every believer is going to hear a shout. And those who are dead in Christ will rise first. Why is that? Why do the dead get a head start? Well, most of them are six feet under, so they deserve a head start!

Now notice that Scripture says the rapture will happen when Jesus *shouts*. That's why I'm not so much looking for *signs* as I am listening for *sounds*. You see, there are only three times in the Bible when Jesus shouts: The first time was when Jesus was standing in front of the tomb of his beloved friend Lazarus who had died four days earlier. John 11:43 records that "Jesus called in a loud voice, 'Lazarus, come out!'" I like what the old country preacher said: "If Jesus hadn't called him by his first name, every dead man in that graveyard would have gotten up!"

The second time Jesus shouts is over in the book of Matthew when he was on the cross, and Jesus shouted with a loud voice and the tombs of the saints opened and corpses began strolling around the city of Jerusalem.

Well, one of these days, Jesus is going to shout a third time. And when He does millions are going to emerge from their graves. Imagine it! Cemeteries will have the pungent, putrid stench of putrefying flesh wafting in the air as graves burst open and the dead arise to their reward. Battlefields will look like plowed fields as dead warriors arise who have fallen in wars throughout the ages. They will be coming from everywhere. Out of the depths of the seas, out of the tropical jungles where planes have been lost and missionaries have died serving Jesus Christ. Every child of God who has been buried in Christ will be raised one of these days as the poet said, "Up from the sea, Up from the sod, All will arise, And go to God!"

But only those who died in Christ are going to be raised. This will be a *selective* resurrection. It will be like this: Imagine that your front lawn is covered with all kinds of metals. There is iron, lead, silver, gold, tin, copper, brass and zinc. Some of the metals are beneath the surface of your lawn. Other fragments are piled on top of the surface. Imagine that a giant electro-magnet is lowered over your front yard and suddenly, a commotion occurs! From under the soil certain metals arise and from on top of the soil other pieces of metal leap. All at once, you see metal being attracted to the giant electromagnet which then carries the metal away.

When you examine the yard, you make a remarkable discovery. You find that the zinc, brass, lead, silver, gold, tin, and copper are all *still there.* The only metal missing from the field is the iron. Do you know why the iron is missing? Iron has the *same nature* as an electromagnet. Only the iron arises because the magnet only attracts that which corresponds to its nature.

One of these days Jesus is going to return, and when He does, only those with a corresponding nature are going to be taken. The Son of God is going to catch up the sons of God. The Light of the world is going to catch up the lights of the world. The Lamb of God is going to catch up the lambs of God.

Next comes...

3. THE RAPTURE OF THE SAVED

In 1 Thessalonians 4:17 we read,

> After that, we who are still alive and are left will be caught up

together with them in the clouds to meet the Lord in the air. And so we will be with the Lord forever.

The phrase "caught up together" is where we derive the word rapture. In the Latin *Vulgate* edition of the Bible, that word is translated *rapio*, from which we get the English word "rapture." It really means "a catching away." When millions disappear from this planet, life is going to continue on the earth, but the rapture will mean that God is cutting off diplomatic relations with the world by calling the nationals home. And the war to end all wars will soon begin.

For the Christian, what a wonderful day that's going to be, because you are going to receive a wonderful new resurrection body. It's exciting to get a new suit for your body, but how would you like to get a new body for your suit? First Corinthians 15 describes this incredible transformation:

> Listen, I tell you a mystery: We will not all sleep, but we will all be changed—For the perishable must clothe itself with the imperishable, and the mortal with immortality.

What will the resurrection body be like? Philippians 3:21 says that when we are changed, we will inherit a body just like Jesus' glorious resurrection body...what does that mean? We can deduce the following:

First, since Jesus had a shape, we'll have a shape. Therefore, you won't look like some other creature. You won't sprout wings or appear like cupid.

Second, since Jesus retained his individual identity, you will too. People recognized Jesus...just as they will recognize you. What's more, you'll retain all the experiences and memories you have now.

Third, Jesus' body was solid, so you will be solid. You will never be Casper the Friendly Ghost. You will not be some amorphous vapor or merely consciousness or thought.

Fourth, Jesus ate food, so you'll be able to eat. Scripture never tells us that Jesus had an appetite (indeed, he probably didn't hunger, since every kind of pain vanishes in heaven.) Nevertheless, I'm persuaded that you and I will be able to consume food in our resurrection bodies – without having to diet!

Fifth, the resurrection body has a great added benefit: Jesus' body could dematerialize. There were times when Jesus appeared and other times when He vanished suddenly. He could walk through solid objects. Imagine being able to walk through a cinder block wall or the walls of Fort Knox!

Some have wondered how old these resurrection bodies will be. After all, does a departed 90-year-old saint get his 90-year-old body back? Or does a child remain perpetually infantile? No one but God knows, of course, but some theologians have speculated that our resurrection bodies will appear to be about 30 to 33 years of age, because certain priests could not begin serving until they were 30. Furthermore, Jesus did not begin His earthly ministry until He was 30 and He died at age 33.

4. THE REUNION IN THE SKY

Forget the potato salad and dominos! This is going to be an exciting family reunion unlike anything you've ever experienced. There'll be joy unspeakable. Not only will you get to meet Moses and Elijah, face-to-face. You'll see Peter, James, and John. There will be that parent you've missed so deeply. You'll be reunited with that mate whose forehead you kissed goodbye in the casket. You'll see that beloved grandparent who left this earth long ago.

But most importantly, you'll see Jesus. With the eyes you're using now, you'll look into His eyes. With the ears you're using now, you'll hear His voice.

You'll touch His hands. You'll feel His embrace.

I love that old song that beautifully describes the soon-coming rapture.

Some bright morning when this life is ore
  I'll fly away,
To a home on God's celestial shore
  I'll fly away

When the shadows of this life have grown,
  I'll fly away,
Like a bird from prison bars have flown,
  I'll fly away

Just a few more weary days and then,
  I'll fly away,
To a land where Joys will never end,
  I'll fly away.

I'll fly away old glory
  I'll fly away
When I die, hallelujah by and by
  I'll fly away!

There is an urgency and emergency in the present hour. Jesus Christ is coming again to take His church home. Are you ready to meet Jesus? In other words, when Jesus comes again in the air, will you be running TO him? or will you be running FROM him. Will he come as your *justifier* or your *judge*?

Friend, make no mistake about it. One day you will answer to God. You may escape him today by rejecting him as Savior, but tomorrow, in the judgment, you're going to stand before him and give an account for every word, for every thought, for every deed that you have ever done.

Ask Jesus to come into your heart today.

Be saved, dear friend, *before* the trumpet sounds.

And you'll be ready to fly away with me.

CONCLUSION

THE ENGLISH LANGUAGE has many expressions and slang phrases, called idioms, and some of them have a fascinating history.

For example, the phrase "face the music."

History records that a musician in China once played in the emperor's royal orchestra. Well actually, the truth is that he couldn't play an instrument at all. But because he knew all of the right people and had political pull, he had acquired a seat in the orchestra, which was a prestigious and high-paying position.

For years, the imposter would sit there as the orchestra played, and he would raise his instrument and pretend to make music. But the truth was that he wasn't making a sound. He was only going through the motions.

Then one day the emperor asked for each member of his orchestra to appear before him for a solo command performance, which meant that this musical fraud would be unmasked. Naturally, the imposter was petrified, for he knew that he couldn't play a note. He had been pretending for too long. And even though he tried to get lessons, his fingers were much too old and unaccustomed to the instrument to play.

The imposter postponed his appointment as long as he could, but alas, he couldn't delay the engagement any longer.

So, in depression and desperation, he took his own life...because *he couldn't face the music.*

Friend, one day soon you will stand before the righteous Judge all alone.

The judgment you face will be a solo command performance in which your life will be reviewed hour-by-hour, minute-by-minute. Many good people won't be able to face the music that day, because they won't truly be saved. Oh, it's not that they didn't know about religion or occupy a pew. It's not that they didn't have many wonderful Christian friends or have great appreciation for the teachings of the Bible. It's just that they pretended to be saved when in reality they were not.

You have an appointment with God. Hebrews 9:27 declares that "...it is appointed unto men once to die, but after this the judgment." The day of God's judgment could be sooner than you think. *Are you ready to face the music?*

If not, the 31 preachers of this compendium invite you once again to pray a simple prayer of repentance and faith to be eternally saved:

> *Dear Heavenly Father,*
>
> *I acknowledge that I am a sinner. Right now, I desire to turn from my sin and follow Jesus Christ as Lord and Savior of my life. I believe that Jesus died for me on the cross and arose again the third day. Thank you, Lord, for saving me. In Jesus' name I pray, Amen.*

If you just prayed that prayer in earnestness of heart, welcome to the family of God! Now, let us encourage you to find a Bible-believing, Bible-preaching, Bible-teaching church where you can profess Christ through baptism and begin your journey of faith.

And start looking up! When the curtains of time have fallen and the last page of the last volume of history has been writ, there will be a final exclamation point...and Jesus Christ will come again.

Who knows?

Maybe Jesus will come *tomorrow.*

Printed in the United States
105741LV00002B/278/A